NEW american plays 2

JUDEVINE David Budbill
DAYTRIPS Jo Carson
PILL HILL Samuel L. Kelley
AWAY ALONE Janet Noble

with an introduction by Peter Filichia

HEINEMANN *Portsmouth, NH*

Heinemann Educational Books, Inc.
361 Hanover Street
Portsmouth, NH 03801-3959
Offices and agents throughout the world

Library of Congress Cataloging-in-Publication Data

New American plays / with an introduction by Peter Filichia.
    p.   cm.
    Contents: 1. Starting Monday / Anne Commire. Yankee dawg you die / Philip Kan Gotanda. The bug / Richard Strand. Interrogating the nude / Doug Wright — 2. Judevine / David Budbill. Daytrips / Jo Carson. Pill Hill / Samuel L. Kelley. Away alone / Janet Noble.
    ISBN 0—435—08604—9 (1). — ISBN 0—435—08605—7 (2)
    1. American drama—20th century.   I. Filichia, Peter.
PS634.N364   1992
812'.5408—dc20   91—32100
                                                                CIP

Series design and cover by Wladislaw Finne
Printed in the United States of America
92 93 94 95 96 7 6 5 4 3 2 1

contents

introduction PETER FILICHIA

So what do *Judevine*, *Daytrips*, *Pill Hill*, and *Away Alone* have in common that got them nestled together in an anthology? Well, all have characters who are in a state of flux, be they emigrating from Ireland to New York, from Mississippi to Chicago, from the big city to a small Vermont town — or moving from a rational mind to one disabled by disease. Each also has people looking for a promised land, whether literally or figuratively.

Work plays a big part in each of these four new plays. The characters in *Pill Hill* are decimated by working at a mill, those in *Away Alone* would welcome working anywhere, and those in *Judevine* long for the days when their town *had* a mill. Meanwhile, the daughter in *Daytrips* would find the most arduous job much easier than dealing with relatives who are losing their minds.

All of the characters have their points, and all have their flaws. But the plays you are about to read aren't here together in one volume because of all they have in common, however slight or considerable that may be. They're here because they're good works by new writers who deserve a forum for jobs well done.

JUDEVINE

Ever hear the one that goes, if a tree falls in the forest, does anybody hear it? More to the point, if none of us know about a small Vermont town, is it even really there?

David Budbill shows us the answer is yes. He's been to Vermont, has lived in a town much like his mythically named Judevine — and he's got quite a bit to say about the place.

Madison Avenue long ago learned to use the word "Vermont" on its products, because many consumers associate the state with purity and tranquility. Now of course those qualities exist in the Green Mountain State, but

Budbill knows better than just to oversimplify. He's written a *Spoon River Anthology* for survivors—those "billion billion souls" who have made it through life in a thirty-six-square-mile town, where the eternal flame is a neon *Beer* sign, and flashlights seem to have batteries that are nearly dead.

No, we're not in Judevine's golden age. The mill that provided so much of the economy is now a junk store. Your best chance for a job? Hang around the garage, the town's nerve center, until the owner gives in and hires you. Otherwise, you might get in some "sugarin'" or you can try to ease the rich women off their ski lifts (after you've done some very creative embezzling). But even if you're fortunate enough to work on a Christmas tree farm, it sure isn't Christmas every day in Judevine.

At first, you may assume that the conflict of the play will occur when the hippies move into the sleepy village, but *Judevine* isn't a conventional play with a central conflict. It's a dramatic poem, crafted with minimalist dialogue, that reports on folks who are red-faced from hard work, hard liquor, and hard health conditions. Ma Joad would find kindred spirits among these people who long ago learned how to wait out the winters for the spring, who remember the year 19-*and*-35, and who somehow express their deep feelings for each other by going to church.

In short, Judevine is more complex than it realizes, which is why you'll be glad that you met its citizens; indeed, after spending time with them, you may think that they were princes who at birth were switched with paupers. They're also people in whom you'll see the best and worst of yourself.

David Budbill gives them all a town forum, where we play the other Judevine-ites who will hear what our neighbors really think. They want us to understand their plights, and why they do what they do. Budbill, meanwhile, casts himself as the omniscient. Is he? One townswoman is shown to resent his writing about them, and she at times seems to have a point. Whatever the case, we come to the conclusion that Budbill has a great affection-slash-love for small-town Vermont. He'd concede that nature may have made a mistake when it chose to squeeze a village in between those hills, but he wants us to know that the people who inhabit it are still here.

DAYTRIPS

When a playwright uses a narrator, he or she is in for some heat from drama critics, who often consider it a lazy playwriting device, hardly the best way to tell a story. Nevertheless, many will have to concede that a narrator turns out to be a good and necessary ingredient in Jo Carson's *Daytrips*. The play deals with a mother's Alzheimer's disease and a grandmother's physical deterioration, and we not only see and hear the (grand)daughter's actual, expressed thoughts, but also discover the inner thoughts her frustrated alter ego longs to scream but her compassion won't allow.

How do you deal with a grandmother (Rose) who calls you Helen, and a mother (Irene) who calls you Olivia — when your name, in fact, is Pat? Now, under any circumstances, Pat wouldn't have found it easy to deal with a generation that once believed sockets should be plugged up, lest electricity run out of them. But those difficulties are squared when you're dealing with a mother whose mind is going — though her body is weathering well — and a grandmother whose body is falling apart but whose mind is clear. Add to these the problems of dealing with elders who constantly remind you that they were once in control, back when the child was "just a young'un" — because it's all the leverage they now have left. "Old age cannot or will not hear," Carson writes — and whichever of those two verbs is the more accurate, the problem remains.

Carson doesn't show us the facets of Pat's life when she isn't tending to the women — because caretaking has gotten so time-consuming that she has no other life. Instead, she is condemned to an existence where, when she talks with her mother, she never knows what's going to come out next. How do you answer her when she asks if she can go home — when she *is* home? Pat must be totally specific —

when asked how much something costs, she can't simply say "twelve"; that gets the response, "Twelve *what?*" When the afflicted can no longer read the denominations of bills, Pat takes a loss rather than argue.

And then the deluge. Was that last mistake just a slip of the tongue or an indication that the condition's getting worse? How do you prevent a woman from opening the car door when you're speeding along at sixty-five miles per hour? There's the poignancy and pain of hearing your mother say "I've got brains I haven't used yet" while you see the unpleasant symbols of her disease: apples she's taken bites out of and then forgotten; spoiled food she didn't notice; her remembering that something must be mailed, but not remembering what.

Small wonder that Pat tells as dinner conversation a story about a man who killed his sick mother. Carson takes her time in showing us how awful the illness is before raising the other painful if inevitable issue of euthanasia. When Pat decides that she'd rather be dead under these circumstances, her mother must, too, right? But how does she feel during one of her mother's rare lucid moments, when the woman suddenly comes alive to say "You think about me dead"?

But if you're assuming this is the mere chronicle of a debilitating illness, look again. It's not just daughter-to-(grand)mother devotion that keeps Pat going or keeps her around. She's felt the struggle of being the unfavored child, trying not to notice, attempting to deny it, finally admitting it, continuing to offer succor in the face of "That time I told you I loved you best, I said it to make you sit still."

Daytrips, then, also asks us to question those relationships we have with our parents. Ironic that Pat should still need such validation from a woman who's lost control of her mind; Carson may be suggesting that looking for such answers may be pointless and the sooner we come to terms with that, the better off we'll be.

Is the play too depressing for its own good? One of the best facets of theatre is that by watching an unpleasant situation, we become better prepared for the event should it ever happen to us. It's impossible not to sympathize as Irene and Rose face manifestations of getting old, such as finding that a pharmacist they've trusted all their lives has retired. And though each may be getting on, neither is dull; when Rose says of a handful of beans, "They're so old they're not going to have no taste," she isn't, double negatives aside, subtextually speaking about herself or Irene — not the way Carson has drawn them. The sad truth is that there's an excellent possibility that Pat's dilemma will someday be ours — and seeing her confront it with dignity and courage may, in future, make it easier on us.

PILL HILL

Wouldn't you like to quit your job? So would the guys in *Pill Hill* who work at the mill. The words together may sound euphonious, but they hold no music for the men in their going-nowhere jobs. Some defend the place in order to justify the lives they've made for themselves, but others have gotten out and will forever stay out. And another has bought an encyclopedia.

Remember encyclopedias? There was a time when we thought that those big, intimidating volumes represented the entire knowledge of the world, a testament to all there was to know and an indication of how very much we had to learn. Today, we may view the encyclopedia as an academic dinosaur, but these tomes are still an imposing presence in Samuel L. Kelley's play on the lives and hard times of contemporary young American blacks. The character who's bought a set (from his friend the encyclopedia salesman, naturally) prominently displays them in his apartment. They're proof that he'll soon do something with his life, that, yeah, he'll quit the mill.

Of course it's hard for all of us to walk away from our jobs, no matter how much we hate them. We can convince ourselves that whatever we do for work, some people have worse jobs. It's a rationalization that keeps us where we are—though we're sure that's only until we're "a few bucks ahead." The truth is, even if the comforts our jobs give us are only adequate, we like them better than no comforts at all.

Perhaps taking a leaf out of Chekhov's book, Kelley structures his play over a long period of time; the second act takes place five years after the first, and the third five years after that. It's plenty of time for much to happen—or for nothing to happen—to six characters in search of a better life. Some do acquire lakefront condos, drink scotch and water, and offer conventional handshakes instead of "soul shakes"—and have even taken on the white man's fear of the neighborhood. But despite the advances, the system devised by "the MAN" (Kelley always puts the phrase in capital letters) still keeps the contemporary American black a little behind. Now the Cadillacs aren't as large as they once were, and even Pill Hill, the neighborhood that once represented his wildest dreams, can be construed as the white man's hand-me-down.

Kelley knows the young black man's joking hyperbole, and lets us hear it. He isn't afraid to show his characters' unpleasant qualities; they're still adolescent in the way they insult one another's mothers, brag about whose car is longer and whose has the most options. And though some readers will be uncomfortable with one character's blatant wish for what he'd like to be in his next lifetime, we don't doubt that Kelley knows the person who said it.

By the end of the play, some men have advanced, some have not, and one has somehow managed to do both. Yes, the times, they are a-changing; the difference between yesteryear's Mississippi sheriff and today's is literally the difference between black and white. What a headlight wiper was to the "Negro" of yore is, happily, poles apart from the headlight wipers that the upwardly mobile black talks about late in the play. And though *Pill Hill* admits that ambition alone can't solve problems—and that opportunity doesn't knock forever—it still urges its characters and audience to keep trying.

AWAY ALONE

Is there "no place like home"? The first Irish immigrant we meet in *Away Alone* has, within minutes of his arrival in America, a place to live and *two* jobs. He doesn't find the streets paved with gold, but manna is often available, if not from heaven, then as leftover truffles from the trade show his friend works. He can buy black-market goods, "work" on his tan, experience the pleasures of Boston and Trenton (!), and wear T-shirts expressing the opinions that he thinks the real Americans would like him to have. That's America.

But so is gutting a house of its original ornate work, or casually throwing away perfectly fine goods into the garbage. It's not long before Janet Noble's characters lose the wildly incorrect preconceptions with which they arrived — probably around the time they see dogs wearing boots walk around people who have no shoes.

Our immigrants also find that the luck of the Irish doesn't travel well. They're victimized by under-the-table employers and scorned by workers who see them as interlopers out to get their jobs. But Noble's characters were aware before they embarked that they'd be exploited and hated, and still had the courage to make the trip. The thrown-together friends live you-and-me-against-the-world, sometimes romanticizing and yearning for the country they left and are already forgetting. Everyone, though, is afraid to ask the questions they're secretly thinking: *Why did it take my family so long to make the move that other families have been making for over a century? Do I feel treasonous for having left? And did I come to a promised land where there is no promise left?* Noble's progress report reminds us of how very lucky we third- and fourth-generation Americans are to have had forefathers who long ago fought these battles for us.

Away Alone also has time for problems that plague every nationality — for instance, the battle between women who look for love and the men who often bolt the moment they find them needing it. The characters also face the questions of whether or not to romance their way up the social ladder, to remember that the wife and chilren are back home, to relate to the sexual slice of the American pie.

Noble set *Away Alone* in the present, but the allusions to Darryl Strawberry's exploits with the Mets now put the play in the recent past. Would there were an equally speedy solution that would render the immigrants' struggles obsolete — struggles we might not give a thought to if Janet Noble weren't such an incisive writer.

david budbill

judevine

author's introduction

Judevine grew out of a series of narrative and dramatic poems and an hour-long play, *Pulp Cutters' Nativity*, written over the past twenty years, about the people in an imaginary town in the mountains of northern Vermont called Judevine — an out-of-the-way place full of people whom the hip consider nonexistent, invisible, but who are, in fact, sacred, unique, unrepeatable individuals, the equal of anyone in God's sight. Judevine is a third-world country within the boundaries of the United States where, as in so many third-world countries, there is incredible physical beauty, great suffering and hardship, and a tenacious and indomitable will to survive. The evolution of this play has been long and arduous, and the script presented here is radically different from the script with which the evolutionary process began more than ten years ago.

Pulp Cutters' Nativity and some of the Judevine poems were first given a staged reading at the McCarter Theatre in Princeton, New Jersey, in 1980 and moved on to a fully mounted production, with an ensemble of four, also at the McCarter, in 1984. *Judevine* then began an odyssey of six more years of additions and deletions, rewrites and reorderings: a production at Vermont Repertory Theatre, in Burlington, Vermont; staged readings at The Boston Athenaeum and The Performance Place in Sommerville, Massachusetts; a fully mounted production at The Western Stage in Salinas, California; a revival at Vermont Rep; a reading at The Gloucester Stage in Gloucester, Massachusetts; a production at Old Castle Theatre Company in Bennington, Vermont; a revival at The Western Stage; a staged reading at Florida Studio Theatre in Sarasota; and finally another staged reading at Arena Stage in Washington, D.C., and another revival at Old Castle Theatre Company.

There are five hours of this Judevine material suitable for staging, so the temptation to try out something new was and is almost irresistible and the possibilities nearly infinite. Yet, as the number of productions and staged readings mounted, and the years passed, it became clear that, given the constraints of a two-hour evening of theatre, some kind of final collection of scenes and an order for those scenes had inevitably presented itself. When, in January of 1990, *Judevine* opened for a six-week run as a Mainstage production at the American Conservatory Theatre in San Francisco, I quit rewriting the play. French poet Paul Valéry said, "A poem is never finished, only abandoned." It was time to take his advice.

Perhaps someday a venue will present itself in which all five hours of the Judevine material can be done. Until that time, however, this evening in the theatre stands as the play called *Judevine*. All the original Judevine material, by the way, is now collected in one book called *Judevine: The Complete Poems*, published by Chelsea Green Publishing Company (P.O. Box 130, Post Mills, VT 05058−0130). I suggest that people involved in producing this play get and read this book as background material for understanding the characters and the place from whence they come.

As a playwright *and* a poet, I am intensely interested in the music of common speech as spoken by "ordinary" people, and because my plays are about "ordinary" people, they concern themselves with political and social, as well as personal, concerns for justice and opportunity. All the characters in all my plays are crippled and hurt in some way, because we are all crippled and hurt in some way.

It is my hope and belief that the theatre is a place where we can give up our smart defenses and brittle sophistications, and dare to be open and vulnerable with each other, where we can feel secure enough, for a moment, to watch our lives being exposed. The theatre is a place where we *pretend* in order to reveal to ourselves what is most meaningful and most real. And since we all share a common bond of woundedness, it is a place where we can look at our delights and joys, our sadness and sorrow and laugh and cry about them — together. In the theatre when our make-believe helps us see and feel what is most important and most real something can happen that we could call healing. This is an old idea, as old as a tribal poet telling a story in the center of an African village or a play presented in the open air in ancient Greece, but it is an idea which is being drowned in our incessant need to be diverted and entertained and by the ubiquitous, hard-edged sophistication of our time.

The great strength of theatre is its ability to gather people together in a place, make a play, a "pretend," and have it become as actual as anything out there in the "real" world. In *Judevine* this pretending takes the form of an ensemble of actors (in recent productions as many as ten or a dozen) who reach back to an earlier time when it was fun to get together in the back yard with a box of old clothes and put on a play. Hopefully out of all this pretending, this *play*, comes a very real *work* in which we learn something about our predicament in this life, our connection to each other, and our common humanity.

I believe that theatre, like poetry and music, is about feeling, about being healed through feeling. It is not about language or technique or even ideas. Language and technique and ideas are all only tools, means to an end, and that end is vivid pictures, real people, honest conflict, powerful emotion, musical expression — in short, cathartic emotional experience. Theatre, like poetry and music, is a path to the emotional articulation of the joys and sorrows of this life, and when that articulation is good we are somehow, mysteriously, if only momentarily, transformed and healed.

I hope that *Judevine* somehow helps us all better understand and feel how each one of us is a sacred, unique, and unrepeatable individual, helps us understand and feel that, as Tommy says to Doug, "We are all in this together." I hope that *Judevine* reveals some of the joys and sorrows of this life and does so in a musical and healing way.

characters

There are twenty-five identified characters (sixteen male, nine female), as well as various other unidentified town's people.

author's production suggestions

The most useful kind of set would be either a raked platform with areas down left and down right containing benches where ensemble members can gather, or a modular arrangement of platforms creating numerous levels for the actors to sit, stand, and climb on, move over and across, up to and down from. Either alternative is simple and can still suggest hills, various sections of an interior, distance and intimacy. (If using modular platforms, it is a good idea to provide enough playing space so that there is room for actors to move around the island of platforms, and room also for a place down left and/or down right where ensemble members can sit while not in the action on or around the platforms.)

Things should be kept simple. This is a play of the imagination and the fewer props there are the easier it is for people to see the actual things of this world in the words and mime of the play. (Some productions have used no props whatsoever. All objects were mimed, and all sounds were generated by the actors with their bodies and their voices.)

Keep in mind that there are three scripts here: (1) the words people say, (2) the constant mime which illuminates, illustrates, and expands upon the words, and (3) the world of nonverbal sounds — wind, numerous kinds of birds, water, songs, insects, a truck backing up, sung chords, fire, a truck passing in the night over wet pavement, dogs, welding shop noises, etc. All three scripts are created and performed by the acting ensemble. Wherever a speech is designated ENSEMBLE, the director should divide the sentences and phrases among the ensemble members in the way that is best for that particular group of actors.

Since *Judevine* depends on the cohesiveness of the ensemble, it is important to make every effort to create a unified group. To that end I suggest beginning rehearsals by playing theatre games and by working on the ensemble sections of the play first. It is also quite effective to keep the entire ensemble on stage throughout the play and let them make their simple costume changes on stage at the ensemble centers down left and right (or anywhere else for that matter), but in full view of the audience.

Cast size can vary, from six to a dozen or more. Each actor must play numerous roles plus be an active and constant member of the ensemble. Numerous characters have their physical size and shape described in detail in the narrative. It is not necessary, and in many instances impossible, to cast actors to these sizes. Part of the pretend of this play is actors playing people with sizes and shapes they personally do not have.

Also, these characters are not mired in downtrodden, proletarian agony, they are simply the rural poor, full of despair and joy, hope and fatalism, like the rest of us. These people are to be loved and respected, but not idealized in any way. They are as wonderful and lousy as are we all. Actors should not confuse their sympathy for the characters with their characterizations of them. The audience should laugh loud and long *with* these characters, but they should never laugh *at* them. No amount of technique can replace love for the humanness of these people.

It is in the nature of this piece that the fourth wall doesn't really exist. Anything that can be done to involve the audience directly in this story, in this town, in these lives is good. We all live in Judevine. Therefore, I encourage directors and actors to break the fourth wall extensively and often.

In addition to speaking their lines, all actors should participate in making the sound effects that are such an important part of this play. This is an ensemble piece and the sounds of our world, the cries of joy and anguish from humans and animals, the mechanical and natural sounds created by neither human nor animal—in short all the sounds we live with—should be generated exclusively by the ensemble of actors on stage, and a lot of time and attention should be devoted to creating these sounds.

If you would like to use objects to create some of the sounds, I suggest locating these "musical instruments" at the ensemble centers down left and down right. These objects could include a fifty-five-gallon steel drum, a smaller, maybe thirty-gallon drum, perhaps a section of cast-iron radiator, and other objects that when struck with mallets, ball peen hammers, drumsticks, brushes, etc., produce different sounds, timbres, and pitches. These items can be used throughout the play but will be especially useful during the welding shop scene. These items can also serve as scenery for Jerry's Garage and Roy's welding shop, among tires, bottles, mechanics' tools, etc. There should also be a triangle, ideal for chiming the hour when appropriate. Feel free to incorporate other metal, wooden, plastic, or glass objects and instruments that will create useful sounds when struck, rubbed, blown into or across, grated, or scratched.

Mime is critically important to *Judevine*, and because it is, the location of things such as camp fires, a wood stove, a coffee cup or a couple of bolts in someone's hand, a bag of fertilizer over someone's shoulder must be carefully and exactly pinpointed, completely realized, "actually there." The reality of the existence of these imagined objects needs to be as accurately delineated by gesture as it is by word. Define the mimed object precisely and then maintain the definition exactly. One of the director's biggest jobs will be to decide what will and will not be mimed. The mime should illuminate, illustrate, and expand upon the words, but not obstruct them. (It is impossible to mime all of the narrative.)

There are a few additional notes, of a more specific nature, at the end of the script.

act 1

PRELUDE AND FUGUE

Houselights down. Preset down. Dark. Then from places
throughout the theatre the actors begin. Each actor, in character,
delivering his or her line in the following group.

ENSEMBLE. Shitagoddamn, all da years me t'ink ah be nathin'
  but a goddamn drunk, ah be high class alacholic just
  like the President!
Christ, if I had the money, the first thing I'd do is buy her
  a funeral.
Shiftless bum is what he is. All he ever done reg'alar is eat.
Are you gonna tell your story or stand around and dump
  on me?
Alice has a bike: a Harley Davidson.
Well, if you can leave half your clothes still on the hook,
  I guess I can leave half mine still in the drawer.
I didn't mean to hurt her! She's my baby, ain't she?
You're crazy old woman! You're crazy! They been gone
  for forty years!
They're up there in that trailer all day long, naked and
  drinkin' beer and smokin' dope!

Now the lines come faster and closer together until, toward the end
of this next group, all actors are speaking at once so that they create
a cacophony in which no particular line can be understood. The
cacophony ends abruptly as the final line rises, is shouted, above the
noise. All sound ceases abruptly with the word "again!"

Nelson Beaudry got twelve trout out of his cellar that day.
Last summer she cut off her finger in the baler, paid her
  farmer's dues.
I'm lookin' for a handful of three-eighths-inch, fine-thread,
  reverse-turn bolts.
The kids at school all say the Hopper kids have bugs and
  worms.
Which they do.

It'd make it nice. To have a place to take a bowl of soup, a
    sandwich, a place to sit and visit.
My son's in the war, you know, in the Navy!
I try not to work too much in the winter,
    it gets in the way of my snow machinin'!
I told you I was sorry about bein' late!
Mister, don't you ever come in here again!

*The ensemble begins an ascending glissando, at the top of which
there is a hold. The lyric for this glissando and hold is: "AH!"*

WHERE AND WHO AND SPRING

ENSEMBLE. North to ancient, rounded mountains, all ledge
    and rock outcropping.
Yet softened green by forest.
Mountains and hill farms,
valleys and bottomland,
and in the bottom,
water —
a river or a stream
and in the bottom also, villages, because —
grist mill, saw mill, creamery, power, log course,
sewer.
One village of the many —
call it Judevine.
Thirty-six square miles, a billion billion souls,
six hundred human souls,
two-thirds in the mountains, two hundred in the village,
squeezed between sharp-rising hills,
room only for the highway, railroad, river,
and what houses could be put amongst the three.
And through the valley flows the river.
For two hundred years we've been coming here,
not in a steady stream, but in waves —
like all migrations, conquerings.
(*Now with an English accent*) First, Anglo stock from the
    colonies to the south:
Stanton, Mead, Middlebrooks,

Taylor, Crocker, Sedgwick, Pixley, Shed.
(*French Canadian accent*) And very shortly after, from the
      north, the French came,
down across the border from Quebec:
Devereaux, Patenaud, St. George, St. Jacques,
Turcotte, LaMotte, Bassette and Gelineau.
(*Italian accent*) Again later in the century
stone cutters come to work the quarries:
Italians:
Scrizzi, Faziano, Albrizzio, Tortilini.
(*Spanish accent*) Spaniards: Gomez, Echeveria.
(*Greek accent*) Greeks: Rublacabla, Vlahos, Katzenzakis.

Then again, just twenty years ago,
another wave of young out of suburbs and cities and into
      these hills:

Maybe someone is giving the peace sign, someone else is saying
"Peace, Brother," others assume a posture of disgust.

Hewitt, Landi, Klein, Liberman, Solomon, Plent.
Hippies!
Lewandowski, Katzenberg, Bernstein, Coe.
Goddamned Hippies!
So who's native? Don't talk to me native.
Because you got here early makes you more?
Witch grass, zucchini, tomatoes, you and me —
all immigrants is what I'm talking.
Native is dirt and stones, mountains.
What else?
We, love, are water.
Just passing through.
We are always here and always leaving.
We are water, like the river, just passing through.
And we endure, year after year, season after season,
waiting out the winter, waiting always, for the spring.
(*In unison as if it were a sigh*) Ah! Spring!
(*Some bird sounds, chickadee, white throated sparrow, etc.*)
Light hovers longer in the southern sky.
Brooks uncover themselves.

Alders redden.
Grosbeaks' beaks turn green.
Chickadee finds the song she lost last November.
Earth softens to the touch.
Buds stand up like nipples.
(*A flock of geese passing over going north.*)
The geese return.
Their long vees plow the fields of cloud.
The trees loud again with birds.

In the morning Whitethroat sparrows cries:
    The sun! The sun!
    I bring the sun in the bright spot beside my eye!
In the evening there are Veeries dreaming they are falling
    water.

*A minor seventh chord begins and continues until the last line in the
scene. Some in the ensemble sing the chord, others deliver the
following four lines.*

Lilacs in the dooryard bloom.
The air is sweet as honied tea.
The orchards hum.
Seeds break ground, stretch up, stretch down.

*The chord becomes another ascending glissando, then turns into the
words: "SPRING! AH!"*

ANTOINE

*Antoine and David enter. Spring sounds: spring peepers, other
frogs, robin, phoebe, crow, etc.*

DAVID. Spring, twenty years ago.
    My first day as a laborer on a Christmas tree farm.
    I pulled my pickup to the side of the road,
    hopped over a drainage ditch running full
    and started up a slope toward a man
    standing about a quarter of a mile away.
    Even now, the first of May,

the woods still stood in better than a foot of rotten snow,
but here where the earth tilted south the ground was bare.
Above the grays and browns of last year's matted grass
the young Christmas trees seemed iridescent
in the morning sun.
Antoine stood motionless, watching me come up the hill.

ANTOINE. You da new mans? Taut you was. Mike said you
was caumin'. Ah'm Antoine LaMotte! Ah live alone
ina trailer up on Aiken Pond. Shitagoddamn!
good to be in da sun again!

DAVID. Antoine is a small man, five two or three.
About his cheeks there is that unmistakable alcoholic
sheen.
His neck moves in deepening shades of red toward the
back until
between his hair line and his collar it is the color of wild
strawberries.
His hair is thin but black and his dark eyes dance
when he talks, which he does incessantly.
His whole body moves to the rhythm of his words;
his hands flutter in front of him as if they were
dancing to the music of his speech.
He walks like a duck.
He bangs around the house of his body like a baby.
He is small, feather-light, delicate and infinitely tender.
We stood for a long time looking out
over the mountains.

ANTOINE. Wall! you mus' be crazy fauckin' basterd to take
a job like dis! Bull an' jam like da rest of us
for two an'a korter an' hour. Your crazy as me!
By Chris' an' Saint Teresa don't say ah didn't
warn ya. Before you're done, your tongue hang out,
touch hole hang daown. You pull and tug till
you cas' your withers. Your mamma roll over in 'er grave,
cry out, "Oh! by Jesus! how ah fail you
as a mudder!" When you go home tonight, your little
wimens she gonna have to take a raincheck.
She gonna hate you tanight!
And you gonna start ta hate dese friggin' trees.

You gonna wish your mudder was a baby girl!

DAVID. We set off down the hill toward a tractor and a wagon
piled with eighty pound bags of Old Fox fertilizer.

ANTOINE. What you really do, David? I know somebody like
the likes of you
ain't gonna spend his en-tire life makin' love to dese friggin'
trees!
What's really why you be here on dis earth?

DAVID. I was afraid you'd ask.

ANTOINE. Dat bad, eh?

DAVID. Yes.

ANTOINE. Well, you can go ahead and tell me, 'cause I known
plenty criminals
in my day, and I know how to keep my moud broken
down an' ou' da order
when I haf too. Some day whan we got more time an' less
money,
I'll tell you what it be like around dese parts back in da
prohibition days.
Den you see how not much you could be could be so bad
compared to then!

DAVID. I'm a ... writer. (*Now mumbling*) I'm a poet.

ANTOINE. What's dat yew say?

DAVID. I am ... a poet. I write poetry.

ANTOINE. Shitacatsass naow! You be?
Oh, goddamnit to shit, I am a proud man to meet you!
Oh, my mudder in heaven look down on me!
I be workin' wid a poet! A man what writes poetry!
Ah, David, we gonna haf a good time togedder!
An' don't you worry none. Yer secret's safe wid me!
Why, when I was a boy back in those Prohibition Days
there was diamond rings buried in the dirt beneath the
porch
an' submachine guns under da hay in da barn,
an' I never new a t'ing about dem.
Ah, goddamnit to shit, I like poetry!

DAVID. When I first knew Antoine he drank a lot,
a six pack on the way to work,
then another couple during the day.

I'm sure he drank himself to sleep.
But he never missed work and he never drank anything
but beer. He swore that if you drank only beer
you'd never become an alcoholic.

ANTOINE. Ah'm no alacholic. Not like Uncle Clyde. He got
an alacholic tumor big as a cabbage in his stomach.
Got to feed it brandy ever' day.
Me, ah ain't nathin' but a goddamned drunk.
Alacholism for dem multitude millionaires. Politicians.
Poor fauckin' basterds da likes a me just goddamn drunks.
David, you like politics? Ah watch dat news
'baout every night. Watch them crazy basterds
jomp around. Goddamn multitude millionaires.
Gangsters. Any of 'em worth a turd get a bullet
in da head. All them Kennedys and that Martin Luther
      King.
Oh Jesus! how ah love dat man! He be like me,
radder be a lover dan a fider.
See how far it got 'im! Naow! White man da biggest
      basterd
whatever live. Steal da country from the Indian,
then make the nigger do the work!
Like me, da white nigger of da nord.

DAVID. Antoine met Shirley.
They lived together in a trailer up in Collinsville with her
      two boys.
About a month after all of us knew what was going on
Antoine finally said,

ANTOINE. David! got me a wimens! Workin' out too.
Workin' out good. Two hundred thirty poun' and not an
      ounce of fat.
Caum up here from Joisey. Dat's how she talk.
She say, "Hoi, Antoine, moi name's Shoiley.
Oi just moved up heah from New Joisey.
Would you boi any chance
happen to have a glass of wudder?"
Dat's how she say it. Shitacatsass, ain't dat funny?
Ah! it make me laugh da way she talk. She is a good
      wimens.

Ah'd marry her tamarra if it weren't for ... hey, ah ...
we lose da welfare an' her wid them two outlaw boys.
Mah rockin' chair money ain't enauf. Was fer me,
get me through da winner, but she got dem bad actin'
    saverges.
Wall, better'n livin' to mahself in dat trailer
with nathin' but mah goddamn dawg!

DAVID. It lasted about a year.
Then Shirley left, went down to a place in Barre.

ANTOINE. David, she left me. Walk right aout. Poof!
Ah'm back in dat trailer with dat friggin' dawg.
On'y friend ah got. Two friggin' dawgs.
Alone again. Ah! goddamnit ta shit, what's the use!
Piss on dat fire, David. Les' go drink saum beer.
Come on, David, drink beer with me.
Les' go drink saum beer.

DAVID. I didn't go and I've been sorry ever since.
Antoine began missing more and more work
until he was showing up about once a week.
That's when Bert fired him.
About a month after Antoine got fired he came over to my
    place
one Saturday afternoon.

ANTOINE. Dawyd, how yu' be? Ah ain't tu good. Fawk,
ah'm 'cinergratin', Dawyd. Caumin' apart to pieces.
Don' know wha' ah gonna do. I di'in't know ah luf
dat wimens so. I di'in't know it. Ah, Christ,
ah wish ma mamma she still be a baby girl.

DAVID. I didn't see Antoine for another couple months.
Then again on a Saturday afternoon, he showed up.

ANTOINE. David! shitacatsass, we back together!
Naow you bedder si' daown.
David, ah'm gonna be a fadder!
By Christ, ah never taut it caum to be. Ah be happy as a
    puppy to da road.
Oh! ah wish to hell I could marry her! She caum home
    from docter's,
sid daown at table, tell me, we both cry all afternoon we
    be so happy.

Next day ah go to docter's say you help me naow ah can't
    be drunk no more,
ah gonna be a fadder! He say, "You are alacholic." Ah
    say, "Naow!
how dat be! Ah taut nobody be alacholic what drink only
    beer."
That's why I never drink the hard stuff. He say, "You
    are."
Ah di'in't know it! Shitagoddamn, all the years me t'ink
ah be nathin' but a goddamn drunk ah be high class
    alacholic
julluk da President!
He say I quit or I never see my baby grow
and by Jesus dat be t'ree week ago an' ah ain't pull a ring
    since.
And ah ain't gonna to nieder. We gonna name 'im ...
    Pierre!
And if he be a girl, we name him Michelle.
Shitagoddamn, David, naow ah be like you book writers,
ah got mah head in da clouds, no more on da graound dan
    da moon,
an' Bert gimme mah job back too. Ah told him,
ah got my reason to work naow. Fauck me!
Ah'll pick bluebird shit off the white cliffs of Dover if I
    have to!
DAVID. Shirley had the baby and Antoine stomped around like
    a banty rooster.
Then it was spring again.
ANTOINE. Graoun's a bullin', David. Time to plant da seed.
You got to make you wedder. Got to do it naow.
Just the right time. It's mudder nature. Like a wimens.
You be like me, last year cabbage and tomato gone to hell,
but I get a side hill a patata and a baby girl! Dis year
Poppa gonna plow da whole goddamn state for his gardin!
Shit, David, we got to get unmarried from these goddamn
    trees!
Ah'm sick of it! Ah'm goin' home. Two o'clock and I don't
    care.
Ah'm goin' to the matinee. Ah be! Ah got to see

my wimens and my little baby. You tell Bert
I ain't functionatin' right today.
Tell him ah be back tamarra! (*They exit*)

JERRY'S GARAGE

Some garage sounds.

ENSEMBLE. In Craftsbury there are two: Raboin's and
    Humphrey's,
down in New Hampshire, in West Andover, it is Thornley's,
in Five Islands, Maine, it's called Grover's,
and from Lake Champlain to the Atlantic Ocean
there has got to be a thousand
known only as The Corner Store.
Almost all have gas pumps, only some
have mechanics or a post office
and I'd wager none still have all three.
Here in Judevine we call it The Garage
or Jerry's.
Jerry's is in, and is, the center of the town.
When there is nothing else to do,
when you are lonely,
you go to the garage and stand around, or sit,
and visit.
CONRAD. Conrad works at the garage,
JERRY. Huh, if you want to call it that.
DAVID. because he may as well.
    If he didn't have a job there he'd be there anyway,
    which is why he got hired in the first place.
JERRY. Hell, if he's gonna be here all the time, he might as
    well be doin' somethin'.
DAVID. Conrad smirks and says,
CONRAD. An' git paid.
    Conrad. Forty-three.
    Works at the Garage, rents a room from Flossie just next
        door,
    has his separate entrance so everything will be
    on the up and up.

Oh ... changes tires, takes the bottles, but never works
    the register.
JERRY. I've urged him to. He doesn't want to, won't.
EDITH. Afraid to's what it is.
CONRAD. Every evening when the valley darkens
    just about the time the lights go on above the gas pumps,
    Conrad begins. Beer ... blackberry brandy.
    By closing time at eight, he hovers in the low and darkened
        room
    like a dazed cat. Jerry locks up, puts out the lights,
    except for the one in the window that says:
ALL. BEER.
CONRAD. And Conrad pads the hundred feet to home
    tilting and weaving
    between broken cars and snow machines,
    headed for his separate entrance.
    Supper? Huh?
    The beer is filling. Think of all those calories.
    The sugar in the brandy gives him carbohydrates.
    His protein comes from television.
    He dines each night on black and white.
    He builds his bone and muscle from
    a two dimensional dream.
    Now he is rugged, handsome, swift and mean.
    There is a gorgeous woman hanging on his sleeve.
A WOMAN IN THE ENSEMBLE. Oh, Conrad!
FEMININE NARRATOR. For years Jerry talked about how he'd
    like to have
    a restaurant hitched to the store —
    there was an empty room out back would do.
JERRY. It'd make it nice ... to have a place to take a bowl of
    soup, a sandwich,
    a place to sit and visit.
DAVID. He talked that way for years,
    then just a couple of months ago his dream got muscled
    out by deed
    and Jerry's got himself a restaurant now —
ENSEMBLE. (*Creating a restaurant*) a Judevine type restaurant —

in the back room, the counter faced in three different kinds
    of paneling,
a meat slicer he picked up at auction,
a hot plate from Alice's junk store
a two formica kitchen tables and some chairs with plastic
    seats from
Beaudry's perennial lawn sale.
They make grinders,
a different soup each day, five days a week,
and you can buy soda in the store to drink with lunch,
but no beer,
unless you're gonna drink it outside,
the license costs too much.
JERRY. Well, it ain't much.
    Got some beat up equipment, nailed together scraps.
FEMININE NARRATOR. He's an ecologist, you see?
JERRY. Just like everything else in Judevine . . .
ALL. half-assed.
DAVID. Which I guess it is and seedy too,
    but such aesthetic judgments depend on point of view.
    From where I look I see something good enough for us or
        anybody,
    a place to visit, sit down, eat and drink together,
FEMININE NARRATOR. even if it is a grinder and a Pepsi,
DAVID. let our caring for each other grow,
    which, as everybody knows,
    has nothing at all to do
    with soft lights and leather booths.

LUCY

Lucy enters Jerry's store.

DAVID. I first met Lucy where everybody meets her —
    at Jerry's Garage, which is the only place she ever goes.
    We hadn't lived here long when one day
    she got me cornered back by the coolers.
LUCY. What's your name? We've got the place, the last one,

just on the edge of town. You know the place?
House is on the right, barn's just across the road.
You ought to stop in sometime; we'll show you around.
We got a nice place. We're all Jerseys you know. It's just
    the three of us,
I mean my husband and my son and me, nobody else. We
    do it all ourselves.
Only don't come today. My husband and son aren't home
    right now, but
they'll be coming back — maybe tomorrow. My son's in
    the war you know.
In the Navy, the only one from here what joined the Navy.
He's on a battleship. He sends us letters almost every day
all about how hot it is, says it's not at all like here.
My husband always wanted to be a sailor but he was
    farming
when the war broke out so they wouldn't let him go.
We been on our place since 19 and 35. Jerseys you know.
We never have anything but Jerseys. You married?
Bring your wife and kids. We'll show you around. Only
    don't come today.
Come by tomorrow — I think they'll be back by then. I got
    to go. Stop by.
They could be back anytime. We'll show you around, only
    not today.
Come by tomorrow.

DAVID. When I paid for my beer, Jerry didn't say a word
    about the woman.
He acted as if what she said wasn't in the least bit unusual.
The second time I saw Lucy she launched into the same
    thing again
almost word for word and again Jerry didn't say anything
    about it.
Slowly, over the years, I heard about her and little by little
the pieces converged until I had her story.
Their son graduated high school in 1942 and within a
    month
had joined the Navy, been shipped out to the South Pacific.
He boasted all over town just before he left that he'd

"Take care of them Japs and be home by Christmas."
That was two years before they got the letter.
He had been their only child.
About a week after they received the news
Lucy's husband hung himself in the barn one morning
    after chores.
Lucy has been living in the house alone since then.
It used to be she'd talk to anyone who'd listen.
She told everyone over and over again how her husband
    and her son
were coming home, maybe tomorrow,
until it became obvious, even to her, she couldn't go on
    doing that.
Since then she has spoken only to strangers who haven't
    heard her story.
(*Youngish Man enters*)
There is a youngish man in town who's been around a
    while.
She was in the store when he came in and she, not
    remembering
he'd heard her dream before, began again.

LUCY. What's your name? We got the place, the last one
just on the edge of town, you know the place,
house is on the right, barn's just . . .

YOUNGISH MAN. Can I just get my beer?

LUCY. across the road. You ought to stop in sometime. We'll
    show you around.

We got a nice place. We're all Jerseys you know.

My son's in the Navy. On a battleship. He sends us letters

YOUNGISH MAN AND LUCY. almost every day about how hot it
    is.

He says it's not at all like here.

YOUNGISH MAN. Listen, Lady, I've heard this story half a
    dozen times before!

They're never coming back!

LUCY. Oh, of course they are, of course they are.

YOUNGISH MAN. You're crazy, old lady, you're crazy.

LUCY. They could be back any time.

YOUNGISH MAN. They're never coming back, woman, never!

LUCY. Anytime. Not today, but maybe tomorrow.

YOUNGISH MAN. They been gone for forty years! They been
dead for forty years!

LUCY. No. No! NO! Don't ever say that!

DAVID. As she spoke, Jerry came out from behind the counter
and seized
the youngish man around the neck the way wrestlers do
and the man's face turned red then blue.
Jerry drug him out the door
and threw him down to the ground beside the gas pumps
and only then did Jerry speak and say:

JERRY. Mister, don't you *ever* come in here again. (*Beat*)

DAVID. Then, in more years than anyone can remember
Lucy spoke to someone she knew and said:

LUCY. Jerry, you sure do get some crazy people in here.

THE POSTMASTER AND THE CLERK

A clock strikes six times. Edgar Whitcomb and Laura Cate enter.

LAURA. Every morning at exactly six, Edgar Whitcomb rises.
He bathes in a basin at the kitchen sink — his face and
hands, his arms,
chest and stomach — down to his waist. He dries himself
and hangs
the basin back on a hook above the sink beside the window
which looks out on the river
which is running, running away.
Then he fills a glass with water, drops his tooth brush in
and shakes
a small amount of dental powder onto the palm of his left
hand.
Edgar Whitcomb is sixty-one years old. He has yet to buy
a tube of tooth paste.
He boils an egg, boils water for his tea and cuts a slice of
bread
from a loaf Laura Cate has made for him. Breakfast ready,
he moves it

to the sink and takes it slowly, standing at the window
in the company of the river
which is running, running away.
He dons his undershirt and shirt, a white shirt, clean and
 fresh,
as each is, six working days a week. He ties a perfect four-
 in-hand knot
in his tie, without looking, while looking out the window
toward the river
which is running, running away.
Now he prepares a lunch, a sandwich and a piece of fruit,
puts it in a paper bag, pours what tea is left into a
 thermos,
puts on his coat and hat, both of which he brushed last
 night,
steps out the door, and walks eastward leisurely the two
 hundred yards
to the Post Office here in Judevine.
He unlocks the door, begins another day as Postmaster to
 this town.
He removes his coat and hat and, pushing his chin hard
 into his neck,
straightens the tiny ceramic pin on his left lapel which
 says:
EDGAR. U.S. Postal Service
Thirty Years.
LAURA. He combs his hair, unlocks the safe, then stands at his
 desk and watches
through the window toward the river
which is running, running away.
At exactly nine each morning Edgar Whitcomb leaves
 what he is doing and
without his coat or hat strides to the town offices just next
 door.
Laura Cate looks up and smiles and —
Good Morning!
EDGAR. Hello!
LAURA. They visit about the weather,

EDGAR. how they are feeling,
LAURA. anything that comes to mind,
and as they do they look deeply and directly
into each other's eyes. (*A clock strikes six times*)
EDGAR. Every morning at exactly six, Laura Cate also rises.
She removes her sleeping clothes, bathes herself, puts on a
dress,
or a skirt and blouse, depending on her mood.
She has never in her life worn a pair of slacks.
She puts on her shoes, which match the morning's clothing,
applies lipstick
sparingly, pats powder to her face and daubs perfume
behind each ear.
She combs her hair, smooths out the wrinkles in her
clothing,
then moves to her kitchen where she prepares her breakfast.
Laura Cate is fifty-two, big boned and stately,
an unseen beauty in an age of bony women.
She takes her breakfast to her tiny dining room and as she
eats it
she watches out the window to the river
which is running, running away.
She rises, puts on her coat, hangs her purse
from the crook of her folded arm,
and as she leaves her house she sings:
LAURA. (*Singing*)
You are my sunshine, my only sunshine,
You make me happy when skies are gray,
You'll never know dear how much I love you,
Please don't take my sunshine away. (*She continues humming*)
EDGAR. She walks down the short path to the road, turns
westward and steps off
intently toward the Town Clerk's Office three hundred
yards away.
For twenty-five years she has been Clerk to the town of
Judevine;
twenty-five years the arbiter of documents, the keeper and
preserver
of all legalities.

When the office is ready for the day's transactions and her
    day's work
lies before her on the desk, she moves to the window and
    with her arms
folded beneath her breasts, Laura Cate watches out the
    window
toward the river
which is running, running away.
At five minutes to nine Laura Cate removes her lipstick
    and her compact
from her purse and touches up her mouth, powders her
    nose,
looks carefully at herself in the compact's tiny mirror.

EDGAR. Good morning!

LAURA. Hello! (*Beat*)

LAURA. Late every winter in a narrow tray at the U.S. Post
    Office, Judevine, Vermont,
Edgar Whitcomb grows the seedlings of pansies and
    calendula.

EDGAR. In the town offices just next door in another tray Laura
    Cate
grows marigolds and cosmos.

LAURA. When spring comes, Laura Cate and Edgar Whitcomb
    meet each other
at the flower bed between the doors to till the soil and
    plant their flowers.

EDGAR. Sometimes on a summer morning you see them there
    weeding between the plants, pinching off the dying
    blossoms
and you can hear them talking, laughing with each other.
    (*Beat*)

EDGAR. Every Sunday Laura Cate walks down the road to
    church.

LAURA. Edgar Whitcomb waits inside his house and watches.
    When the time is right, he strides out the door, across the
    road
and meets her whereupon she takes his arm and they enter
    church

LAURA AND EDGAR. together.

Edgar and Laura and the other ensemble members sing a hymn together; the last stanza of "Faith of Our Fathers" or "Lead On O King Eternal" or "Love Divine, All Loves Excelling" including the Amen.

EDGAR. When the benediction has been said, they leave the church

LAURA. and take their Sunday meal together,

EDGAR. then together walk beside the river,

LAURA. this river,

EDGAR. their blood, their passion and delight, that for thirty years has moved

LAURA. through their lives,

EDGAR. always changing, always new, running,

LAURA. while they watch and stay,

LAURA AND EDGAR. these two who watch and stay,

LAURA. companions to each other, to the river,

EDGAR. while the river runs away.

ANTOINE ON IMAGINATION, WOMEN, LOVE AND LONELINESS

Antoine and David enter.

ANTOINE. Ah, David, ah'm gettin' sick a dis. Ah can't stand it too much longer.

We got to open up dat bowser factoree like we talk about.

Make dem pussy wigs for da wimens.

Red one, yellow one, black kinky one,

red-white-an'-blue one for da pa'tri'its.

Dat be da t'ing!

In dis country, David, you can't get ahead by workin' out like dis.

You got to go it on your own, haf saum 'magination, be da boss,

not just another sla'f like we be here day after day. You and me, David,

put our money all tagetder open up dat factoree. We go 'raound

fraum door to door, sell dem wigs, tell da wimens it be da
    latest t'ing.
An' we be da fidders, you and me! Saum job!
First place we go be to dat hippy girl live up da road from
    our place.
Why, she be saumt'ing like you never see!
Saints in da trees! What we do without da wimens!
Dis life ain't built for to live it all alone.
Ah be forty-five, dat half of ninety, what ah'll never see,
before ah find my wimens. An' all dem years ah livin' to
    myself in dat
tin can wid nauthin' but my goddamn dawg. We ain't
    built to live dat way!
you got to haf saumbody be wid, saumbody talk to, cry
    wid,
roll around da bed, sid across da table from.
You can't live touchin' nauthin' but a goddamned dog!
Da Lord make plenty mistake when he build dis place an'
    us is what ah t'ink,
on'y you don't tell da priest ah say so, but one t'ing he got
    right
was whan he made da wimens. David, you know what I
    mean —
how your hand ache to hold 'er. Dey be so different fraum
    da likes of us.
Like mah cat an' dog what loves each odder an' don't fight
only cuddle up and lick each odder all the time.
Wimens is good for da pecker an' da soul.
And, Mister, you get 'em bot' in one
and you got saumt'in' better 'an da world!
Aow! All dis talkin make me itch to see her,
haf' saum tea an' touch her face. (*Beat*)
So why ah be here wid you all da afternoon? Good-bye!
    Ah see you!

Antoine and David exit.

ALICE TWISS

ENSEMBLE. Beside the brook, below the road, just down from
　　　Jerry's
　　and just above the river, the old grist mill stands,
　　by far the biggest building in town, plain and solid, quiet,
　　　functional,
　　not a single frill.

*Alice enters and assumes her position just inside the door of the
mill.*

　　The mill is Alice Twiss's junk store now.
　　Four stories high and filled to the top, each floor, each
　　　enormous room
　　glutted, crammed, pressed full, mounded to the ceiling
　　with everything anyone could ever pick up and carry away.
　　And narrow passages leading here and there through the
　　　dark.
　　In all of humanity only Alice knows what's there and
　　　where it is,
　　and the place so full the things spill out into the sun
　　between the building and the road,
　　beside the brook, behind, along the river,
　　old drays, sledges, sleighs, Coca-Cola coolers.

ALICE. When her pick-up's there she is too and waiting just
　　　inside the door
　　on a stool in the faint light of a window
　　that hasn't been washed in a hundred years.
　　She: Alice: the Minotaur, returned, this time friendly,
　　creator, keeper, guide to the Labyrinth of Judevine
　　(mythology forever repeats itself but never exactly)
　　this time not half-bull, half-man but half-woman, half-man
　　as you will see.

DAVID. I pull my pickup off the road and stride toward the
　　　mill.
　　For a moment I am Theseus.
　　(*David acts out the Theseus-Labyrinth scene*)
　　I will wander down the Labyrinth unraveling a ball of
　　　string

and when I find the beast I will slay it,
follow the yarn back to the light of day, back to my
    Ariadne,
back to Athens where I will assume the throne, abandon it
    and create:
ALL OR DAVID. Democracy!
DAVID. Nah.
This is another time and I don't like such fantasies.
What's here is good enough. What I want to say is what I
    see.
This is not Epidaurus, nor am I the prince. Besides,
you don't need string. Alice has a flashlight.
I mount the granite steps.
Hi Alice.
ALICE. Hi.
DAVID. I'm looking for a handful of
three-eighths-inch, fine-thread, reverse-turn bolts.
ALICE. Yuh.
ENSEMBLE. She rises, turns on a flashlight whose batteries are
    almost dead
and follows the yellow glimmer down passages so narrow
    sometimes
the searchers must move sideways, stoop and duck,
    passages
more like tunnels, vague shapes looming on all sides,
    dangling overhead,
lost in gloom. Then, turning in the chill, she stops, reaches
    through the murk,
extracts, from a heap of chairs, snowshoes, old tables,
    electric motors,
overcoats, hammer heads and ax handles,
a rusted metal box and out of it she takes a handful of
three-eighths-inch, fine-thread, reverse-turn bolts.
ALICE. Two dollars.
DAVID. At the door again, I pay her, and with business done
    her taciturnity dissolves and we have a visit.
DAVID. You been fishin' lately?
ALICE. I was out at daylight just this morning up on Pond
    Brook,

but I only got enough for breakfast.

DAVID. Usually you do better than that.

ALICE. Usually I get my limit. But Sam Hines has got that brook cleaned out.

DAVID. He doesn't!

ALICE. He does! He don't stop when it's time to quit, ya know. You know he takes too many.

DAVID. You don't do so bad yourself.

ALICE. But I stay within my limit. It' ain't right the way he does.

ENSEMBLE. Like many women in these parts she loves to hunt and fish.

Her pick-up has a camper on the back and in the rear window a gun rack

from which she hangs, depending on the season,

a shotgun, a 30/30 or a fishing pole.

She catches more trout than Sam Hines and between them every summer

there is a not-so-private competition.

DAVID. Alice has won Jerry's buck pool more than any man in town.

ALICE. Alice has a bike, a Harley Davidson,

which she rides to work each day the weather's good.

ENSEMBLE. She keeps the bike as clean as she keeps herself,

wheels free of mud, chrome gleaming. The bike has saddlebags,

the rigid kind, and rear view mirrors looming above the handlebars.

From each mirror flows a raccoon's tail off animals she's shot herself.

Alice claims she's had the thing up to a hundred and twenty ...

David laughs quietly but incredulously. Alice and the ensemble give him a hard stare.

DAVID. I believe her!

ALICE. Although Alice deals hard and won't dicker, once you get to know her

you can tell her what you want and she will dig for it,

      bring it 'round
and be fair about the price.
DAVID. I love Alice. Unlike visiting with a man, I never feel,
     when I'm with her,
that twang of competition. And unlike visiting with a
     woman,
I never feel the discomforting, exciting dance of sexuality,
the aching in the fingertips.
Being with Alice is undistracted relaxation, unmitigated
     pleasure
in the presence of another being whom I can love and she
     love me,
no strings attached.
I know this simple, crippled joy with no other human in
     this world.
I was down to Jerry's not long ago and Alice was there
which is not unusual since it's where she goes to warm
     herself in the winter
when the mill's too cold to stand the place for long.
There was a woman with her, older than Alice and slight,
     but taller.
She wore a dress.
I said, hello, paid for my things and left, aware of an
unwanted, disconcerting jealousy.

TOMMY STAMES

Tommy Stames enters hunting deer.

ENSEMBLE. Tommy Stames spent eighteen months in Vietnam,
     Pleiku, Danang, Hue.
Names, strange, not at all like Judevine.
Folks around here didn't say much about his being in the
     war, mostly
they just tried to make him feel at home.
But some said he was nervous, he had changed.
Or maybe it was they who moved around him at a distance
circling like dogs around a bear
wondering what it was was in their midst.

When deer season came, Tommy got his deer as he had
     always done
every year since he was twelve. He was the greatest hunter
     on the hill
and now everybody knew
he was somehow even greater.
(*An ensemble member strikes a slap stick or snaps a board*
to the floor to create an imitation rifle shot)
One shot dropped his buck, as always, and
as always, as the seven times before,
he dressed his deer in the accustomed way, opening the
     belly
from sternum to vent, his knife slipping cleanly
through the hide and flesh.

The ensemble begins a high pitched, strange, eerie, discordant, only
slightly musical chord, which, once established, begins to change
pitch randomly.

Then a new maneuver.
His knife wrung the genitals, extracting the penis and the
     testicles
and with them a tab of belly skin.
He hung them by the fleshy ribbon in a tree
just as he had done in Vietnam.
(*The strange sound quickly stops*)
When the people heard of it, the men snickered and said
they'd have to try that next year,
(*The strange sound begins again*)
and the circle widened and we moved at a distance
like dogs around a bear, wondering
what it was was in our midst.

GRACE

David and Grace enter.

DAVID. Grace lives in a trailer on the edge of town, down
     along the river.
She's got three kids. She had a husband, but he split.

I saw a questionnaire once that she'd filled out asking
   parents
if they'd volunteer at school. All she said was,
"I'd like to, but I go no time."
GRACE. Well, we get up at half past five, my husband and
   myself I mean
and he is out the door by 6:15. Then I get up the kids and
   them and me
we all leave together a little after seven. I take Doreen to
   school,
then drop the other two to Mrs. Fairchild's and then I go
   to work myself.
When I get done I pick up the kids to Fairchid's and we
   get home by six.
My husband, he gets home about an hour later.
By the time we get our supper there's no time left for
   nothin'.
We live like this six days a week, even Saturdays.
And Sundays, we try to work around the place,
you know, get in the wood
or fix the goddamned car.
DAVID. Since her husband left she's given up her full-time job
   and things for Grace and for the kids have gone down hill
   which is no doubt one of the reasons she got into so much
      trouble . . .
but, ah . . .
Grace will speak for herself.
GRACE. The hell I will.
DAVID. Well, she can speak for herself.
GRACE. You're goddamned right I can.
DAVID. Will you? Please.
GRACE. I got nothin' to say.
DAVID. You do too.
GRACE. Why do you want me to do this anyway?
DAVID. It's your chance to have your say, to tell your side
   and tell it like you want it told.
GRACE. Why should I bother? Nobody'll listen anyway.
DAVID. I will.
GRACE. Big fuckin' deal.

DAVID. Thanks. Are you going to tell your story?

GRACE. Alright, alright, Mr. Poet, only maybe you won't like
   it.

DAVID. Maybe.

GRACE. It ain't no Vermont picture postcard.

DAVID. Good.

GRACE. I suppose you want to hear about the time I had to go
   to court.

DAVID. That'd be a good place to start.

GRACE. Voyeur, ain't ya?

DAVID. Yes. Just like everybody else.

GRACE. True enough. Only everybody else don't write it down.
   Where do you get off anyway, undressing all of us in
      public?
   I've heard about those poems you write. I've heard that's
      what you do.
   I know how you do it. Fiction. Fiction, shit. I can barely
      read
   but I know fiction. Those people read your stuff really
      think
   you made us up?

DAVID. I made up you!

GRACE. Bullshit to that! How could you?
   I'm talkin' to you, ain't I?
   Christ, you're stupider than I thought!

DAVID. Are you going to tell your story or stand around and
   dump on me?

GRACE. Maybe I'll do both.

DAVID. Fine!

GRACE. You just want me to embarrass myself don't you?

DAVID. No! I just want you to have your chance!

GRACE. Okay. But nobody will listen. Nobody around here ever
   listens.
   Everybody around here ...

DAVID. You already said that.

GRACE. Shut up! I'm talkin' ain't I? Everybody around here
   already knows
   what they think of me. They think I'm a beast or some-
      thing. They think

I'm not sorry for that time. Well, maybe I'm not. Huh?
Maybe I'm not sorry. How about that!
I didn't mean to hurt her! She's my baby, ain't she? She
    came out of me ...
All I wanted was some quiet. What's so wrong with that?
She was screamin', I mean screamin'. She'd been doin' it
    for days.
You can only stand so much of that. I stood as much as I
    could stand
and then I hit her. I hit her. I hit her and I hit her! I
    wanted to ...
(*Grace means to say "I wanted to break her face,"*
but she can't bring herself to say it)
Do you understand?
No. No. You don't ... because you can't,
because you are always in control, you always got yourself
    together.
No. You could never understand. I love my baby. I love
    her and
I wanted to break her face. Both. Both! Both those things,
    not just one.
Goddamnit, not just one!
That's what I told the judge, but he's just like you.
DAVID. Anymore on that?
GRACE. No.
DAVID. What ... ah ... what about the way they say you
    sleep around?
GRACE. What! Gimme me a break, will you, David? Who says
    that? Edith?
How could I? When? You know what my life is like.
I would if I could, if I ever got the chance. Why not?
You think I'm made of stone or somethin'? You think I
    wouldn't like
to have somebody I could be with, share all my troubles
    with,
do chores and keep this place together with?
You think I wouldn't like that?
To have somebody to sleep up next to, to hold on to? ...
You're goddamned right, Mister, because it's comfort!

It's warm and good, I mean, sometimes it can be.
Fun is what I mean. Fun!
We could stay at home all day someday in the middle of
the week,
just him and me, and lounge around all morning, have
lunch together,
take a bath and get in bed and make love, and stay in bed
together,
naked, and watch TV all afternoon until the kids come
home from school.
You don't think I'd like that? By Jesus, you are a fool!
You and everybody else in this goddamned place.
I hate this place! I hate it!
And I hate you!
I'd get out of here tomorrow if I could. I'd go someplace
if there was someplace I could go. I'd take the kids and I'd
go. I mean it.
I don't care what people say, to hell with them, and you,
and this goddamned place to ...
Vermont! Vermont. Fuck Vermont.
And fuck you too. I'm not sayin' any more.

Grace and David exit.

HI!

*Conrad enters. A pretty, young woman, a novice cross-country skier,
her clothes demonstrating obviously that she is from down-country,
enters and crosses over. Conrad stops, watches her. The skier passes
Conrad. Conrad watches her with that mixture of envy, lust,
disdain, hatred, self-hatred, incredulity and rage that the poor
always feel for the rich. As she passes Conrad, the pretty, young
woman warbles: "Hi!" Conrad watches her go off, then turns and
looks at the audience.*

JERRY WILLEY'S LUNCH

CONRAD. Before Jerry got the garage
we worked for the Mountain Company down in Stowe

helping New York ladies off the lifts,
all day on top the mountain freezing our asses off
for two and a quarter an hour.
(*Jerry enters and begins miming the narrative*)
We never brought a lunch, not once in all those years,
just six pieces of bread, a jar of mayonnaise and sodas
    which
each morning when we reached the mountain top
we placed inside the warming hut beside the skiers' lunches
left there so they wouldn't freeze.
As always Jerry said:
JERRY. Hell, I ain't eatin' salt pork and macaroni when I got
    these!
CONRAD. Then he'd unwrap half a dozen skiers' sandwiches,
    extract a slice or two from each — roast beef, corned beef,
    ham . . .
Whoa! . . . pastrami!
rewrap them carefully and fix our lunch.

DOUG AND BOBBIE

Doug and Bobbie enter.

BOBBIE. Doug is better than six feet,
    weighs more than two hundred and fifty pounds.
He has a couple of teeth missing up front
and his voice is high and pinched. It doesn't belong to his
    body.
DAVID. When Doug laughs he sticks his enormous stomach
    out,
    throws his head and shoulders back and laughs loud, with
        his mouth open,
    like a picture I saw once of a Russian peasant, in *The
        Family of Man*
    Until recently Doug jumped from job to job never keeping
        one
    more than a couple of months.
EDITH. Shiftless bum is what he is. Only thing he ever done
    regalar is eat.

BOBBIE. But he always had work.

DAVID. People hated him for that, and for his saying,

DOUG. I try not to work too much in the winter.
Gets in the way of my snow machinin'!

DAVID. Doug has cut logs and pulp, worked at the Firestone
store in Barre,
been a mechanic in Burlington, worked for the highway
and the railroad,
been a farmer, a carpenter, trucked gravel, pumped gas,
driven a school bus,
been a janitor down to the elementary school, a security
guard at Ames
and worked on the lifts for the Mountain Company
and in all the years I've known him he's never been fired,
he always quits.

CONRAD. Doug worked on the lifts when me and Jerry did.

JERRY. Yeah. We drove to work together;
eighty miles a day round trip so we could
freeze our asses off

DOUG, JERRY, CONRAD. for two and a quarter an hour.

JERRY. All day on top that mountain bowing and smiling,
helping those New York ladies off the lifts.
But we got the turkeys too didn't we?

DOUG. Well I guess.

JERRY. As the chair topped the rise, we'd reach out, offer the
skier a hand ...

DOUG. (*Incredulous that a grown man could have such a job*) That
was our job.

JERRY. Then at just the right moment, we'd give a little jerk
and down the turkey would go.

DOUG. Oh! Pardon me ma'am! Excuse me! You alright?
Then we'd help her up, grab a little tit, get her goin',
step on the back of her ski and down she'd go again!

BOBBIE. Doug and Bobbie started farming. But the milk check
is too small!
They can't get by on only cows.

DAVID. The last time I saw Doug he looked serious and sad.
He asked me, *me*,
if I knew of any work. I haven't seen him throw his

stomach out,

his head and shoulders back and laugh in a long time.

BOBBIE. For years Bobbie drove the pickup truck to Morrisville

to sew the flies in men's pajamas at a factory down there.

When you spoke to her about the job, she'd blush and
turn on a heel

like a little girl. She was good. The best one down there. It
was piece work

and she was fast. She quit the sewing when she and Doug
went to farming.

DAVID. Bobbie is beautiful, or could be. Under thirty years of
work and plainness

you can see her body, see her face, those definite, delicate
features glowing.

DOUG. She strides like a doe.

DAVID. In spite of two brown teeth her smile is warm and
liquid.

BOBBIE. Last summer she cut off a finger in the baler,

DOUG. paid her farmer's dues.

BOBBIE. Now she holds her missing finger behind her when
she talks.

She's got something new to blush for.

DAVID. Doug told me once,

DOUG. (*Seriously, with great regret*) I always wanted to go to
college, study, get a certificate,

be a math teacher or somethin'. (*Beat*)

DAVID. Well! We've got a new roller rink down in Morrisville
now

and it turns out Doug's the best one there.

(*Roller rink organ music.*

Entire ensemble skates as David continues)

Six foot, two hundred and fifty pounds, the biggest pot
you've ever seen,

but he moves across the floor so light it seems he isn't even
touching.

He can skate backwards, do a spin.

When he and Bobbie start to dance everybody watches.

They glide and twirl. Bobbie smiles her shy smile,

then Doug draws away on one skate,

a loop, a spin, alone — across the floor.
You can hear his squeaky laugh rise above the noise
of skate wheels and organ.
He spreads his arms and legs apart and floats across the
        floor
smooth as cream,
his body open, leaning on the air.

GOSSIP AT THE RINK

*The skaters come off the floor and converge on the benches and begin
taking off their skates.*

CONRAD. Way to go, Dougie, way to go. I want to tell ya, you
        skate good.
DOUG. You ain't so bad yourself, Conrad.
CONRAD. Well, thing is, I can skate, but I can't twirl like you
        can.
        You're good at twirlin', Doug.
DOUG. You should practice.
CONRAD. Speakin' of twirls, here comes Edith. Hi, Edith, how
        you doin?
EDITH. No better.
CONRAD. Figures.
EDITH. I guess you could see how Grace was hangin' all over
        that Tommy Stames here this afternoon.
CONRAD. I'm kinda glad ...
EDITH. Slobberin' all over each other, right now, out there in
        the parkin' lot.
CONRAD. I'm kinda glad ... to see them two together.
EDITH. I think it's disgusting.
DOUG. You think everything's disgusting, Edith.
EDITH. You can make all the fun you want, Doug ...
DOUG. Why, thank you, Edith, I think I will.
EDITH. but I heard they're shackin' up together.
CONRAD. I know they are, Edith.
DOUG. They been livin' together about a month now, Edith.
        By Jesus, Conrad, Edith here is slippin'.
        She ain't keepin' her ear tight enough to the ground.

CONRAD. I know it! Hey, Edith,
    you got to keep that thing pressed tight
    if you're gonna keep up with the news!
EDITH. Go ahead you two, but you'd think she'd have a little
        shame or modesty
    or something after that awful trial and . . .
DOUG. It was a hearin', Edith, not a trial, it was a hearin' and
    it was a long time ago.
EDITH. Well, I think the two of them hitchin' up together is
        gonna be nothing' but
    T.R.O.U.B.L.E.

*Conrad and Doug look up stupidly from undoing their skates. They
look at each other:*

BOTH. Trouble.
CONRAD. Why is that, Edith?
EDITH. You know very well why.
    Vietnam did something to that boy's inside brain.
    You heard what he did with that deer up in the woods.
DOUG. What'd he do, Edith? What'd he do?
    I want to hear you spell it. What'd he do?
EDITH. It's no use with you two. There's children involved
        here.
    I'm thinking about the children.
DOUG. Gawd!   CONRAD. You're thinkin' about yourself,
                        Edith, like you always do.
EDITH. That boy is a potential madman.
CONRAD. Why he's not!
EDITH. He's a sick boy.
    He's a stick of dynamite ready to go off in somebody's
        face.

*Etc. etc. ad lib for Edith, continuing until Conrad gets to ". . .
calm yourself!" All three talking at once here.*

DOUG. He's a good man.
CONRAD. Calm yourself, Edith, calm yourself!
    (*Edith is finally quiet*)
    Why, you're off the handle!
    I see Tommy with them kids and he treats 'em right.

He loves them kids just like he does Grace. You can tell.

EDITH. There are lives at stake here, children's lives!

Why, you know what they do.

They lie around all day in that trailer naked

and drink beer and smoke dope.

DOUG. Aow! It sounds like heaven to me!

EDITH. You know they're doin' that.

DOUG. Conrad, they're doin' that!

CONRAD. They're doin what?

DOUG. They're doin' that!

CONRAD. They're doin' that?

DOUG. Oh, my God, they're doin' that!

CONRAD. I wish to hell I was doin' that!

Beats roller skatin', don't it, Bobbie!

EDITH. I am thinking about this community.

I am just standing up for what is right.

CONRAD. Oh, yeah, yeah, sure you are. And you're an authority
       on what's right too,

aren't ya, Edith? Why, of course you are. Why ...

you watch that Bill Donahue Show!

EDITH. It is not Bill. It is Phil.

CONRAD. Bill. Phil. What's the ...

EDITH. What's the matter, you got trouble with your inside
       brain?

CONRAD. Hey. I ain't got cable.

EDITH. That's not all you ain't got.

DOUG. Edith, why don't you leave them two alone?

Probably they got troubles of their own. Why don't you
       figure out somethin' else to do with all your extra
       spare time?

CONRAD. Why don't ya ... learn to skate? Learn to skate,
       Edith. Save us all and learn to skate.

EDITH. Bobbie, I'm surprised at you. Why don't you speak
       up?

This is a terrible thing that is happening here.

DOUG. Come on, Bobbie, let's go home.

BOBBIE. I agree with you.

DOUG. What?

BOBBIE. I agree with her!

DOUG. You would.

BOBBIE. All you guys ever think about is Grace. I'm thinking about the kids!

EDITH. That's right.

DOUG. Jesus. Two of a kind.

BOBBIE. And I don't like all that dirty talk either.

CONRAD. Gawd! for awhile there I thought we were having fun.
You sure know how to ruin a good time!

DOUG. Come on, Bobbie. Let's go home.
Snip, snip, snip, all the time Edith. Fer God's sake!
Snip, snip, snip.
Snip, snip. Jesus Christ, Edith. Snip, snip, snip. (*Bobbie and Doug exit*)

TOMMY. I made a little poem for you.

GRACE. You did?

TOMMY. Yeah. You ... ah ... want to hear it?

GRACE. Sure.

TOMMY. It's called "A Fleeting Animal."
When you abandon everything
    and give yourself to me
when I abandon everything
    and give myself to you,
we make a fleeting animal
    of such beauty, passion, nakedness and grace
that I am glad it slips away when we are done
    because this world is hurt and cruel and nothing
that naive and loving and unashamed
    could possibly survive.

ARNIE

Bird sounds: crows, a hawk, maybe a little wind.

DAVID. Arnie and I harvested Christmas trees three falls together.
Arnie is emaciated and always dirty. He shaves only on Saturday nights
before he goes to the bottle club. His face is more wretched than any I have ever seen. (*Arnie enters*)
All I remember about those falls together

is how much Arnie knew about the Second World War
and how his nose dripped. He'd stand in the snow and
     shiver
like a popple leaf and his nose would drip. He never
     bothered to wipe it
except maybe two or three times a day he'd sop it gently
with the back of the glove on his right hand.
He had a filthy, ragged, black and green Johnson Woolen
     Mills jacket
he wore summer and winter. He stole it from the Mount
     Mansfield Company
when he worked there on the lifts, which is okay with me
since those in Stowe steal more from the likes of Arnie
than the likes of Arnie could ever imagine stealing from
     them.
I remember one day. It was warm and we'd eaten lunch
and were lying around with our boots off and . . .
(*The sound of geese going south*)
talking about everything and laughing and somehow I
     said,
because I am who I am, "Life's really good, most of the
     time."
Something like that anyway.
And Arnie began shaking his head slowly and his eyes got
     sad:
ARNIE. Naw. Naw. Not fer me. Most athe time it ain't.
DAVID. Then Arnie raised his head quick, or as quick as slow
     Arnie could,
and his face had been transformed. It was ghoulish,
     terrifying,
as if the gates of hell had tried to swallow him and he had
     got away.
Then he bared his rotten teeth and said, slow, with a grin,
while his nose dripped,
ARNIE. But ah'll survive.
DAVID. Arnie will survive, in spite of the Mountain Company.
     (*The rest of the ensemble surround Arnie and David*)
They will all survive hidden away from down-country
     skiers

and the big money. They will survive, wretchedly, but
they will survive.

And when everybody thinks the gene pool has withered to
a ski bum
and his après-ski bunny, then, unknown to everyone
who's supposed to know, the ways of staying alive will still
be known
by a few outlaws living in shacks along the banks of the
Wild Branch.

ENSEMBLE. Arnie went down to Massachusetts for a couple of
years
to work in a shoe factory.
He made pretty good money,
but he couldn't stand it down there.

DAVID. One fall we were cutting trees up on Elmore Mountain
when color was still in the hills. It was a clear day
and we were up toward the top of the lot looking out over
the Lamoille valley at Eden Mountain about twenty miles
away.

ENSEMBLE. That's when Arnie,
Arnie the Wretched,
the Ugly,
the Stupid,
the Outlaw,
the Poor,
that's when Arnie said,

ARNIE. Lookit that. That's why I live here.

ENSEMBLE. And we looked across the ancient
green and brown
and red and yellow
mountains
and the sky was blue
and some fleecy clouds
and an Osprey hunted the Lamoille
and we stood there
and listened to the wind slip through the spruce trees.

The sound of the wind blowing through the trees. Sound fades.
Lights fade to black.

act 2

GHOSTS

ENSEMBLE. Dangling from a branch nine feet off the ground
in a Balm-of-Gilead that stands beside the mill
below the road down by the river in the center of the
  village
is a baby carriage
which is the high water mark for the flood of seventy
and is why nobody has ever taken it down —
a reminder of the day we were cut off.
We paddled a canoe down the road to Jerry's,
tied up at the gas pumps and watched
cars and porches going down the river.
Nelson Beaudry got twelve trout out of his cellar that day,
but that high water was nothing like the flood of twenty-
  seven.
Then the river washed this place away
and some people say what was left and what's here now
isn't a town at all.
They say it's only ghosts of what once was.
The only people who think this place is real, they say,
are folks who live here;
the rest of the world doesn't even see it,
drives through and doesn't even notice —
which they say is proof
Judevine and all of us who live here really don't at all,
that we and this place are dead
and have been dead for years.

ROY MCINNES

Welding shop sounds. Roy McInnes is working in his welding shop.

DAVID. Roy McInnes is a welder.
He spends his life with chains and block and tackle, steel
  and torches,
lives his days inside a hood looking like a medieval warrior,

peering through a small rectangle of blackened glass,
watching light brighter than the sun.

ENSEMBLE. He listens to the groan of generators,
the crack and snap of an electric arc liquifying steel.
His hands are always dark and on his upper lip
there is a mustache as if wiped there by a greasy finger.
(*Shop sounds stop*)
Roy McInnes speaks quietly and slowly and moves that
way.
He seems at ease inside his body, comfortable there.
When you shake his hand his grip is warm and gentle
and you can feel the calm he carries in his person flow into
your arm.

DAVID. Roy and I were visiting one day, years ago,
after we had got to know each other some,
and we got to talking about work and I said, because
I was afraid to tell the truth, that I'd just about rather
garden
than do anything, to which Roy responded,
and there seemed to be some sadness in his voice,

ROY. Well, I don't know about just about.
All I know is what I'd rather do than anything:
I'd rather weld. (*Shop sounds begin again*)

FEMININE NARRATOR. Roy McInnes is a carpenter who builds
with steel,
with boilerplate and torches. In place of nails he binds his
dream
with hydrogen and oxyacetylene.

DAVID. Shaper, moulder, alchemist, intermediary, priest,
his hands communicate a vision, they create with skill and
grace
an act of intercession between reality and need.

FEMININE NARRATOR. Roy's house and shop are on the edge of
town.
The shop was built in stages. The tall center section
with its steep-pitched roof is sided with slabs from the
local mill,
whereas the lean-to shed on the left is particle board;
the one on the right is homesote.

ENSEMBLE. Summer people say it's ugly,
   but what they can't, or won't, understand is:
   the sidings write a history of its construction.
   Rome wasn't built in a day either.
DAVID. When Roy built the center section he needed an
      opening large enough
   to admit big trucks, like loggers' rigs, but he couldn't
      afford the kind of
   rising, jointed, overhead doors gas stations and garages
      have
   so he found a way to use ordinary storm doors, the kind
      with glass
   so he could get some light in there, by hitching them with
      hinges
   side to side and stacking them three high so that now he's
      got
   two folding doors which make an opening fifteen feet wide
   and seventeen feet high: two doors made from eighteen
      smaller doors.
FEMININE NARRATOR. Roy heats the shop with a homemade,
      quadruple-chamber, oil-drum stove:
   four fifty-five-gallon drums: two side by side above one,
      the fire box,
   and one above the two: a glowing diamond of cylinders
   all welded to each other and held apart by rods and all
      connected by a pipe
   which leads the smoke from one drum to another and
      finally,
   when it has bled the smoke of heat, exits to the chimney.

*Shop sounds begin a crescendo so that by the time David reaches
". . . human speech is pointless" he has to shout.*

DAVID. This is a place where—against the grinder's scream
      and whine,
   the moan of generators straining, the crackling spit of
      metal rent asunder—
   human speech is pointless,
   drowned in a cacophony of unearthly voices.
   (*Shop sounds stop*) And when the machines get still,

it is a place to see through the smoky fog something
    medieval,
brooding, dark, fantastical.

FEMININE NARRATOR. It would be so easy to see this place as
    sinister,
to see the wizard/priest who rules this lair as evil, that
    would be so easy
if you didn't know that he is Roy—
the one who lets the calm of his body flow into your arm
    when you touch his hand.

DAVID. Stand in the highway; look at the shop straight on;
    pretend it isn't what it is; get beyond its function.
Look at its lines, at the proportions of height to width,
    sheds to center section—
an early Christian basilica, or something Gothic.

Some members of the ensemble begin singing medieval music.

FEMININE NARRATOR. The tall center section, narrow, steep-
    roofed — the nave
the sheds — the aisles, roofed over flying buttresses.
And those doors of doors are cathedral doors.

DAVID. There are no rose windows, and it's ratty, but it soars —
    not too high or very gracefully, but it soars!

FEMININE NARRATOR. It is a January day. The doors of doors
    fold open.
Roy appears in hood and grimy apron.

*A large old log truck in need of a tune-up and a new muffler is
heard in the distance and getting closer.*

DAVID. Then just down the road, smoking through the village,
    the penitent comes,
the one who seeks the healing touch of fire.

*Guy DesJardins appears driving a log truck and making log truck
sounds.*

FEMININE NARRATOR. Guy DesJardins, trucker of logs and
    lumber, who just this morning
while loading the biggest butt-log beech he ever saw in his
    life,

snapped the boom.

DAVID. The truck lurches down the road, clam and boom
    dangling,
a wounded beast, Gargantua's broken arm.
Guy shifts down, pulls to the doors of doors and in.

FEMININE NARRATOR. There are no acolytes, no choir,
but the engine sings its cracked and pulsing song
and the censer spurts heady clouds of smoke to the rafters.

DAVID. The truck shuts down and for a moment Guy and Roy
    stand before the diamond juggernaut of cylinders,
their hands outstretched in ritualistic adulation,
a prelude to the mass.

FEMININE NARRATOR. The boom is jacked and steadied,
readied for the altar of cutting flames:
this Mass of Steel and Fire.

DAVID. From the clutter of his accidental reredos Roy brings
    angle iron.

*Shop sounds again appropriate to the action. A quick crescendo and
decrescendo so that all is quiet by the time Feminine Narrator gets to
"the healing touch."*

FEMININE NARRATOR. A ball peen hammer bangs, generator
    moans, light arcs and snaps,
steel flows a second time — a liquid, balm, metallic salve
    and
. . . the healing touch.

DAVID. When the clanging mass is finished.
when the groans and snaps and spits have ceased,
when there is silence, when only a spirituous wisp of
    greasy smoke
ascends toward the blue-foggy rafters,
when Guy stands knowing it is done,
the celebrant lifts his hood and says benediction:

ROY. That ought to hold it, Guy.

FEMININE NARRATOR. They drink coffee from dirty cups, eat
    doughnuts with greasy hands.

*As Guy backs out, the ensemble not involved in the action begins
singing the end of the Hallelujah chorus timed so that the last*

Hallelujah is sung in a retarded tempo and after the final line of the scene.

DAVID. Then Guy backs out, is gone, smoking down the road,
  back to the job, leaning on his horn and waving,
FEMININE NARRATOR. in what has got to be plain-song, a canticle,
  praise and joy for the man,
DAVID. a chorus of Hallelujahs, for the reconciling arc of fire!
EVERYONE. Hal-le-lu-jah!

AT THE LANDING

The landing of a logging operation somewhere in Judevine. Late December, early morning, the sun is about to rise. Antoine is warming himself by a camp fire. Antoine talks to himself, then to the audience.

ANTOINE. Shitacatsass! Freeze like a turd!
  Bull an'jam here outin da snow,
  so cold touch hole fall right out!
  An' dese pants ain't wuth two cents,
  so ain't this discount jacket
  an' these boots got cracks
  from last year. May as well be out here
  dressed in mah bikini.
  Freeze like a turd.
  (*To the audience*) Ah'm gettin' old. Ah can't take this
  too much longer. And then what ah do?
  Live on dat friggin' Social 'curity?
  'baout enauf buy a can a peacesoup once a month.
  Ah work longer than the sun ... you lazy basterd!
  Ah be here 'fore you get oudda bed,
  be here still when you gone hum!
  An'fer what? Make friggin' fifty, eighty dollar
  a week, tear my gut out fer dat?
  An'ah work forenoon Saturday
  just for the government. Da snooty basterds
  take it all! Every friggin' penny.
  It ain't no use. Ah never get ahead.

Da friggin' politicians tax da pants
right off mah wimens. Ah got nathin!
Ah never had nathin. My Poppa,
he never had nathin'.
Why, by the Jesus, I'm so poor
I can't afford to cast a shadow.
I tell dat to them Washin'tonians they say,
"That's okay. We take it!"
An'fer what? So they can waltz araound
down there an' fuck dere sec'ertaries
'steada eatin' lunch! Fuck me!
Thieves, all of 'em.
'ceptin you can't tell it
'cause they wear a suit!
Now you take some poor basterd
up in dis godforsaken place, let 'im steal
a chain saw or a caow, see what happen!
Lock 'im up right naow!
Mister man, I mean right now!
An' why they do that?
'Cause he be a thief? Poof!
They lock him up 'cause he be stupid!
He be too daum ta wear a suit!
Okay. You take me. Say I write my Senater,
say, "Ah'm sorry, sir, but ah be too poor
ta pay da taxes so don't you bother
send a bill." Ah wake up nex' mornin'
in da clinker wi' da chicken thief,
an' mah wimens and da babies be alone.
An' da ones we got right here ta hum,
da ones down to state capitol,
is even worse. Come time dey be elected
they caum 'raound shake mah hand say,
"Ah work fer you, ah be yer sla'f
daown to da capitol." Talk about straight
as serpent did to Eve. Then they get elected
an' you see how their noses get a funny color
from bein' up da touch hole a da millionaires
too long. You see 'em on da street say,

"Ho! ah be Antoine, 'member me?"
Dey push you raound like you be stick of pulp!
Ah, what's dah use? It never be no diff'ernt
'an it be right now. It never was. It never be.
No use. Piss and moan is all I ever do,
'cause it's all there is for da likes a me.
At least it make me feel a little better some.
Preach at dis pile a wood.
Fifty, eighty dollar a week,
an' a hernia every day! Shit.
Basterds. Crooks. Two cylinders.
No use.
Bull and jam. Freeze like a turd.
(*Doug enters*) By Jesus, where ya been? It's
da middle of da afternoon.

DOUG. Couldn't drag myself outta bed.
My back is killin' me. That goddamn crawler
is about to do me in. Pinched a nerve or somethin',
Hurts like hell.
And this weather don't help neither.
I always thought that Conrad was a crazy stupid fool,
but maybe he ain't; maybe he knows what he's talkin'
'bout.
He was sayin' t'other day he thinks this ugly weather's
'cause
of all that walkin' on the moon or 'cause
that air pollution's eatin' holes into the sky. Hell,
you know it's somethin' what ain't natural.
Spring comes too late, fall comes too early,
but it's worse than it ever used to be,
and the birds ain't actin' right.
Too goddamn cold too soon!
Why, this morning when I stepped outside to blink
my eyeball froze right open and my feet froze to my shoes!

ANTOINE. Ah, Dougie.

DOUG. It don't make it easy.

ANTOINE. Dat be da Bible truth!

DOUG. Well, there's only one thing worse than all this crazy
weather

and that's what's called the holy state of matrimony.
Holy, hell! It's like livin' with the devil!
You go out and get yourself a hen, she clucks around
for about a year or two, then she gets broody
and she begins ta cackle; you get too close that hen'll
peck ya. She'll sit around all day, watch them soaps
and all the time be eatin' up your money.
Christ, if I'da known I'da never done it.
It's a terrible price to pay for rollin' 'round the bed.
Jesus! how I wish I'd been smart like Tommy. Stay away
from church and all that marryin' stuff. I wish I'd been
like him. Stop in at night, see his little lady, dip in
and go. That kid is free!
He ain't locked inside a hen house every night.
Hell, it's too late for me. I'm a domesticated cock,
and what's worse there's only one hen in my flock.
By Jesus, I'm a slave for life.
(*To the audience*)
Listen boys out there, stay the fuck away from church.
Don't be like me and spend your life
wishin' you were someplace else and cryin'
to yourself 'bout how you didn't know how it would be.
Take it from me, she can catch you in a minute,
then she'll be done, but you'll have the chain
around your chicken leg for all your days!
You catch one and you think you've got
a sweet young thing, soft as a puffball on a tree.
You get her home and mister you have got a witch!
She'll change into a bully spruce so rough
it hurts to look. And ugly! Christ!
you just don't know! She'll drink your booze
and eat your food, get fatter than a sow.
She'll piss and moan and scream at you.
She'll belch and fart and lock you out!
Don't do it boys! Don't you get caught!
By Jesus Christ, I wish to hell
I'd run until I'd lost her.
ANTOINE. Shitagoddamn! Soun' like you climb onto
    Canadian thistle. A burr in yer ass this mornin'.

Ah always taut your little wimens
be gentle as a doe. What happen to you?
DOUG. Ah, things ain't workin' out just right.
ANTOINE. Wall, ah be here ta listen
if yew wanna talk.
DOUG. It's nathin'.
It'll all blow over, maybe.
Where the hell is Tommy!
Damn near seven o'clock.
If he'd work that dink a little less
and run the chain saw more
maybe we'd get somethin' done.
ANTOINE. Caum on now, Doug.
You take it easy on dat boy.
He be a good worker and you know he be.
You wass a kid once too.
Caum on.
we warm our han's before we go ta work.
TOMMY. (*Enters*) Sorry I'm late. Hard to get up.
Christ, it's cold!
That bed is better than this place.
DOUG. Oh, sure it is, 'cause Grace kept sayin',
"Don't go! Don't go! I want some more!"
You sharpen them saws?
TOMMY. I sharpened 'em.
DOUG. Where's yours?
TOMMY. Down to the woods.
It didn't need it.
Only needed touchin' up.
DOUG. That's no surprise.
It don't dull if it don't cut!
TOMMY. Leeme alone, Doug.
ANTOINE. Tommy, he have bad night.
His back is sore.
DOUG. That ain't it! We're losin' money
with this equipment standin' here.
We got to get goin'!
And this kid here better make up his mind
if he's gonna cut pulp or fuck around.

He's been late all week!

I ain't out here for my health you know.

TOMMY. I told you I was sorry about bein' late.

DOUG. Yer always sorry and yer always late!

ANTOINE. You boys stop dat now!

There be plenty time ta cut da trees.

They be here hunnert years,

mus' be they be here at least till noon.

Dey ain't gonna raun away.

You both sit down, warm up by dis fire,

den we all go to work.

DOUG. Where's that log truck? Where's DesJardins?

We're plugged right up in here.

I got no room to move around.

When's he comin? You call 'im, Antoine?

ANTOINE. Yas! Yas!

He say he be here end da week!

TOMMY. Either one of you got anything to eat?

I ain't had my breakfast yet.

DOUG. You hain't ettin' yet? Well, ain't that a shame!

You're supposed to eat before you come!

Shit, boy, this ain't a picnic!

Why didn't you have your woman for breakfast?

ANTOINE. Doug.

DOUG. You're the one who's always sayin'

how full of vitamins and minerals that stuff is.

Ought to be you could go all day on just ...

ANTOINE. *Doug!*

TOMMY. You're leanin' on me hard, man.

You'd better lighten up.

DOUG. Yeah?

TOMMY. Yeah. Really.

DOUG. Is that right?

TOMMY. Yeah, That's right. (*Beat*)

DOUG. I seen those Darkies you got hangin' around your place.

TOMMY. What are you talkin' about?

DOUG. I'm talkin' about those Junglebunnies you got visitin'

you.

TOMMY. What about 'em?

DOUG. Them your . . . *soul brothers* from Vietnam?

ANTOINE. Caum on, you two. Stop it naow.

TOMMY. Yeah. They are.

That's exactly what they are.

DOUG. Well, we don't like Niggers around here,
and we don't like Nigger Lovers either.

TOMMY. Is that right?
You and who else.

DOUG. Me and that's enough!

ANTOINE. Stop it, Doug!

DOUG. Shut up, Frog!
Why don't you and your nigger friends go somewhere else?
Why don't you take that cute little piece of pussy of yours
and all them Nigger friends and get the fuck out of here!

TOMMY. Oh, Jesus! why can't you wake up!
We're all in this together!
We're all gettin' fucked over in the same way!
Can't you see that?

DOUG. What?

TOMMY. How come you never finished school?
How come you're not a math teacher somewhere
like you wanted to be?

DOUG. What are you talkin' about?

TOMMY. I'm talkin' about
you got more in common with those
"Nigger" friends of mine
than you do with all those white folks
you're always workin' for.
I mean, people like you and me and my friends.
We're in this together! The Man is after your ass too.
Why can't you see that?

DOUG. Are you sayin' I ain't white? You sayin' I'm not white?
You are fuckin' crazy, man. Edith's right. You're crazy.
I'm white, Mister. I am white!

TOMMY. Yes. That's right.

DOUG. No black man is my friend.

TOMMY. That's right. You're right.

DOUG. I ain't no Nigger and I ain't no Gook.
   I am white.
TOMMY. That's right. You *are* white.
DOUG. (*To Antoine*) He's crazy.
ANTOINE. It's you! (*Doug moves away*)
   (*Antoine approaches Tommy*) Let it go, Tommy.
   Caum on. I got saum breakfast here for you.
   Here's saum coffee an' saum bread da wimens make last
      night,
   and saum apple jelly, and . . .
   Ah! and lookie here! Ah got a leg a chicken too.
   Caum on, Tommy, eat. Eat, Tommy. Eat.
   How be your little wimens?
TOMMY. (*With a mouthful*) Good.
ANTOINE. Good. You babies ever t'ink baout maybe you get
      married?
TOMMY. We're talkin' on it.
   But, Antoine, it's a scary thing,
   especially for . . . well you know . . .
   for Grace and me.
ANTOINE. Wall, yas, I know.
   but if you don't try to start again . . .
   why be alive?
TOMMY. Yeah, well, we been talkin' on it
   and pretty serious, too.
ANTOINE. Good. Dat be da t'ing ta dew: get married.
   Betterin livin' to yourself, Tommy.
   Ah be forty-five, what's half of ninety
   what I'll never see,
   before I find my wimens.
   It be da best t'ing dat ever happen to me.
   You need saumbody to be wid,
   talk tew, share. It gets to be
   like bein' just one person.
   It's no good to be alone.
TOMMY. Jesus, don't I know.
ANTOINE. We were meant to go two by two.
TOMMY. Thank you, Antoine.
   Well, I better get to work.

Tommy starts his exit toward the woods. Doug has been watching from a distance.

DOUG. Tommy. What I said ... that weren't right.
I'm ... sorry. I'm sorry, Tommy.
It's just ... it's just we're earnin' nothing out here
but our deaths!
Ah! never mind. (*Tommy exits. Arnie enters*)
ANTOINE. Ho! Look who it be!
DOUG. Aw, Christ, hang on to your wallet!
Lock everything up! Here comes Arnie.
ANTOINE. Wall, Arnie, how you be?
What you up to 'sides no good?
Workin' naow?
ARNIE. Naw. Can't find nathin'.
DOUG. I bet you ain't lookin' too hard neither.
Can't afford to have a job, old Arnie can't,
always gettin' in the way of his goin' to jail.
Christ, this country's goin' broke just buyin' grease
to lubercate the jail house door
he's in and out of there so much.
ARNIE. I was wonderin' if you could take me on.
Things is terrible narrow just right now.
DOUG. Oh, no! Oh, no! Antoine, I'm warnin' you.
He comes, I go. I ain't workin' with him anymore.
We'll go broke just puttin' back all the stuff he steals.
That bastard'll steal the shirt right off your back,
won't ya, Arnie? Why not tell 'im
where you got that jacket?
ARNIE. Mountain Company give it to me
when I got done.
DOUG. Give it to you, shit.
You stole it and you know it.
ARNIE. Wall ... I had it caumin'.
DOUG. Sure you did. So did we all.
Only maybe you should say how come
you got one big enough for me.
ARNIE. Only one I could get a holt of.
DOUG. Bullshit to that! You're a liar too.

That's the one you stole from me.
I ought to tear that thing right off your back
right now only I couldn't stand to touch it.
It smells too bad. (*Doug exits*)

ARNIE. Ugly ain't 'ee.

ANTOINE. He ain't functionatin' right, today.
Got a splinter in his pecker.
Ah wish we had a place for you, but just now
we ain't. Da boy down to da woods,
Doug bouncin 'raound on dat crawler
an' ah be here at da landin'.
Nathin' you could do. Ah wish dat we could
help you out. Ah don't know how long we be here
anyway. Dat crawler just about to come apart to pieces.
When that happens we be done.
How be your little wimens? I hear da two of you
be back together.

ARNIE. Yas, we're back together, but it ain't no better.
Just like it used to be. She's just as ugly
as she always was. Mister, she drinks whiskey
like you used to drink that beer.
I'd be better off livin' with a bobcat.

ANTOINE. Wall, dat too bad. A man shouldn't haf to wear
'is hard hat in da house.

ARNIE. I know, Christ, if I had the money
the first thing I'd do is buy her a funeral.
Wall, I won't keep ya.
Lemme know if you can use another hand.

ANTOINE. Ah will. (*Arnie begins exiting*)
Arnie ... ah be sorry. (*Exit all*)

WHAT I HEARD AT ROY MCINNES'S

Roy's welding shop again. Roy and David are in the shop.

DAVID. I was down to Roy McInnes's one other time the
winter that
Antoine, Doug and Tommy worked together in the woods,
and Guy DesJardins stopped in that time too.

I think Guy stopped in every time he passed through
    town,
just to warm himself, have a cup of coffee, say hello.
(*Guy enters the shop*)
Guy came through the door within the doors of doors
    stomping
and doing that little wintertime dance we all do
where you exhale rapidly and hop back and forth from
    foot to foot
while you pat your hands and say,

GUY. Jesus! Roy, is it cold enough for you?

DAVID. I can't remember what Roy said to that
but you're supposed to think of something funny.
Guy said "Hi" to me and I said "Hi" to him and the three
    of us
gathered around Roy's quadruple-chamber, oil-drum stove.
They began to talk and I began to listen.

ROY. Where you workin' now, Guy?

GUY. I'm drawin' logs and pulp off the landing up to where
Antoine and Doug are cuttin', the old Mead place,
on the other side of Bear Swamp. You know the place?

ROY. Well, I guess I do. My grandmother lived up there
when she was just a little girl.
before my family came down off the mountain
and settled down here in the village and got civilized.

GUY. They did, did they? How come it never took with you?

ROY. I've wondered that myself. Speakin' of wild ones,
is that Stames boy still workin' with those loonies?

GUY. Yes, sir, he still is. He's been workin' with them steady
since early this past fall.

ROY. Huh. He's stuck with them that long. Huh.

GUY. Yes sir.

ROY. It may be that that boy is settlin' down.

GUY. Well, you know, he's got himself a family now.
What with Grace and the kids and all that kind of thing.
I think it gives him something to look forward to,
something to go to work for, and Jesus Christ,
you know a woman's good for any man.

ROY. No. I didn't know.

TOMMY'S DEATH

Jerry's Garage.

FEMININE NARRATOR. Antoine and Doug and Tommy cut logs
  and pulp right through that winter
  and into spring. When the black flies came out they gave
    up
  working in the woods and each went his separate way,
    found summer jobs
  or no jobs at all.
  Tommy went on living with Grace and they both seemed
    happy
  as far as anybody could tell and Grace's kids did too.
DAVID. I saw Grace down to Jerry's once that next spring and
  she had a pretty bad shiner but nobody said anything
    about it, of course,
  and what people thought, if anything, I can't say.
FEMININE NARRATOR. Then it was summer, the middle of
  July ...
DOUG. (*Entering, to the others already there*) Tommy Stames shot
  himself.
CONRAD, ALICE. What? What?
DAVID. What'd you say?
DOUG. Tommy Stames killed himself.
CONRAD, ALICE, DAVID. What? What'd you say? Oh, my God.
DOUG. He shot himself up to his camp.
CONRAD. Where? Up to his camp?

Jerry enters or comes out from underneath a car or something.

DOUG. (*To Conrad*) Up to his camp. Antoine came and got me.
CONRAD. (*To Jerry*) Tommy Stames killed himself. He shot
  himself.
JERRY. Where?   DAVID. Oh, my God.
CONRAD. Up to his camp. He killed himself.
DOUG. Antoine came and got me.
  He left a note for Antoine. All it said was:
  "Thank you, Antoine. You know where to find me."

JERRY. He shot himself?

DOUG. Antoine came and got me. We went up.

We ... we brought him back.

Antoine knew. He knew.

Tommy killed himself. He killed himself.

DAVID. Tommy went up to his favorite place, that little clearing
in the woods.

CONRAD. He had a little camp up there, a fireplace,

a little lean-to made of spruce poles and hemlock boughs.

Why, he camped up there.

JERRY. It was a little clearing in the forest.

ALICE. You go up through the woods and you cross a little
stream

and you come to this clearing in the forest where the light
comes in.

DAVID. Before he killed himself

he made a circle out of stones he'd gathered from the
stream

and in the circle there were bits of bark and twigs,

little signs or symbols, something.

JERRY, DOUG, ALICE, CONRAD. (*All together, each taking a line*)

You go up through the woods and cross a little stream.

Antoine came and got me. We went up. We brought him
back.

A clearing in the forest where the light comes in.

He camped up there. Spruce poles and hemlock boughs.

DAVID. He put himself in the middle of that circle.

FEMININE NARRATOR. He was sitting down.

DAVID. He took his army carbine ...

JERRY, DOUG, ALICE, CONRAD. (*Together, each taking a line*)

You go up through the woods.

He left a note for Antoine

You cross a little stream.

A clearing in the forest.

FEMININE NARRATOR. ... and he shot himself right through
the heart.

He knew exactly where his heart was at.

He didn't miss.

Jerry, Doug, Alice, and Conrad all begin talking continuously, repeating lines and fragments of lines from earlier in the scene until they all abruptly stop as the Feminine Narrator says, "with the pebbles from the stream." Grace enters.

DAVID. He fell backward on the ground.
He was laid out on the ground . . .
Like Jesus on the cross, with his arms spread out.

FEMININE NARRATOR. He died right away and right inside
that stone circle he had made
with the pebbles from the stream.

The others stop talking. They all see Grace.

DAVID. You could tell he didn't suffer.
He looked so peaceful, like he felt good . . .
like he . . . finally felt good.

SOMEONE FROM THE ENSEMBLE. In the forest where the light
comes in.

FEMININE NARRATOR. And on his shirt he had pinned a little
piece of paper
and on it he had written:
Grace and Peace be with Me.

All turn and stare at Grace.

GRACE. *No!*

THE HOPPER PLACE

ENSEMBLE. Down Creamery Street just across the tracks
there's a burnt-out cellar hole full of rusting junk and charred
remains—
what's left of where the Hoppers used to be.
Yeah, they're in a shack now, up on the bank behind the
ruin.
There's the Hopper woman, two of her men, six kids and a
goat all in that shack,
or so people say anyway; I dunno.
Always, summer and winter, three snow machines
and at least that many kids are scattered in the dooryard.
Those Hoppers have it good bein' as they're on Welfare,

Food Stamps and every other give-away you can get.
Oh, I know it. I wish I could just sit around on my ass, ya
    know, wouldn't have ta work,
just get hand-outs given to me an' things like 'at.
At school the kids all say the Hopper kids have bugs and
    worms.
which they do,
and the kids won't get near them except to call them names.
Well, I wish I had one of them big old color TV sets . . .
(*Now everyone talking at once*)
Yeah, and I hear they got a couple of VCR's, two stereos and
    everything.
And what about all those snow machines they got around
    there all the time.
They get a new car about every six months is what I heard.
Why they got gold plated fixtures in the bathroom, in the
    sink and shower both!
I just don't know where they get all that money.
Jesus, I just don't know how they do it.
Somebody said they go down to Florida or someplace every
    winter and live in a big hotel and on government money
    too! (*All abruptly stop together*)
ALL. Them Hoppers have it good.

SAM HINES AND THE CHRISTMAS MITTENS

Jerry's Garage.

DAVID. About a week or so before Christmas last year I saw
    Sam Hines —
you remember him, he's the one who's such a fisherman,
the one Alice Twiss claims poaches trout out of Pond
    Brook
something wicked — well, what goes on, what's gone on,
between Sam and Alice over the years is more than we've
    got time for here —
anyway, as I was saying — I saw Sam down to Jerry's
    Garage one morning
about a week or so before Christmas last year
and while we were visiting he said,

SAM. Look at these!

DAVID. And he held his hands out palms up
   to show me a new pair of deer skin choppers
   with hand knit liners made of brown wool.

SAM. The kids give 'em to me for Christmas.
   Little Sam bought the choppers with the money he made
      sugarin' last spring
   and Jenny knit the liners. I got 'em now because they
      couldn't wait.
   Ain't those the nicest pair you ever seen?

DAVID. A few days after that, Sam and all the other parents in
      town
   came down to the school for the Christmas open-house
      and exercises.
   When Sam went to leave his mittens were gone.
   Then a couple of weeks later, Sam was driving through the
      village
   and saw the littlest Hopper boy walking down the road
   with a pair of mittens on so big one of them could have
      been his hat.
   Sam pulled over, rolled his window down, and said,

SAM. Nice lookin' mittens.

THE LITTLEST HOPPER BOY. You mean these?
   Yeah, nice ones, ain't they?

SAM. Where'd ya get 'em?

THE LITTLEST HOPPER BOY. My mother give 'em to me fer
      Christmas!
   She even knit the liners, see?

SAM. Yes, sir, those are *fine* mittens.
   Nicest pair I ever seen.

DAVID. And he rolled up his window and drove away.

*The sound of Sam's pick-up truck fades away then modulates to an
eighteen-wheeler, diesel in the distance. The eighteen-wheeler gets
closer, passes through the village and fades away.*

CAROL HOPPER

Carol Hopper enters and sits on the steps of the Farney place. Truck sounds, now and then, passing through town on wet pavement going both east and west. Horn noises.

ENSEMBLE. Almost any night you can see Carol Hopper on the street,
  out to flee the noise and clutter of the shack,
  her brothers, her mother's boy friends.
  Tonight, November 9th, 8 P.M., thirty-eight degrees,
  an inch of snow in the village, the highway wet,
  headlights and street lights glistening in the road's black mirror.
CAROL. There is a quiet here Carol comes to meet, to be with, almost every night.
ENSEMBLE. She sits in the dark on the steps of the abandoned Farney place.
  She is sixteen, her blond hair, alight in the street lamps,
  is prettier than her face.
  Trucks shift down and grind through the village.

The diesel truck sounds begin again quietly.

CAROL. Westward and eastward, their red and yellow, square-rigged lights
  vanish in the dark and Carol Hopper listens to the engines fade.

Truck sounds fade as sound of wind begins. Sound of the wind.

GRACE SPEAKS

Grace enters. David enters. David sees Grace first.

DAVID. Hi, Grace, I'm ... I'm sorry, Grace. I'm sorry.
GRACE. I don't want your sympathy.
  I don't want to talk to you or anybody else around here either.
  I heard what Edith said about Tommy bein' a stick of dynamite
  ready to go off in somebody's face. Well, she was right, wasn't she?

Only thing that she got wrong was whose face it was
    gonna be.
It's the people around here drove him to it.
They all had him figured out, didn't they? They didn't
    want to listen
to anything except what makes 'em feel all warm and gooy
    or righteous
or somethin'. Nobody ever wants to listen to the truth!
Nobody ever wants to know what Tommy thinks and feels!
(*Grace stops, realizing that she's switched tenses*)
You and your kind can only keep this up for so long.
You can only keep us down for so long, and then one day
    we are going to ...
How are my kids ever gonna get anything better'n what I
    got!
How they ever gonna .... They got to live! ...
You can only make us your servants and your slaves for so
    long
and then we will rise up and swarm all over you
like spiders, like napalm! I am warning you! I'm warning
    you!

DAVID. Grace, I'm not ...

GRACE. You're not one of them? You got land, don't ya?
    You live up there on the hill, don't ya?
    You inherit some money so you could buy that land?

DAVID. Well, I ...

GRACE. I knew you did. I knew you did.
    You know what I inherited?
    A kitchen table, with the formica already worn off.
    You keep sayin' how you want to give me my chance,
    how you want to stand up for me.
    You don't. I know you don't.
    You don't give a shit for me, David.

DAVID. No, Grace.

GRACE. You look at me and you don't even see me.
    All you see is what you want to see.
    I am invisible to you.

DAVID. No! That isn't true!

GRACE. You know what I would like to do?

I'd like to tear out both your eyes!
Then maybe you could see me.
I'm doin' houses now. I mean in addition to working
down to Stowe.
Maybe I could do your house for you. Call me if you want
to.

RAYMOND AND ANN

Raymond and Ann's farm. Raymond and Ann enter. They begin doing the things they do around their place. David and the Feminine Narrator enter.

FEMININE NARRATOR. Raymond and Ann kept to themselves
and because of that
some people thought them snooty and aloof.
DAVID. It wasn't true.
FEMININE NARRATOR. Other people theorized perhaps there'd
been some great pain in their lives,
more than the stillborn child buried on the knoll above the
house,
that kept them from the usual sociability. No one knew.
DAVID. Personally, I think when they came to this mountain
fifty years ago
they wanted only silence and each other and having found
these things they were happy.
FEMININE NARRATOR. Raymond was God's gardener. He grew
the best of everything.
DAVID. His garden always free of weeds, rows so straight
it seemed he planted with a transit.
FEMININE NARRATOR. Although they were poor and everything
about the place homemade,
their farm had a neatness and an order reflective of people
who know what to do and how to do it and who
do not overstretch the limits of their land or themselves.
DAVID. By the time I knew them they were old and didn't
have a team,
only Sandy, middling size, mostly Belgian, who weighed
maybe seventeen-hundred pounds and was so intelligent

if she'd had hands she would have harnessed herself,
intuited the day's work and done her jobs unattended.
I always had the feeling that, though there were other
    animals on the place,
cows, chickens, sheep, a pig, there was an absolute equality
between the man, the woman and the horse.

FEMININE NARRATOR. Raymond was tall, angular and bony.
He carried himself upright to his dying day.
He cackled when he laughed and when he told a joke
he always laughed before the punch line so he could be the
    first.

DAVID. Ann was slim and quick, full breasts and hips,
and although her face was plain, she was to me unspeakably
    beautiful.
She wore her white hair and wrinkled skin the way a
    summer flower
wears its bloom. And in her eyes, even at the age of
    seventy, burnt a fire
so bright and fierce, a passion so intense, it made me feel
    old and worn.
In her presence I was sick at the slackness of my life.

FEMININE NARRATOR. Every afternoon after dinner Raymond
    and Ann lay down together
on the large sofa in the living room, wrapped themselves
    around each other
and took a nap. (*Some few bird's songs begin quietly*)

ANN. Sometimes we slept, sometimes we only lay in the stillness
    listening.

RAYMOND. In the summer we listened to the wind and the
    birds' songs. (*Bird songs end*)

ANN. In winter we listened to the wind and the mute birds'
    little feet
scuttling across the feeder on the windowsill.

DAVID. Often they fell into a half-sleep in which they dreamed
    waking dreams
or they let their minds go still as the room.

FEMININE NARRATOR. They napped like this each day because
    it was a time

when they could come together, these two distinctly separate
people,

touch each other and be very nearly one being in that
place.

DAVID. They had an unspoken understanding that during these
times

they would not talk, but one day Ann said,

ANN. You know, we've been more than fifty years, doing the
same things

day after day, changing only with the seasons and I've
never got tired of it,

oh, angry and frustrated plenty, but never tired. I wonder
if we ever will.

RAYMOND. Well, we had better get to it if we're going to.

FEMININE NARRATOR. They both then saw clearly and briefly
the end of their lives

and they laughed quietly and held each other.

RAYMOND. I was thinking just now about that time, years ago,
after we built this place.

We were young and new and I held you here as we are
now

and I was thinking, I wonder what it will be like to be
here when we're old,

the two of us in shrinking bodies wrapped around each
other.

I think I knew then, fifty years ago, pretty clearly

what it would be like today. I knew how it would feel.

Do you think that means our lives have been too
predictable?

ANN. (*Threatened*) Why should it?

RAYMOND. Well, to see that far ahead and then to get to where
you saw

and look back and see that you were right

seems so strange, predictable.

ANN. Have you enjoyed it?

RAYMOND. Why, you know I have.

ANN. I have too.

DAVID. Toward the end of the sixties and into the early seventies

every summer
there was what Antoine called a "hippy invasion" around
here.
Young people from the cities poured into these hills.
I remember one spring Antoine saying,

ANTOINE. Watch out, boys! Dere really caumin'in dis summer.
Dere's gonna be a million of 'em wash in here like a tidal
wa'f.
Dis place use'd ta be more caows 'an people,
naow we're gonna be more 'ippys 'an caows!

FEMININE NARRATOR. Raymond and Ann became mentors to
them,
elders with Confucian knowledge, replacements
for the parents the kids had left behind.
Raymond and Ann were visions of another way of life.

DAVID. But the influence went both ways
and Raymond took to working in the garden barefooted,
then he went shirtless and got a summer tan, then
he removed his cap and the traditional bronzed forehead
with abrupt demarcation between the sunburn and ashen
skull disappeared.
It was the talk of the town.

EDITH. What's he doing at seventy-something acting like a
kid?
I think it's disgusting!

DAVID. It tickled Ann, and what other people said
didn't bother her at all. It never had.

FEMININE NARRATOR. One summer afternoon Raymond came
in from the garden,
approached Ann from behind, put his arms around her
middle
and kissed the back of her neck. Then his forearms touched
her breasts
dangling unsupported beneath her shirt. And her shirt
was open from the top a few buttons.

RAYMOND. Goodness, what is this?

ANN. What is what?

RAYMOND. This.

DAVID. His hands moved to her breasts and held them.

ANN. Well, maybe you shouldn't be thinking you're the only
one
can learn from hippies. If you can go around with half
your clothes
still on the hook, I guess I can leave half mine in the
drawer.

RAYMOND. Well, I guess you can!

FEMININE NARRATOR. Raymond rested his chin on her shoulder
and gazed down her shirt.

RAYMOND. Does it feel good?

ANN. Sort of strange would be more like it.

RAYMOND. Do you like it?

ANN. Some.

RAYMOND. Would you go out in public the way you are right
now?

ANN. Raymond Miller, you know I'm not a hussy!

Raymond and Ann begin shelling peas.

FEMININE NARRATOR. Early July, the height of summer, clear
and warm and a light breeze
to stir things, cool things, an idle day filled with ease,
gentle and sweet
and a rarity in this ungentle place. A half-dozen days a
year like this,
no more, the others always with some kind of edge to
them, a harshness,
which makes it all the more wonder-filled that this place
should yield
two people such as Ann and Raymond.

DAVID. They were under the dooryard apple tree
at the summer table shelling peas
when they heard the noise.
(*The sound of motorcycles in the distance*)
At first a dull roar in the distance, then closer and louder
until when it passed through the sugarbush just down the
road,
it had to it the sound of war. (*Sound much louder now*)

DAVID AND FEMININE NARRATOR. Then they were there:
(*Ensemble members playing the motorcyclists enter*)

THE FOUR IN DARK GLASSES. Four of them.

> *The following lines divided between the four in dark glasses. As each says his or her line the others continue the motorcycle sounds.*

Four steel helmets gleaming black,
four faces with dark glasses,
four faces pale, ashen,
as if they had been powdered.
In black they came:
black leather jackets,
leather pants,
leather boots,
leather gloves with gauntlets to the elbows
and silver rivets gleaming everywhere.
Their bikes black and silver too—
choppers,
handlebars in the air,
seats leaning back—
they roared into the lane and toward the house and garden.

ANN. The chickens scratching in the dooryard screamed and
     ran away.

RAYMOND. Sandy reared and bolted, broke through the fence
and disappeared into the woods.

> *From here until the motorcycles leave the lines are divided between ensemble members other than Raymond and Ann.*

ENSEMBLE MEMBERS. In black they came, into the garden,
     into the rows of corn, over tomatoes, down rows of broccoli,
     through the fence of peas.
     They wheeled and turned and came again through the
          garden flowers,
     over squash and cucumbers, dill and thyme, carrots,
          potatoes, beans.
     One rider singled out an errant hen and ran her down.

TWO ENSEMBLE MEMBERS TOGETHER. They came again through
     the garden,

ANOTHER TWO. their tires churning and digging the earth,
     spewing soil and broken plants into the air.

ENSEMBLE TOGETHER IN UNISON. They roared toward the two

old people . . .

ENSEMBLE MEMBERS. (*One at a time*) then veered away,
down the lane,
down the road,
over the hill and away.

*Evening birds begin singing, but very quietly as heard from inside a
house with the windows open: barred owl, wood thrush, white
throated sparrow, veery. Some crickets.*

DAVID. After supper on a summer evening.

FEMININE NARRATOR. They were sitting in the cool house, she
in his easy chair.
She looked up at him quizzically; already she had left him,
was in a strange place, alone.

DAVID. He watched the life drain from her face.
She said nothing — not even good-bye.

FEMININE NARRATOR. He sat for a time in the growing dusk
and stillness. Then
as the sun headed down behind the mountains,
he scooped her up into his arms the way you would a child
fallen asleep somewhere away from its bed
and laid her down on the couch where she liked to nap.

*Raymond exits to the barn. As he leaves the house the bird songs,
etc. get a little louder.*

DAVID. He went to the barn and finished chores, then stepped
into the evening
and felt the cold air spilling down the side-hill all around
him.
He listened to the crickets, the barred owl and white
throated sparrow,
the wood thrush.
Then he came inside and went to bed.

FEMININE NARRATOR. In the first light of morning he dug a
grave on the knoll
behind the house next to the child's grave, then went to
the barn
and built a box of rough pine boards from his store of
lumber.

He harnessed Sandy and she drug the box to the knoll
and with her help he lowered it into the grave.

DAVID. He went into the house and picked her up,
he wrapped his arms around her middle and carried her
   upright,
her head rising above his head because she was stiff.

Raymond exits with Ann.

FEMININE NARRATOR. He put her in the box, put on the lid and
   nailed it down.

He covered her over. He filled in the grave.

DAVID. He sat down on the freshly mounded earth and began
   rocking slowly
back and forth. And then he wept. His tears poured down.
He moaned and wailed. He rolled his head and wept.
He shook his fist at heaven. He rose and paced and wept.

FEMININE NARRATOR. He held his face in his hands. He clawed
   his pants, tore at his shirt.
He stomped the earth and smashed a fist into an open
   palm.
He turned his face toward heaven clinched his teeth
and screamed. (*From off, Raymond screams*)

DAVID. When there were no tears left, when he was weak and
   trembling,
he led Sandy to the barn, unharnessed her, turned her out
   to pasture
and went into the house. (*Raymond enters*)

FEMININE NARRATOR. He stood at the window then looking at
   the mountains
and he wept again, this never-ending, accumulated grief
for the inevitable.

ENSEMBLE. You can see him in his house sitting in a chair
his hands folded in his lap his mouth slightly open.
You can see him in his house standing at a window
one hand of fingers pressed gently to his lower lip.
You can see him in his house moving from room to room
his hand trailing his wife's ghost like a child's blanket.

*Slight beat. Remaining lines divided between ensemble members
exclusive of Raymond and Ann.*

ENSEMBLE. The end of summer
and Raymond feels the sun that baked his head pass coolly
now
across his shoulders.
September: red leaves turn white bellies to the rain and
wind.
November: Five o'clock and raining. Chimney smoke lies
down,
crawls across the meadow like a slow, soft snake.
Raymond, having killed a deer, leans against the woodshed
door
and stares at the carcass hanging there. He strokes the
murdered head,
speaks softly words of comfort and wonders why he took
this life.
ANN'S GHOST. (*From off*) Raymond. Raymond! Dinner!
RAYMOND. I'll be right in, Ann.
AN ENSEMBLE MEMBER. There are too many lives in this life, too
many deaths,
and no amount of thought can save him from his grief for
dying things —
not even knowing resurrection sure and green as spring.
ENSEMBLE. (*In unison*) Ah!
ANN'S GHOST. (*From off*) Raymond?
RAYMOND. I'm coming.
ENSEMBLE. Raymond died last spring.
With the man gone the place dies
like an old pine dying bit by bit, from the tips inward.
The outward sign of inner forgotten death.
(*Some bird sounds, a quiet coyote howl in the distance*)
The garden goes to witchgrass, timothy, aster, hardhack,
grey birch, red maple. Balsam, spruce begin
their long reach through the roof of his old car.
One night coyote sits on Raymond's porch and howls;
notice to the rest:
this again is nowhere.
Mullein grows midroad
The roof lets in rain.
Joists buckle, floors warp,

rafters groan and sag.
All give up geometric pretense,
go pulpy soft.
Chimney brick dilapidates.
Someone steals the windows.
Porcupines come in.
The house fills with quills and shit.
Two dead porkys in the sink.
The sofa is a nesting bird's delight.
A broken chair.
Then down. Disheveled nest. Pile of sticks.
There is no in, no out. (*Sound of the wind begins*)
Raspberries sprout from Raymond's sodden mattress.
What boards are left turn black. (*Sound of the wind*)

GRACE AGAIN

Just outside Jerry's Garage.

DAVID. It must have been at least a year between the time
        Tommy died
    and when I saw Grace next.
    I had just pulled in to Jerry's, gotten out of the car
    and was headed into the store, my head down, thinking
        about something,
    as Grace was coming out.
    She saw me first.
GRACE. Oh! Hi, David. Hi.
DAVID. Well, I'll be . . . . Hi, Grace. Boy, it's been a long time.
GRACE. Yes, it has.
DAVID. My gosh, it's good to see you.
GRACE. It's good to see you too.
DAVID. Ah . . . how you doin'?
GRACE. Good. Real good.
DAVID. That's good. I'm really glad to hear that.
GRACE. I got a new boy friend now.
DAVID. Well that's good news.
GRACE. Yeah. We been goin' together, let's see, must be, hell,
    since last winter sometime anyway.

I was workin' as a chambermaid down to Stowe —
at the Edelweiss, you know. He always stays at the
Edelweiss
when he comes up to Stowe.

DAVID. That's good.

GRACE. Yeah, and it's workin' out too. He's good to me, and
good to the kids too.
He always brings us presents, the kids and me, I mean.

DAVID. He's got money?

GRACE. Oh, David, he's got pots of money. I mean, he is rich.
Like you don't know.
He runs an import business in New York or somethin',
I don't know what it is. I mean, he is rich!
He's got an apartment in the city, up on the upper east
side. Eighty-third Street.
It looks out over the East River, thirty-fourth floor. And I
mean, big too.
With big, wide, floor to ceiling windows that look out onto
the river
and across to Queens and Brooklyn.
God, the Brooklyn bridge is so beautiful at night.
The Queensboro bridge is too, that's the one right close to
where we live,
but not so much, not so much as the Brooklyn bridge.
I just love to stand at those windows
after the kids are all in bed
and watch the river and all the lights
and all the lights reflected in the river.
I never thought I'd like New York, but, David,
it is beautiful.

DAVID. (*Sadly, realizing the extent of her fantasy*) Yes, I know. I
used to live there.

GRACE. Well, ah ... that's right, isn't it.
Well then you know ... I mean ... how beautiful it is.
I mean ... at night ... with the lights.

DAVID. Yes.

GRACE. Of course, he won't let us come while the kids are
doin' school.
He says they've got to get their education. He's very big

on education.

But when the kids are out of school, he sends his plane right up here

to Burlington and we fly down to LaGuardia. His chauffeur and his limousine

picks us up and takes us right up to the door of his apartment building.

It's nice, David. I mean it gives me a chance to get out of here.

DAVID. (*Somberly*) That's good.

GRACE. He says my kids have got to get an education so they don't end up like me

and have to spend their whole lives working by the hour down to Stowe.

I mean he is big on education.

DAVID. (*Trying to call her back from her fantasy*) Grace!

GRACE. Oh, Jesus! Look what time it's got to be!

Every afternoon about this time, he calls me on the telephone.

No matter where he is, he calls me on the telephone.

If he's in his limousine he calls me on the mobile phone.

He always wants me home to get his call. I got to go.

It's been good to see you, David. How you been?

You still livin' up there on the hill? I got to go.

DAVID. Okay.

GRACE. It's been good to see you.

I wish we could talk a little longer,

but he calls me every afternoon.

Take care, David. It's good to see you.

As Grace exits, The Youngish Man enters. They bump into each other. David watches the encounter.

GRACE. Oh. Hi .... Hi.

I got a new boy friend now. It's workin' out too.

THE YOUNGISH MAN. What?

GRACE. It's workin' out good.

THE YOUNGISH MAN. (*With his usual cruelty*) You don't know me.

GRACE. (*Realizing he is a stranger and while exiting*) Oh. Oh. Oh.

Grace exits. The Youngish Man continues entering as David watches.

THE YOUNGISH MAN. Jesus! What is it with this place?

REPRISE

The sounds of a summer morning along a river; bird calls: chickadee, white throated sparrow, various warblers, cedar waxwing, morning dove, crow, ducks, an osprey. David enters carrying an imaginary fishing pole and begins fishing. Summer-morning-on-the-river sounds continue.

DAVID. Dawn. A summer morning, and I am fishing on the
    river in Corot's Pool
  which is just upstream from Singing Bridge, a bridge with
    iron grating
  on which your tires sing. I call this place Corot's Pool
    because
  it is a deep, still stretch of water with overhanging trees
  and the hand-laid stone abutments of an old bridge on
    either side,
  and on a sunny morning the light through the trees falls
    upon the water
  and makes a dappled quietude of irresistible tranquility.
  It is the kind of place where Corot would be if he were
    here instead of me.
  For as long as we have been here people have fished here,
  walked here, watched here. (*The cry of an osprey*)
  I cast a lure into the water, then watch the sky more than
    the river.
  I can hear the cry of an osprey: out to find her breakfast.
  But I neither hunt nor work, instead, I climb out of the
    river
  and sit down on the quarried stone of an abutment,
  pour a cup of coffee from my thermos and relax,
  from what was already relaxation, and I think.

The ensemble begins to surround David.

ENSEMBLE. No matter who lives, who dies,
  the seasons never rest.
  Creatures take their turns,
  and the year turns

and turns
and turns.
In spite of all that could be wrong and is,
in spite of all the pain ...
Summer and winter,
and summer and winter,
and summer again.

DAVID. All is change. There is no constancy.

ENSEMBLE. The farmers on the hills and in the bottomland,
what farmers there are left, are already doing chores.
In the village everything is quiet, but soon ...

CONRAD. Conrad will pad the hundred feet from home, unlock
the garage,
turn out the light in the window that says BEER,
put on the coffee pot, turn on the gas pumps and the air
compressor
and then stare out the window
at the empty, early morning road.

ROY. Soon also, just across the railroad tracks and over the
meadow from here,
Roy McInnes, a mug of coffee in his hand, will move from
house to shop,
swing open the doors of doors and begin the day.

ALICE. Alice and her lover will roll over under the covers and
embrace each other.

LAURA. Edgar Whitcomb

EDGAR. and Laura Cate, both retired,

LAURA AND EDGAR. in their separate houses, will rise, prepare
their separate breakfasts,
and go about the things they do to get ready for another
day.

LUCY. And there are those who live their lives alone. Lucy.

CAROL. Carol.

CONRAD. Conrad.

GRACE. Grace.

FEMININE NARRATOR. And there are those who left.
Arnie went back to Massachusetts.
Bobbie and Doug lost the farm and got divorced.
Lucy finally got sent to Waterbury.

And Jerry, good old boy Jerry, remember Jerry?
He dumped his middle-aged wife
and ran off to New Jersey with a twenty-two-year-old girl.

EDITH. I could see that comin' a mile away.

DAVID. And I remember Antoine dancing in the house of his
    body and saying:

ANTOINE. Ah, David! What would we do widout each other?

DAVID. And I remember the ghosts.

ANN. Raymond?

RAYMOND. Ann.

GRACE. Tommy! (*Beat*)

ENSEMBLE. No matter who lives, who dies ...
    Summer and winter.
    And summer and winter.
    Creatures take their turns
    And the year turns
    and turns.
    All is change. (*Beat*)

ENSEMBLE. Midnight. Outside the car it is fifteen below.
    A foot of new snow.
    The village is deserted, dark —
    except for eight street lamps
    and the light in the window
    at Jerry's Garage that says:

ALL. BEER.

ENSEMBLE. The smell of woodsmoke seeps into the car.
    Judevine, ugliest town in northern Vermont,
    except maybe East Judevine!
    disheveled, wretched Judevine —
    is beautiful in the night.
    It is beautiful because
    its couple hundred souls
    have given up their fears,
    their poverty and worry,
    and for a few hours now
    they know only the oblivion of sleep,
    and the town lies quiet in their ease.

The sound of the wind. The wind fades.

additional production notes

CADENCE AND TEMPO: The script for *Judevine* is more like a score for a piece of music than it is a script for a play and it needs more to be conducted than to be directed. It would be good to think about it as a symphony with numerous movements rather than a play with numerous scenes. Therefore, a production of this play rises and falls on the musicality with which this script is approached. This is especially true in the first two scenes, "Prelude and Fugue" and "Where and Who and Spring." These scenes establish the mood and pace, the cadence, of the play. They are the runway on which the play gathers speed and takes off. By the time you get to the last "Spring! Ah!" at the end of the second scene the play needs to be off the ground, full of energy and delight, up in the air and soaring.

SOUNDS: In general, the ensemble-created sounds, bird calls for example, should come *before* the mention of them in the narration. Thus, the geese fly overhead before the line "The geese return." We hear the osprey before the narrator says he hears it. Etc. (However, in scenes like Roy's welding shop, where the sounds and the narrative are so intertwined, this does not necessarily apply.) If you design the set so that there are ensemble areas both down left and down right, then the possibilities for fantastic stereophonic sound effects become unlimited. Various sounds can travel back and forth between ensemble areas or from one area to another: the geese, cars and trucks passing by, a lure being cast into the water from one location and landing in the water at the other location.

HOW MANY DAVIDS? The script is laid out so that one person can play David throughout. *Judevine* has been produced many times, however, with David's part being distributed between all or many, both men and women, in the ensemble. Should you choose to cast *Judevine* with multiple Davids, it is important that David have some kind of defining clothing or object that can be passed from one ensemble member to another as each assumes the role of the poet. In productions where David's part has been shared, the ensemble has used a cap, a pair of glasses, or a pencil as the definitive piece of David's gear, passing it from one narrator to another.

FEMININE NARRATOR: The Feminine Narrator should be close in age to David. Both should be fairly young, so that they make a couple in the scenes they narrate together. This is especially important in "Raymond and Ann."

ACCENTS AND DIALECTS: *Judevine* is most effective, I think, when "New England" accents are avoided altogether. The only character really in need of a little accent is Antoine, and his can be slight. Fake, generic accents are worse than none at all.

INDIVIDUALS, NOT TYPES: The people in this play are unique. Tommy is not the typical Viet Nam vet, Grace is not the typical poor white single mother, Alice is not the typical butchy lesbian, Doug is not the typical fat redneck. Although each character can be placed more or less within a group of people he or she is first, foremost, and always, before any representation of a class or a type, a sacred and distinct individual.

jo carson

daytrips

author's introduction

This piece is for Marie; it is, in great part, autobiographical. It was very hard to come by.

It is the first thing I've written that is autobiographical since bad poems in junior high school. I'm not much inclined to autobiography. I do write out of things that concern me, things I find wondrous or troubling or funny, and I'd heard people speak of writing like treading water, you do it or you drown, but I'd never written anything that way before.

I wrote *Daytrips* to tread water.

We kept my mother, Ree in the play, in my parents' home for eight years. She is still alive as I write this essay; she is in a residential home now. When she cannot walk anymore, we will have to make other arrangements.

Rose is also alive as I write this and in a nursing home. The week after we put my mother in a professional care facility, Rose had a stroke (and fell) and was partially paralyzed. Rose has recovered some use of her right side but not enough to come home without full-time care.

My life had never before changed so radically as it did the week we were no longer directly responsible for their day-by-day care.

And I was never the primary caregiver. I had the leisure to come home and write. And I did write. At least three times the material in the play. And other stuff.

My father was the primary caregiver.

He is not in the play because I don't want to put words in his mouth. He is very much alive and can speak for himself.

The play is out with his blessing. He said, when I finally had the courage to show it to him, "I'm glad you wrote it."

It uses the three women because I wanted the piece to be about more than Alzheimer's disease — there is a victim in it so it runs that risk — and the generations are a study in duty and madness.

Duty is always tough stuff.

And the madness is not just of the two older women, all three are mad, Pat is considering murder except murder might really be the greater kindness and then, what is the duty?

I didn't know then. I don't know now.

I've come to understand *Daytrips* is a version of *No Exit*. I didn't know what it was writing it.

I was collecting pieces, lots of them, journalism, fiction, monologue, dreams, poetry, scenes, some with references in them that skipped all over forty years and no intent except treading water. Four or five years worth of pieces.

I woke up one morning and it had achieved critical mass. It was a play. So I set about making a play of it. I spent a year on and off trying to make the narrator go away. I know perfectly well that readers for theatres hardly crack plays with narrators in them. For good reason.

Except I couldn't beat this one off with a stick.

And past tense in the theatre doesn't work, so, if a narrator was going to be there, there had to be two present tenses somehow. And then it had to be present tense over forty years with nothing linear about it except emotion.

Oh, hell.

So I made an arbitrary decision.

Don't worry about two present tenses and forty years, just tell the story. A friend says "don't worry about the mule going blind, just load the wagon." And this script, three productions later, is what has come of it.

The first reading was done by a small, grow-your-own-plays sort of theatre I work with sometimes called The Road Company. We did it for an Alternate ROOTS (Regional Organization Of Theatres, South) annual meeting and people laughed and wept through the whole thing. I was shocked and honored.

The first production was by The Road Company with the theatre department of the University of Virginia/VPI at Blacksburg, directed by Bob Leonard. The second, billed as the world premier, was at the Los Angeles Theater

Center, Los Angeles, directed by Steve Kent. The third, the east coast premier, was at the Hartford Stage Company, Hartford, Connecticut, directed by Michael Engler.

I've been told I should be put in jail for saying some of this stuff out loud.

I've been told by a woman who was a caregiver for eighteen years that I speak for her and she is grateful. She was weeping and laughing.

I've been told "It's not dark enough yet, the South is a dark and terrible place, I know James Dickey, I saw *Deliverance.*" I was weeping and laughing.

I've been told it cannot "be sat through by normal people."

I've been told I had no right to make something that serious the least bit funny.

Take your pick.

It won the Joseph Kesselering Award in 1989. I was on a pay phone in a motel parking lot at the edge of the Navajo Lands in Gray Mountain, Arizona, when I heard the news. I was jumping up and down, weeping and laughing one more time. A truck driver asked if I was all right. "Fine," I told him, "fine!"

He said, "Lady, you could have been bit by a snake and made it to a telephone and that'd be true."

The big things I learned about writing from writing this play are (1) that comedy is about survival and (2) that if I am not scared of what I am trying to write, I'm not working hard enough.

The things I've learned about me from living the stuff of it surface on a day-by-day basis. Some of them I like, some of them I have to live with.

characters

PAT/N(ARRATOR): Forty or so. They are the same person and *two people play her.* There is a rational and an irrational world in this piece. Pat is caught in these stories. The narrator has the perspective to tell them and to comment. The narrator speaks with the audience.

REE/IRENE: They are the same person and one person plays the part. Ree is a victim of Alzheimer's. Words do not say what one visit with a victim can say. Ree is seven or so years into her illness. Ree is not old (65 or so) but she is so unsure of herself it looks like the same thing. Ree lists to the left. Ree is sometimes like a ghost herself. Ree keeps her distance. When she comes close to someone, it is an agressive move. Ree has a sound track which does not make logical sense and cannot be stopped in the middle. There are moments in which the emotional content makes good sense and the logic does not make sense at all, other moments of surprising lucidity. Irene is about 40, healthy. Irene is the same age as Ree in the dreams, but they are Pat's dreams: Irene can be whatever she needs to in them. Irene is the mother of Pat.

ROSE: Very old, plenty more than 90. Rose is not steady but she does not shake. She has trouble with her balance but it is not a problem in her knees. She stares at things to see but she does not squint. She needs more light, not less. Her voice sometimes comes from odd places in her register but it does not quiver. She resists the easy sort of help that is an affront to dignity. She's hard, she's not mean; she's raw, for age strips the social graces, but she is also comic because of it. Being Rose is the hard part. Rose is the mother of Irene, the younger of two daughters. Helen, the ghost, is the older daughter.

production notes

The set should be simple, with levels and movable pieces that can become the seats in a car, a sofa, and a hospital bed. A real hospital bed and a real sofa are too big.

The props are also small and simple. An apple, a scarf, a medicine bottle in Rose's pocketbook, money, a bag with stuff to go in it for souse meat are appropriate. A coat tree is useful.

Costumes should be in keeping with the character. What I mean by that observation of the obvious is that the four people who play the show should not be in some variation of a uniform. Pat and the narrator can be similar.

Women of a variety of ages can play the parts. Or women of close to the same age can play the parts, with the transformations of age and infirmity acted in the body and the voice. Don't paint someone to look old to do Rose.

There is a moment the play calls for in which the actors switch roles. In effect, they become one another. The transformations are critical. The play can be complete without the moment, and it is preferable to keep the same characters and play the lines as written than to play the moment if it doesn't work.

The play has in it several levels of what is real, and it is anything but linear in time. Ree is a motor of sorts, her presence is sometimes like what happens when you put an animal on stage. Her reality is different and Pat has to deal with it.

a note on this edition

The version of the play included here is the literary edition and differs slightly from the acting edition published by Dramatists Play Service.

the play

PAT. (*Holds a jacket*) Hey, buddy, I got your jacket.

REE. Am I going home, Olivia?

PAT. You are home.

REE. My mother lives at home.

PAT. You live with your husband. Remember good old Price?

REE. I know Price, I married him. And there's a man who says he's Price but he isn't. He's one of the Carson boys but he's not the one I married. It's that other man ...

PAT. Ree. Don't start.

REE. Price does whatever that other man says, he told Price not to let me have another dog ...

PAT. We have to put your jacket on.

REE. And he told him not to let me drive and Price won't let me. I can drive. Oh Olivia, you don't know what it's like not to have a car. And he said I couldn't have a dog. He calls Price and Price just goes wherever that other man wants.

PAT. Ree! Your jacket.

REE. Oh.

PAT. OK. Other arm.

REE. Olivia, you've got to help me with my money.

PAT. Your arm, buddy.

REE. Price takes it.

PAT. Price does not take your money.

REE. He spends it on that other man and they play golf and they won't take me home. Are you going to take me home?

PAT. Bend your arm! Good. We're going to see your mother.

REE. My mother ...

PAT. In Kingsport.

REE. My job is to take care of my mother and Price won't let me drive. (*Ree struggles with the jacket*)

***

N. This is Ree. She used to be Irene. Irene was my mother.

REE. I don't have children.

N. She has Alzheimer's now.

REE. My brain is turning into jelly.

N. This is her joke.

REE. Grape.

N. This is my grandmother, Rose.

REE. She's my mother, I take care of her.

N. Her mother was Patricia. I am named after Patricia. I am —

N AND PAT. — we are Pat.

ROSE. You are Helen. I know Helen.

PAT. Helen is dead.

REE. This is Olivia.

ROSE. It is not.

N. There is a real Olivia, my great aunt Olivia. Ree confuses me with her. I am gone from Ree's memory but I fit somehow in her memory of Olivia. Tomorrow or next month, I will be somebody else. Someday I will be mother because her mother will be all she remembers.

PAT. What was she like, Grandmother?

ROSE. Who?

PAT. Your mother.

ROSE. She was a mule. All she knew to do was work.

N. Old age has fragile flesh that makes it hard to pull on shoes or unlock doors or stand up from sitting or bend over. Old age hurts in the joints of bones. Old age cannot see except at a certain distance.

PAT. Grandmother, you light matches to plug the heater in?

ROSE. You have to be so careful of the juice.

N. Electricity. She used to be afraid it ran out of sockets if they didn't have something in them. Old age cannot or will not hear.

ROSE. What'd you say?

REE. Mother, this is Olivia.

ROSE. You mean Helen. What does she want?

PAT. I said you are confused sometimes.

ROSE. Your time's a comin'.

PAT. Is this a prophecy?

N. She and her husband bought the second model T in Hancock County, Tennessee. She drove it down Clinch Mountain with no brakes but the hand brake. It was the only time she ever drove. They kept their horses to pull it with when it wouldn't start.

ROSE. Or Floyd ran it out of gas.

N. She is old enough to have been old already when men landed on the moon.

ROSE. Old enough I shouldn't be livin' alone. Say that and see if it don't stick in your craw, Princess Helen.

***

N. Helen has been in her grave forty years. Pat speaks to her ghost.

PAT. Helen, she gave you birth, she held you as you died . . .

ROSE. I took care of you.

PAT. Is this what you hear?

***

N. Ree speaks to the ghost of Burkett.

REE. Ohhh . . . . You pulled my ears, I loved you.

N. Ree speaks with ghosts every chance she gets. Burkett is a favorite uncle also years dead. He pulled my ears too, said it made more room for brains.

REE. And Margaret! She's not bent. Margaret!

N. Burkett's daughter Margaret died of polio.

PAT. Where, buddy?

REE. (*Points to a place*) Margaret, you want to dress up paperdolls?

***

PAT. Mother, which jacket do you want?

IRENE. The one that makes me look like Grace Kelly, the one that was much too expensive so I charged it, the one that makes me feel like I just received a Nobel Peace Prize for hazardous service as a high school librarian and I am on my way to meet the king of Sweden instead of being on my way to take the queen of East Center Street to the grocery store. (*She has it on. It is the jacket from the opening scene*) This one. You should try it on sometime. (*A transformation. Ree is three years sick. There are not big physical changes, there is a new uncertainty in her bearing and an edge in her voice that turns to panic*)

REE. Where did I put . . . I swear people take things. Pat takes my clothes, I used to have good clothes, I had a jacket that I really liked and I now see her with it on like I wasn't even here and she just walks around in it. What have you done with my jacket? Why did you take it. (*Pat shows Ree the jacket she has on, then hugs Ree. A transformation begins from the hug, Ree wants loose, Pat lets go. Ree struggles with the jacket. There are physical changes. Ree has a tilt, her eyes don't exactly focus. She cannot get the jacket off. Same as the end of the opening scene*) Olivia . . .

PAT. Leave it on, buddy, you'll need it. We're going to Kingsport.

***

ROSE. (*She was on this subject last time she spoke*) I need somebody to live with me. Helen.

PAT. You don't want me, you don't like the way I live, Grandmother.

ROSE. You'll change.

PAT. When I change, I'll come live with you.

ROSE. Lord, just take me home. I want to go back to Kyles Ford. You reckon anybody's still alive?

***

N. This daytrip started with a picture Grandmother had had for years. She never hung it anywhere that I remember but as a child I was allowed an occasional rummage through the closets so I had seen the picture.

PAT. The closets were where I learned about Helen — Helen who haunts us all — but that is another story.

N. The picture is a hand-tinted photograph of Kyles Ford, Tennessee. It was made by a man who came through with his equipment in the back of a horse drawn wagon. He took the photograph on speculation and sold copies to the residents of Kyles Ford. There weren't many people but most every family bought one. There are two houses in the scene the man chose and the further one is the house where my mother was born.

PAT. I had been there or so I was told.

ROSE. You were just a young'un. It was when those people came that nobody knew and it turned out they'd come to the wrong reunion. They should have gone to the Kesicks. Cusick is a C. Cusicks can all read.

N. It was Sunday after Thanksgiving, one of those November

gifts, a beautiful, almost warm day. Grandmother wasn't
going with us ...

ROSE.   Lord, what do you want to go back there for?

N.   ... but when we stopped to ask again, she decided she
might come after all.

PAT.   I took the precaution of bringing a map.

ROSE.   What do you need that for? Just start like you was goin'
to Rogersville. I'll show you.

N.   And when we got to Rogersville ...

ROSE.   Turn around, Helen, we've gone too far.

REE.   This is Olivia, Mother, Helen is dead.

ROSE.   Well, she better turn the car around.

PAT.   A mile or so back up the road where the map suggested,
I turned off 11-W.

ROSE.   This ain't it, ain't no road like this to Kyles Ford.

PAT.   Just be patient.

ROSE.   I know where I come from.

REE.   Maybe we should go back home.

N.   We came to a crossroads with an arrow that pointed across
the mountain to Kyles Ford ...

ROSE.   You're just lucky. They done cut another road. Even a
blind hog gets an acorn once in awhile.

PAT.   We started up the mountain.

ROSE.   Lord, let's turn around. I don't want to do this.

REE.   Mother ...

ROSE.   We're a like to die ... you have to start in the mornin'
if you're gonna' get across Clinch Mountain in the daylight and you done took your own time and eat dinner
already.

N.   Once, you probably needed to start in the morning if you
were going to get across Clinch Mountain in daylight.
Clinch Mountain is one of those ridges with a backbone to
it and the gaps are few and far between. It's not much of a
gap on the road that runs into Kyles Ford. It's a thirty,
forty minute drive and a series of curves that might prove
harrowing to the uninitiated.

PAT.   We topped the mountain and started down the other
side.

ROSE.   Robert Wilcox built that house. His wife's family had some money and Robert built him a fancy house with it. George Holms lived in that house yonder. His wife left him and she left his young'uns with his mother. Said she'd married the devil and birthed two little devils but she wasn't goin' to raise 'em. Said she walked into Rogersville and caught a ride to Knoxville and took up being one of them street preachers they had down there on Market Square. You believe that? I don't. But that's what they said. Nobody'd pay a woman preacher. Now your daddy's cousin . . .

N. My Grandaddy's cousin.

ROSE. . . . lived there but he wasn't no 'count. Your daddy would of moved in over here if I'd a' let him.

N. The road began to follow the Clinch River.

ROSE. Wes Johnson and Charlie Levisay had the ford. One of them lived on either side and they run the ferry back and forth. Made right smart money till the county put the bridge in. They set 'em up a toll booth at the far end of it but the county made' em take that down. Neither of 'em ever amounted to nothin' after that. There was people that still took the ferry in the winter when the bridge got iced up. Not your daddy.

N. We crossed the bridge that put Charlie Levisay and Wes Johnson out of business.

PAT. On the other side was a rock road that turned off the highway and ran along the river.

ROSE. Lord, ain't that a road.

REE. Mother, what?

ROSE. I said ain't that a road.

N. I thought she wanted me to turn up it.

PAT. I had to stop the car and back a ways before I could make the turn.

ROSE. What do you think you're doin'?

PAT. (*To Rose*) Backing up.

N. I turned onto the road.

ROSE. Where do you think you're a goin'?

PAT. You said you wanted . . .

ROSE. Stop this car! You stop right this minute!

N. I stopped the car.

ROSE. I'm gettin' out. If you go up this road you're goin' without me.

N. She got out of the car.

ROSE. Now you just go on if you're so dead set on drivin' somewhere! Go on!

PAT. I drove.

N. I could see her in the rearview mirror standing in the road with her cane, holding her coat about her with the other hand.

ROSE. Go on! Both of you ...

REE. Olivia?

ROSE. Go see for yourselves ...

REE. I can't be like this ...

PAT. I put the car in reverse, backed the ten yards and stopped beside her.

ROSE. I'm not goin'.

PAT. There's a law against leaving the likes of you standing in the middle of the road.

N. She laughed. And got back in the car.

PAT. Grandmother, what's on this road?

ROSE. You sure do want a lot, don't you?

PAT. I'd like to know what's on this road.

ROSE. Well, yonder's where I was born, and that's the house we moved into after daddy got it built. I didn't live in it very long.

PAT. Why?

ROSE. Just ride on a little.

N. On up the road, a quarter of a mile, alone in a field overlooking the river, are the graves of my grandmother's father and the great-grandmother I'm named after.

PAT. I'm going to walk over there.

ROSE. You just sit tight.

PAT. That's Patricia ...

ROSE. You're not gonna pay respects to a man that was that mean.

PAT. I've never been here.

ROSE. I loved my mother but she lays next to an awful man and she laid with him ever' night that he was home that she was married to him.

PAT. Maybe she loved him.

ROSE. Well, I didn't.

PAT. Maybe she was scared of him.

ROSE. Maybe I'm still scared of him.

N. And sitting there in the car, looking at the river across a field she helped to work,

PAT. she told me how she eloped with the man who was her school teacher.

ROSE. It didn't take no ladder, I just knew where Floyd was waitin' for me and I got in bed and stayed till everybody was asleep and I walked out the door.

N. They moved as far as they could afford to go, which was a half mile away, down on the main road, to the house in the picture where Helen and my mother were born.

ROSE. I did not go back till he was dying.

PAT. She said two sisters, both younger, came to live with her and Floyd two weeks after they married.

ROSE. He was a bad man. And my husband was a good man. Floyd was good.

PAT. What was so bad about him?

ROSE. Let's just go home.

N. I turned the car around and started back out the road.

PAT. Did he beat you?

N. We rejoined the main road. It felt like being safe.

ROSE. He beat all of us if somebody didn't do what he wanted.

PAT. What did he want?

ROSE. There are things people don't say to each other, Helen.

REE. Mother, this is Olivia.

***

ROSE. I stand here at night and look out and it's the same man every time, it don't matter how cold. He's under Ida Cole's tree. Ida Cole should of cut that tree. Nobody needs a tree that big. But Ida Cole didn't hardly cut his grass. Your daddy cut the hedge. Fifty years. And Ida Cole just let that tree grow. The man lives in it. Don't that beat anything you ever heard? Floyd told me once about a man lived in a tree, could throw mules over a fence. I don't think this is the same man. I think I know this man. He got mad when Irene's Skippy Dog run out in front of him and now he's waiting for your daddy. It was Skippy Dog that died. I wrote him a note and I went over and left it at Ida Cole's tree. Said "Floyd Cusick is dead. Leave me alone." I don't know if he can read. I should of put some money in it 'cause now he's out there every night studying this house. He looks right here at me. He hollers for me to come outside and some night I have to go.

***

PAT. Ree and I were on our way to Kingsport in the car. I had fastened her seat belt and she didn't like it.

N. She never likes it.

PAT. But she had settled down and she was watching things go by. Watching things go by is not looking at scenery. Her head moves to try to see specific things by the side of the road.

PAT. Look up, buddy ...

REE. Don't tell me what to do.

PAT. I found my own thoughts.

N. A friend had given me a mess of rhubarb. I love rhubarb and when I remembered it, I thought I might find strawberries.

REE. I haven't had rhubarb in I don't know how long.

N. I had not said rhubarb.

PAT. What made you say that?

REE. I got brains I haven't used yet.

N. Price says she's got brains she hasn't used yet. Ree usually thinks it's funny and laughing sometimes helps her sit or eat but she was not just being funny when she said it.

REE. Rhubarb in the tummy.

N. She's got brains she's just now using and she knows it. We were driving again, to Kingsport.

PAT. When we are driving together now, we are usually going to Kingsport.

REE. What are you putting in it?

N. I planned to buy a quart of oil. I saw myself in K-Mart's parking lot putting oil in my car. She did too.

REE. I have to send something.

PAT. What?

REE. I don't remember.

N. I did. I had an overdue electric bill ready to mail in my pocketbook.

PAT. I tested her.

N. I'd think "dog" and get nothing. I'd think of my dog, a specific dog I could see in my mind.

REE. I pat dogs I like.

N. Sometimes it was involuntary on her part.

REE. Wash the dishes! Do I have to say that?

PAT. How do you know what to say?

REE. What do you think I say?

N. She couldn't tell me and she couldn't do it all the time. It happened most when she was sitting in the passenger's seat and the car was in motion.

PAT. Going to Kingsport.

REE. You don't like my mother.

PAT. It was a day I didn't want to go to Kingsport.

REE. You're making me fall.

N. I see her levels of competency like plateaus. When she comes to an edge, she falls again. She was falling.

PAT. I don't think you're any better, Ree, that's all.

REE. You think I'm stupid.

PAT. I think your memory is bad.

REE. You think I'm worse.

PAT. How do you know that?

REE. You stop it!

PAT. (*To change what she is thinking and to distract Ree*) Look at the mountains, buddy, look at the sky ...

REE. I can't go away just because you want me to.

PAT. Look at the clouds in the sky.

N. She did look and the conversation was as lost as my name.

***

N. There are the dreams.

PAT. We three are at Watauga Lake.

N. Watauga is so beautiful, steep and deep and clean. People have been lost in Watauga, fallen out of a boat never to be found.

PAT. I cut my foot there once, a cut that took stitches to close and I bled into the lake.

N. I think of that sometimes when I'm there, that thirty years

later, swimming, molecules of my blood may still be there.
Mine and other people's, I don't forget them. In my dream,
Watauga is the red of the sunset and it makes me think of
blood but the day is hot and I wade into the lake.

PAT. Mother and Grandmother are there.

N. They don't ever come when I am swimming, playing with
friends, but they are there in my dream. They tell me to be
careful and I say I am careful.

PAT. I am careful.

N. I have on plastic shoes so I will not cut my foot again. As I
wade into the lake, I say

PAT. you come too.

IRENE. We don't have plastic shoes.

PAT. I offer to pull mine off and give them one each.

N. My shoes would not fit their knotty feet.

IRENE. No, we'll do it anyway.

PAT. And they sit on the shore and take off their shoes and
both of them in their afternoon dresses wade into the lake.
They hold hands.

N. I walk further into the water. My jeans get wet. I call to
them.

PAT. Come on!

ROSE. Our dresses will get wet.

PAT. I'm wet, it feels good.

N. I am waist deep, I am chest deep, my feet no longer touch
the bottom and I kick gently in my plastic shoes to stay
afloat.

PAT. Come on.

N. And they come. But they do not swim. They walk. Holding
hands. They walk past me. I see their heads beneath the
surface of the water.

PAT. I told you it feels good ...

N. And they walk. Further than I can see, further than I feel
safe to swim and they are gone. I do not call

PAT. come back,

N. I say

PAT. good-bye.

N. And I swim back to shore and I pick up their shoes and

PAT. I bring their shoes home.

REE. Look at the naked people.

PAT. I don't see any naked people.

N. Ree speaks to the ghost of her father, Floyd.

REE. Daddy ...

PAT. We were walking. We don't walk very well.

N. Ree hurt her feet for vanity before her father died. She went from three-inch spike heels to Wallabees and the librarian's desk in a county high school because she didn't ever want to be as dependent as her mother. Now, she wears bedroom slippers and on pretty days, we sometimes get as far as the end of the block.

PAT. No clothes, buddy?

REE. They have clothes on. I can see inside.

PAT. Transparent?

REE. (*Confirms*) Naked. Oh, no .... My daddy is naked. No! You're supposed to come and get me! Come and get me! Come and get me! (*Ree falls to her knees. Pat tries to hold her up*)

PAT. I can get you!

N. A car pulled to a stop because we were in the middle of the street. I knew the woman driving ...

REE. My daddy was supposed to come and get me but now I have to stay and dance!

N. ... but she sat like she was at a stoplight waiting for us to change.

PAT. Ree! You don't have to dance, there's no music, the band's gone home already. ...

REE. Oh.

N. We moved and the woman in the car drove on.

REE. Why did I sit down, Olivia?

PAT. You got tired.

REE. My feet hurt.

***

N. Ree listens to Pat.

PAT. There was a piece I heard on the radio about a woman who was lost in some big city department store. Her husband took her to get her hair fixed at the beauty salon where she had been a customer for years. (*Ree plays with her hair on her fingers. Ree spent time in beauty salons, she got permanents*)

REE. She got a permanent.

PAT. He saw her to the main door of the department store. Until this time, she had negotiated the rest of the trip with no problem. This time she got to her appointment a week late. Seven days. Nobody knows where she was and she doesn't remember. The police assumed she left the building when they searched for her but she was found wandering in a storage area of the same department store. She was very thirsty.

REE. I am not.

***

N. It was another daytrip.

PAT. We call Grandmother before we leave Johnson City so that while we drive the twenty miles she will get out of bed and begin to get dressed.

REE. I go to Kingsport and I take Mother to the grocery store.

ROSE. I don't need to go to the grocery store. I have to go to the drug store.

N. She never needs to go to the grocery store.

PAT. But we always go and she always buys food.

N. A quart of milk. Three bananas. One potato. A carton of Cokes, classic. A handful of beans.

ROSE. They're so old they're not gonna have no taste.

N. Every other week, we add a box of Ralston, a pound of bacon, a loaf of bread, a dozen eggs and a quart of ice cream. Ree always shopped for groceries too. She bought the smallest ham in a can—a ham because Grandmother won't eat beef . . .

ROSE. I like cows.

N. . . . and a box of peppermint sugar sticks.

PAT. Now I have the ham and sugar sticks in my basket and I manage to leave them in Kingsport.

ROSE. Your mother forgets ever'thing.

PAT. And they are consumed.

N. Ree used to forget she already had a ham in her basket and get a second ham. Those came home with her. There was a stack of them in her refrigerator.

REE. We can't eat those, they're for Mother. I forgot and brought them home.

N. It was a light week at the grocery store. We had the potato, we had the quart of milk. In another bag, we had a little ham and the candy.

ROSE. I have to go to the drugstore.

N. So I drove downtown to the drugstore that had been her drugstore since Kingsport only had one drugstore.

ROSE. This ain't it. My pharmacist has moved.

PAT. What is it?

ROSE. Lord, I don't know. Ask Irene.

REE. Price knows.

ROSE. My pharmacist moved and Price found him for me.

N. The new pharmacist in the old drugstore didn't know where the old pharmacist had gone.

PAT. Grandmother, do you have any idea?

ROSE. Out that ways somewhere. On the highway.

PAT. Which highway?

ROSE. Like you go to Bristol.

PAT. 11-W.

N. It is the only road Grandmother concedes might be a highway. The four-lane to Johnson City is just a road. I would have done well to remember that, but I didn't, I had a revelation.

PAT. Let me see that bottle.

ROSE. It ain't a gonna point you nowhere.

N. But it did.

PAT. Revco.

ROSE. Well, ain't you somethin'?

PAT. A Revco on 11-W towards Bristol.

N. Piece of cake.

PAT. I found one.

N. I even found a parking place directly in front so we didn't have to walk very far. I guided Grandmother back to the part of the store where prescriptions are filled. She handed me the empty bottle, I handed it to the pharmacist. He punched up the number of the prescription on his computer, read the screen and began to fill it. Grandmother studied him through her cataract glasses.

ROSE. That's not the man.

PAT. What?

ROSE. That's not my pharmacist.

PAT. But he can fill your prescription, he's got it on the computer ...

ROSE. He don't know me, Helen. That other man gives me a senior citizen discount.

N. The pharmacist who was working on her prescription assured her he could do that too. He handed Rose the filled bottle.

ROSE. He don't know me. How does he know what medicine I'm supposed to take.

PAT. He's got it on a computer.

ROSE. I don't care what you think he's got it on, he's not my pharmacist. (*She opens or mimes opening the bottle and pours pills onto the counter*)

PAT. Grandmother?

ROSE. He might be a nice man but he's not my pharmacist.

PAT. What the devil do you think we're going to do?

ROSE. You don't talk to me like that! We're going to find my pharmacist. Price did it. I have to have my medicine.

N. For a moment, I just looked at the man who seemed to me to be a perfectly good pharmacist. (*As the pharmacist*) "Does her man work at Revco?"

PAT. I think so ... the bottle says Revco.

N. (*As the pharmacist*) "What's your man's name?"

ROSE. What does he want, Helen?

PAT. Your pharmacist's name. What's his name?

ROSE. Lord, I don't know.

N. There are four Revco Drugstores in shopping centers on highways in Kingsport.

PAT. I counted them before I tore the page from the directory.

N. I wouldn't have torn the page out if the pay phone had been in order and I could have spent a quarter each time and asked if the man who used to be the pharmacist at Freels was now the pharmacist at that Revco. And I didn't realize the pay phone was out of order until I'd already put the first quarter in, but I couldn't get a dial tone and then I noticed that the receiver wire was hanging loose where it should have been connected to the body of the phone.

PAT. So I got back into the car with the page from the phone book . . .

ROSE. You shouldn't have done that, what if somebody has to look up Revco?

PAT. . . . and we drove

N. and at each Revco, we spent the agony it takes to get out of the car and go in and peer at the pharmacist back of the counter.

PAT. I offered to go in and ask if the man had previously worked at Freels so she wouldn't have to get out of the car and I wouldn't have to wait.

ROSE. He don't know you, why should he say?

PAT. And at the fourth and last Revco in a shopping center on a highway in Kingsport, Tennessee, Grandmother and I walked with five legs between us, Ree lost behind on two of her own, towards the high counter where the pharmacist stood above us.

N. (*As the pharmacist*) "Well, hello Mrs. Cusick, good to see you. You gonna' get some medicine today?"

ROSE. I am.

PAT. She handed her empty bottle to him. He punched a number on his computer, read from the screen and filled the prescription.

ROSE. We had a right smart time a findin' you.

N. (*As the pharmacist*) "Oh, I'm here, I'm right here every day."

PAT. He handed the bottle back.

ROSE. I want the discount you get for senior citizens.

N. (*As the pharmacist*) "You got it."

PAT. He took her money and made the change.

N. (*As the pharmacist*) "I wish you well, Mrs. Cusick."

ROSE. Lord, don't wish me that. If you're gonna wish somethin', wish I could die and get it over with.

***

N. Ree listens to Pat.

PAT. There was a piece in the newspaper about a middle-aged man who was a carekeeper for his ailing mother. Her condition deteriorated and he killed her, cleaned up the mess — the murder weapon was never found — and wrapped the body in plastic bags. His neighbors said he was meticulously clean. (*Ree understands this is about her indirectly and she is drawn to Pat. The move is also aggressive, like a child invading another's territory*) He called the rescue squad and told them there were two bodies and a donation for them at the address. When the rescue squad arrived, there was three hundred dollars on the table in the kitchen with the mother's body and a note that said he found his health failing too and he didn't want either of them to be a burden on anyone else. The note directed the rescue squad to the backyard where they would find his body and asked that they turn the garden hose on the place he had bloodied with his dying. When they got to him, the garden hose was laid beside him, all they had to do was turn it on.

REE. Turn it on.

***

N. There is more to the story about Kyles Ford, going back to where my mother was born. As we were leaving, I asked,

PAT. Is there anybody you want to see?

ROSE. Lord, no.

N. So I drove half a mile, maybe a mile ...

ROSE. Stop here, Helen, turn in here.

REE. Mother, this is Olivia.

ROSE. It is not.

PAT. I turned in the driveway of a weatherbeaten little farm house.

N. An old woman stuck her head out the door to welcome whoever was disturbing the peace of her lonely Sunday afternoon.

ROSE. This is your Great-Aunt Bee. Now, you keep your mouth shut 'cause Bee'd as soon bite you as she would to talk to you.

N. Bee, the vicious, hobbled down her front walk to get a better look. When she saw Rose sitting in the back seat, her face broke into a smile that stretched muscles that hadn't been used for a while and she allowed as how she'd open up her front room if this company would come sit in it.

ROSE. I ain't gettin' out of the car. If you want to talk to me, you're gonna' have to sit in it.

N. So Bee climbed in and for the next hour and a half she filled Rose in on who'd married who, who'd bought what, who'd lost what, who'd died, who's young'uns had gone to jail and who was likely to die any time now. She included herself in that list and they both spoke about what ails them, what ailed their dead husbands and what kills us all in the end, whatever it is. Bee fussed with her hands the whole time. She had tiny cuts on the insides of both of them.

ROSE. What have you done to your hands?

N. (*As Bee*) "I made souse meat, I always wear hard on my hands makin' it 'cause I get all the meat off. I don't waste no meat."

ROSE. Oh, Lord. Brain cheese.

PAT. Souse meat.

N. There are other words for it. It's a Thanksgiving delicacy in some places because that's about the time hogs are slaughtered. Bee was late, this was the Sunday after, but the hogs' heads had been a gift and an impoverished old woman will make the souse meat on Friday and give thanks for weeks. (*As Bee*) "You want some? I've got a lot of it, there was two heads."

ROSE. No.

N. (*As Bee*) "I got plenty, I got more than I need, it's so rich."

ROSE. I don't want it.

N. (*As Bee*) "Oh, Rose, take somethin' somebody wants to give you."

ROSE. I don't like it. And I left here sixty years ago so I wouldn't have to eat no more of it.

N. (*As Bee*) "Oh. Well, I don't reckon there's nothin' I can give you then."

ROSE. I don't reckon there is.

N. "Well," Bee looked at scenery that had been familiar for those same sixty years, "Irene, I'm gonna' give you souse meat." Bee struggled out of the car and launched toward the house.

PAT. I followed her into her kitchen. There was a bed in her kitchen.

N. (*As Bee*) "I live in here, I would have opened up the front room if Rose would' a come in."

PAT. She's like that.

N. Bee opened her refrigerator instead. She removed a big platter of brown jellied glob that filled the room with a smell reminiscent of canned dog food. She cut off a generous end, wrapped it in aluminum foil, put the foil package into a plastic bag and the plastic bag into a small paper sack. (*As Bee*) "You give Rose some of this and see if she don't eat it." (*Pat takes a bag from N/Bee*)

PAT. (*To Bee*) Price will eat it. (*To audience*) I thanked her, told her again who I was, rather, who I was kin to — Irene's girl — and I was on my way out the door.

N. (*As Bee*) "You know your grandmother hasn't changed a lick in fifty years. Except she got old."

PAT. I carried the souse meat to the car, waved at Bee who stood in her kitchen door.

ROSE. Don't you put that stuff back here.

PAT. And we drove back north on highway 11-W

N. to the town where Grandmother locks everything that can be locked.

ROSE. Lord, Helen, you have to.

REE. Mother, this is Olivia.

ROSE. It is not.

N. To the town where she is afraid of all the strangers and everyone is a stranger but where she doesn't have to cook or eat souse meat.

***

PAT. The mother of a friend is a victim of Alzheimer's. (*Ree tries to attract something nobody else can see. Ree sees a spaniel-sized dog. Her gestures are odd: Ree might wave to it, she might reach as if the dog were an arm's length away or beckon with a finger. These are not big gestures, they are private*)

N. (*As the friend*) "I never considered assisting her death because she and my father spent their lives believing in the will of God and this was just one more act of the same old will." (*Ree tries to whistle to it but she can't whistle. She can hum but it is no song. She hums to the dog to come*)

N. (*As the friend*) "Taking care of my mother put my father in his grave and for the last eight years she's been in a nursing home."

PAT. How do you pay?

N. (*As the friend*) "Medicaid pays. She's destitute. Took four months to spend their life savings and Medicaid took over. Medicare . . ."

PAT. Doesn't pay for custodial care.

N. (*As the friend*) "Gotcha."

PAT. And my father isn't broke yet. (*The dog is prancing at Ree's feet. She is pleased but she is also frightened. She turns to avoid being licked*)

N. (*As the friend*) "My mother does not open her eyes, does not move except when the nurses turn her and has not made a sound for the last three years. I take that back. She burps and farts. They say when she curls into a fetal position, death is approaching. Her arms are clinched across her chest now. That's been the only change in the past year."

PAT. Do you think about . . . [*assisting death*]?

N. (*As the friend*) "Of course. I think it shouldn't have come this far but I can't do anything now. I'm not even welcome to help turn her over." (*Ree pats the dog*)

PAT. (*To Ree*) What are you doing?

REE. Skippy Dog is back. He's gonna bite you.

✝✸✸

N. I ordered a book by Betty Rollin called *Last Wish*. It came in the mail a day Ree was at my house. I carried the package into my bedroom to open it.

PAT. I knew what the book was about and I did not want to open it in front of Ree.

REE. I like books.

PAT. Betty Rollin's mother had an incurable cancer and asked her daughter to help her die.

N. Betty Rollin's mother knew what she was doing right up to the moment she swallowed the pills and passed out.

PAT. Betty Rollin found a recipe, assisted in getting the ingredients and helped ensure the length of time and privacy necessary to let the pills work. I read the book and wept.

N. When I remembered Ree, she was gone. I hunted for twenty minutes, an arbitrary length of time I read "should your Alzheimer's patient become lost."

PAT. I could not find Ree anywhere so I called the police.

N. She walked a half a mile, crossed a four-lane highway and lost a shoe. She was standing in someone's back yard. They reported her. When we got to the address, a woman waved us around the house.

PAT. Ree seemed glad to see me.

REE. I know you.

N. She wanted to go home but she would not get in the car.

PAT. He's a policeman, buddy ...

REE. I know you, you think about me dead.

PAT. I had to force Ree.

N. The officer stood by and watched. "Happens a lot," he said, "you'd be surprised how many old people wander off. One old boy sneaks away. Has to. We hunt him every other week."

PAT. Wonder what his carekeeper is reading when it happens.

N. Ree had no idea where she had been or that she had been anywhere.

REE. Nobody even takes me to Jonesborough!

***

N. Ree pays attention when Pat tells stories.

PAT. There was another piece in the paper about a man whose mother had it. (*Ree moves to Pat again. She is agitated*) The mother was already in a nursing home. He had cared for her until he couldn't keep her by himself anymore, nine years, he had put her in the best nursing home he could find and he found it awful. So he took her out, parked his car in the garage with her in it, ran a hose from the exhaust through a hole he cut in the trunk and helped his mother to the carbon monoxide. He did it, he says, because he would want death for himself and he could do no less for someone he loved.

N. (*To Pat*) There's more to this.

PAT. The man was also in the car. He says he wanted a murder/suicide but the police think he planned it to look like a murder/suicide where the suicide part got botched. His mother died and he did not.

N. (*To Pat*) He is in jail.

PAT. So he's not had much experience planning this sort of

thing and he turned out to be a lousy planner!

N. He is going to stand trial for murder.

***

N. It was another daytrip. On the way to Kingsport, Ree opened her door to get out at sixty-five miles per hour.

PAT. She was mad at me.

N. A bag of apples for Grandmother turned over as I jerked the car to the side of the road.

REE. I need to leave.

PAT. She was restrained by a seat belt which she spent the rest of the drive trying to bite.

N. The apples rolled, loose and bruising, in the back of the car.

REE. I'm not something you just tie up. I have to go see my mother.

PAT. We're going to your mother's.

N. We pulled into the driveway of Rose's house. I stopped the car, got out and went around to open Ree's door.

PAT. We're here.

N. I unbuckled her seat belt.

REE. I have to go home.

N. She did not want out.

PAT. I collected the apples, put them back in the bag and banged on Grandmother's door until she appeared and began to unlock the series of locks. There are three.

N. It is easier to take apart a window, storm window and standard window on that house than it is to get in a locked door. Price did it last time she lost a key. Now, she wants to board up the reassembled window because someone came in that way. This time, she had trouble with the latch on the storm door. It was hard to open and she kept leaving it to go back inside . . .

PAT. Grandmother! You have to unlock it!

ROSE. Maybe I don't want company.

PAT. Unlock it!

N. When she finally flipped it open, I carried the bag of apples in before I tried Ree again.

PAT. This is your mother's house. Do you want out?

REE. I always want out.

N. She began the series of movements that mean she's trying to make her brain tell her body what to do.

PAT. Put your foot outside the car.

N. She grabbed the seat belt and smiled as though she had done what I asked.

REE. I take care of my mother. I take her to the grocery store. She eats ham.

PAT. Your foot, buddy, put your foot out of the car.

N. But she couldn't so I picked up her feet and turned her in the seat and put her feet out the door.

REE. Out!

PAT. That's it!

N. Except she couldn't let go of the seat belt. It was wet from where she had tried to bite it. I took it from her hand.

REE. I used to like you.

N. Inside, Rose had on one shoe and was working on the second.

PAT. Once in, I got Ree a drink of water because she fell to tears saying her throat hurt. Then I took her to the bathroom which was what she needed.

N. It may have been the problem when she tried to get out of the car. The tears were frustration.

REE. Pieces get stuck in my throat . . .

PAT. She means words get lost in her jelly.

REE. Grape.

PAT. I asked Grandmother what she wanted from the grocery store.

ROSE. I'm going. I have to look.

PAT. You're not dressed.

ROSE. Just hold your horses, I'm getting dressed. Get my coat, Helen.

PAT. You have on your bed clothes.

ROSE. I know that. Get me my coat.

N. It was not a coat over bed clothes that bothered me. It was those bed clothes. They are in shreds. She won't wear her newer ones —

ROSE. They don't feel right.

N. —either.

PAT. Change your clothes and I'll get your coat.

ROSE. I don't have to do what you say.

PAT. You do if you want me to get your coat.

N. But we were a long way from needing the coat. She was still struggling with the second shoe.

ROSE. When I die, write on the stone "her feet swole up."

PAT. I sat to wait. I read jokes from a four-year-old *Reader's Digest*.

N. The "Most Unforgettable Character" in the issue was an elderly woman. *Reader's Digest* should meet mine. The last time we three went to the grocery store together, she stopped a stranger to say I was on my way to hell because I hadn't come to live with her.

ROSE. Her duty and she hasn't done it.

N. And somewhere in Ree's brain, duty proved to be a fighting word — you never know when you are going to say one — and Ree hit Rose to make her hush.

ROSE. What on earth is wrong with her? Helen!

PAT. I restrained Ree and she hit me.

N. That was six months ago. I don't take Ree in stores anymore.

PAT. I watched Grandmother struggle with the second shoe.

N. Her shoes all have holes but we cannot find shoes to buy that she likes. The old ones have this advantage: they are stretched to fit her bunions.

PAT. Grandmother, this is a second thought. It's not a good idea for us all to try to go to the grocery store.

ROSE. Second who?

PAT. Thought. Just tell me what you need and I'll run and get it.

ROSE. I have to look.

PAT. I hoped she meant look in her refrigerator. We do that. "I have to look," she says and we inventory the refrigerator to make a list of missing things.

N. But she was still working on the shoe.

PAT. You could do that after we look.

ROSE. I have to look at the Oakwood.

REE. I have to go too. They cash my check . . .

N. Forty years ago, Oakwood was the first supermarket in Kingsport.

ROSE. Time was I had to carry you around it.

N. She goes there now out of habit. She won't go in anywhere else. And for the twenty years Irene, my mother, was in Kingsport at Oakwood on Saturday morning, she cashed a check for spending money for the coming week. At the name Oakwood, Ree says she needs to cash a check.

PAT. Grandmother, it's not a good idea today.

ROSE. What's not?

PAT. For us all to go to the grocery store.

ROSE. I'll walk if you don't take me.

PAT. Mind if I watch?

ROSE. What's wrong with me a going?

PAT. Circumstance.

N. I can't say because of Ree. Ree erupts for that but Grandmother doesn't see how bad Ree is, so to her, it is not a reason anyway. When we finally went to the bathroom, she watched me pull Ree's pants down, watched me steer her to the toilet by force so she missed the dirty clothes hamper where she was trying to sit and then, she watched me pull Ree's pants back up again. All without Ree's cooperation.

ROSE. Is something wrong with her?

PAT. Yes!

N. But she refuses to see.

ROSE. Irene should come by herself. She'd take me, Irene likes to go to Oakwood.

REE. I need to cash a check.

PAT. Grandmother, you're not dressed, you're not getting dressed fast enough to get there before supper time and I don't want to wait. Now. You need eggs?

ROSE. You're awful to me.

REE. She's mean to me too.

ROSE. I'm not going to give you my money . . .

PAT. Milk? Ralston? Bananas?

N. She did not say yes or no to any of them so I checked her refrigerator by myself, threw away two bowls of food I could no longer name, and left the house as she finished putting on her second shoe and began to pull her night clothes off to put on her corset and slip.

ROSE. I'm a changin' my clothes to go, Helen!

N. I went to a grocery store, not Oakwood. I bought the whole
list I had made. And a ham. I also bought a bakery cake.
When I got back, she was standing at the door, her coat
on over her day clothes, a scarf tied around her head.

ROSE. Put apples on my list, I want some apples.

PAT. I brought you apples. Price sent them.

ROSE. What?

PAT. You've got some.

N. I pointed to them. She uses apples to make jelly that runs
like syrup and never jells. Ree was bumped up against a
chair because she could not find her way around it eating
one of the apples. Ree takes a bite, sometimes two, puts
the apple down and forgets it. I saw, without looking,
another apple with a bite out of it.

REE. When am I going home?

ROSE. You're at home.

REE. I am not!

ROSE. Where'd you get that apple?

PAT. (*Points*) Price sent you apples.

N. This time she looked.

ROSE. I don't care. You still have to take me to the grocery
store.

PAT. I've been to the grocery store. I bought a cake.

N. A cake. A single-layer white cake with white icing. No
coconut, no decorations. There is no other acceptable kind.

ROSE. Well. I guess we have to eat some of it.

PAT. I guess we do.

N. So I put up the cold groceries and cut the cake. Two of us
ate a piece. Ree put hers in her pocket. Or tried. Grandmother watched but she didn't see.

ROSE. Did you drop your fork or your cake?

PAT. Both.

N. I cleaned up the mess. The apple beside Ree's plate had
one bite out of it. Grandmother kept her coat and her scarf
on. It was hard to eat with the scarf on, the ends tied
under her chin got in the way and crumbs collected, snow
on the navy blue scarf, stars in a night sky. We finished
our cake.

ROSE. Helen, it's time we started.

PAT. I've been.

ROSE. I didn't go.

PAT. I went for you.

ROSE. And you're not going to take me, are you?

PAT. Not this time.

ROSE. Dressed up and no place to go 'cause you can't get the princess to take you. Well, what do I owe you?

PAT. Twelve.

ROSE. Twelve what?

N. Pesos. Yen.

PAT. Dollars, Grandmother.

N. I spent twenty but I'd decided to buy the cake and it is somehow accepted that we — never she — buy the ham. The trip she made in her clothes was into the bedroom to find her pocketbook. I waited in the kitchen with Ree who paced, pushing against the cabinets, the refrigerator, hunting for a door.

PAT. Whoa, buddy . . .

REE. I have to go home . . .

N. I tried to remember it is not important that she be still. Grandmother finally returned with three bills in her hand. She layed down a five —

ROSE. Ten.

N. —and two one-dollar bills.

ROSE. Eleven, twelve.

N. I studied her. I know she prefers that she be wronged and I be guilty so I do not think she knew. I preferred to lose five dollars than to explain and wait for her to go look in her pocketbook again. Ree found the door when Rose came through it and she stood on the other side beckoning to me.

PAT. You need to pee again?

REE. I don't want to hurt anybody's feelings but I have to go home.

N. She had another apple with a first bite out of it.

PAT. Buddy, you're wasting apples.

REE. I am not!

PAT. Grandmother, Ree and I are going home.

ROSE. You're not going to stay the night either, are you?

PAT. Don't start that.

REE. I'll stay. She's my mother, I take care of her.

ROSE. Let her stay, Helen. She wants to.

PAT. Don't tempt me.

N. Ree had trouble coming down the steps and was afraid to come any further because she saw things moving in the walkway and she fought the whole distance. Then I had to push her into sitting in the car. Rose watched from the door. Ree didn't want her seat belt fastened. She fought it, too. The day was proving to be hard for Ree. I locked her door, a precaution known to be useless. I got in on the driver's side, waved good-bye to Grandmother and started the car.

ROSE. You be careful driving over that mountain.

N. There is no mountain in our way home. She was thinking of Clinch Mountain on the way to Kyles Ford.

ROSE. And tell Viola I hope she gets better.

N. She meant Ree.

ROSE. I may not be here when you come back. Me and Cissy Johnson's been talking about going somewhere together. If she's rid of Wes. Now, he's not bad, he just don't talk like we do. Sits down there at the ferry and spits.

PAT. You have a good time.

ROSE. We will. Lock your doors so nobody can't get you.

N. She retreated to lock her own doors. The return to Johnson City was without incident.

***

IRENE. Pat, you're not very good to her.

PAT. What do you think I ought to do? Move in? She thinks I should.

IRENE. No. Just go see her.

PAT. I do go.

IRENE. Not once a month.

PAT. I don't go every Saturday.

IRENE. You could go for me.

PAT. She could take a taxi to the grocery store.

IRENE. Pat. She's lonely.

PAT. She could call a friend if she had one —

IRENE. We're all she's got.

PAT. —but she doesn't need one, she has you.

IRENE. What on earth makes you say that?

PAT. Mother. It's true.

IRENE. But it's got no heart in it, daughter, no blood, and you have her blood in you.

***

PAT. A woman I barely know called me at home.

N. (*As the woman*) "I just wanted to say how sorry I am ..."

PAT. I'd seen her the week before at a potluck supper, someone asked about my mother and she had joined the conversation.

N. (*As the woman*) "I know about Alzheimer's, I directed an A.D. unit at a nursing home."

PAT. (*To the woman*) What can you know. (*To the audience*) She said she called to give me a list of services for families and victims of Alzheimer's. I began to understand that this was not what she had called to say. There were long silences. I finally read what I had copied back to her. It is not a long list, there aren't many services. I had it from other sources.

N. (*As the woman*) "The husband of a friend died recently, he had it." (*Ree moves close to Pat again, listens. She is agitated*)

PAT. (*To the woman*) How long did it take? (*To the audience*) This is the first question anyone who has ever been a carekeeper asks. Every year after ten earns stars in heaven.

N. (*As the woman*) "Twelve years."

PAT. Two stars. (*To the woman*) Twelve years is a short case.

N. (*As the woman*) "He didn't die of the disease, he starved to death."

PAT. He didn't eat?

N. (*As the woman*) "My friend quit feeding him. I'm very proud of her, it took a lot of courage. It was the right thing to do, it's how the body would have died years ago if it could have ..."

PAT. How long?

N. (*As the woman*) "How long what?"

PAT. Did it take for him to die.

N. (*As the woman*) "Not long."

PAT. How long?

N. (*As the woman*) "Three months. But he was a horse, he

would have lived another twelve years. His doctor came by the house and asked if she wanted to put him on IV and she said no and he didn't say anything else and he had to know."

PAT. What did the husband do?

N. (*As the woman*) "Do?"

PAT. During the three months.

N. (*As the woman*) "Asked for food. He didn't talk again, he opened his mouth and pointed. After a while, he cried. But he did that already, it makes criers out of people."

PAT. Ree is a crier now.

REE. I am not.

PAT. What did she do?

N. (*As the woman*) "Gave him water."

PAT. And that's it?

N. (*As the woman*) "Took her first vacation in twelve years when he died, went to California to see her youngest daughter's girl get married."

PAT. How does she feel?

N. (*As the woman*) "She did him a favor. He should be grateful."

PAT. How does she feel?

N. (*As the woman*) "She's glad he's gone."

***

N. Don't say it.

PAT. Price, her carekeeper, Price, who is not here because the times I am here are the moments he can take for himself, Price, my father, says

N. Don't ever say it. Don't even think it.

PAT. He does not name "it" but he and I both know. "It" is some way of assisting death. So the hardest question is not even named between us. (*Ree is very agitated. Pat knows and speaks anyway*)

N. Don't begin to think it.

PAT. I do think it.

N. If you can think something, if you can imagine it, you can find yourself doing it.

PAT. I can imagine. (*Ree tries to bite Pat. Pat holds Ree at a distance and Ree does bite Pat's arm. Pat shakes Ree hard and holds her. Ree kicks*) I do imagine. I can name the ways.

(*Pat is obliged to hold Ree up or she would fall. When Ree stands up, Pat lets her go*) I think of it when I think what I would want for myself. (*Ree tries to spit at Pat and cannot spit*) I would not want to come to this.

*****

N. There was a real Helen. I never knew her. Unless it's true that you lose one in this world to get one and we are somehow the same. She was Rose's oldest daughter. She died the year I was born.

ROSE. She was the prettiest girl you ever saw.

N. I have seen pictures. Helen never smiled in them. My mother was always smiling.

PAT. My mother was the beauty of the two.

ROSE. Your mother was all right but Helen was pretty.

N. Helen died for lack of penicillin. It was a product of World War II and available for people in service but not for private citizens when Helen got pneumonia.

ROSE. I begged the Lord not to take her.

N. Helen was married but she did not have children. I suspect she didn't want them. Helen did not tolerate disorder.

ROSE. Helen cared about things like I do. Irene took after her daddy. I give Irene Helen's sofa 'cause she didn't have no furniture in that house they bought in Johnson City and she used it! Put it in the living room and didn't care who sat in it or what they had on the seat of their pants!

IRENE. Mother. It's just furniture.

ROSE. It was Helen's!

IRENE. You gave it to me and I am using it.

ROSE. Well, I want it back! If you got no more respect for the dead than that!

IRENE. It is hard enough to take care of the living.

ROSE. Helen wouldn't have said that to me.

IRENE. Helen never had the occasion.

N. Helen kept sheets on her furniture except when company came. Helen would take apart store bought dresses and resew them by hand because she did a better job than machines.

ROSE. You know I love you best. You're the new Helen. Now, don't tell your brother and don't tell Irene either.

N. She took me through her house and pointed out things — furniture, china, jewelry, clothes — that had been Helen's. She told me about Helen, how she loved these things and how careful she was with them. She said Helen's things would be mine when I was old enough to take care of them. I felt rich in furniture but I was not allowed to sit on Helen's chairs. I never had a bite from a plate that was Helen's. I wanted to want the furniture, I wanted to be as important as Helen but Helen of her memory was not a child and I was.

PAT. I asked to share with my brother and not be the new Helen.

ROSE. That time I told you I loved you best, I said it to make you sit still.

***

ROSE. Irene was sick and Helen died. I expected Irene to die. I could have understood if it had been Irene. She was so sickly when she was little and she had that heart. I wish it had been Irene. You know what Irene done? She took that sofa and had it reupholstered.

IRENE. Good as new.

ROSE. It wasn't Helen's sofa anymore and she brought it back over here and had them movers plop it down in my living room. And yonder it is. And I don't care who sits on it. If it was Helen's I'd care. But it got ironed. [*As though Irene's name were a verb*] And then when Floyd died, I got ironed. I don't know why I've had to live so long. I wish I could of died the day before Helen.

***

IRENE. She wished it had been me that died. She told me. It was one of the Saturdays. We finished her chores as though nothing had happened and I cried going home. I said the things I wanted to say to her. You are a mean woman or stupid, one. You better be glad it's me and not Helen that's alive, Helen wouldn't have put up with this. I was halfway home and I turned around to go back and say them to her. I drove in her driveway, left the car running and banged on her door . . .

ROSE. You forget something?

IRENE. I forgot to say I love you.

ROSE. You drove back here to say that?

IRENE. No. No, I didn't ... I got back in the car and drove away. We never mentioned it. I remember things she's forgotten about Helen, how hard she was, how stubborn, how like her mother, how hard they were on one another. Who will take care of her if I don't?

***

N. Ree speaks to Helen's sofa.

REE. Ohhh ... I know I'm so silly and Olivia just says anything .... Hey! Somebody took the skin off and I don't know where it is but it's the nicest thing you can do for yourself, makes people like you. I know what I'm talking about, I was ... and you came and washed my hair ... (*Ree loses words and stands wringing her hands*)

ROSE. What do you study about?

REE. Me?

ROSE. What are you studyin'?

REE. Studying?

ROSE. You just stand there and stand and study. What about?

REE. Me. What's wrong with me.

***

N. Rose speaks to the ghost of Helen.

ROSE. Well, Lord. You are a sight for sore eyes. This mean you come to live with me? I asked the Lord to send you. You hard a hearin'? I am. Sit down, why don't you? I said you want to sit down? You ain't what I asked the Lord for if you won't sit down. You plan to stand there till I die? I been waitin' a right smart time myself, no tellin' how long you'll have to wait. Get in there and get you a bite of jelly. I made it. It ain't good but you could taste it. You gonna get you a bite of jelly? (*Rose tries to touch the ghost but she cannot*) I have a gun, you know that don't you? If you ain't gonna talk to me, you might as well get in your car and go home.

***

ROSE. How do you get in at night?

PAT. I'm not here at night.

ROSE. Why do you talk to me now?

PAT. I talk when I'm here.

ROSE. You want a bite of my jelly?

PAT. No, I don't.

ROSE. Helen! How do you get in?

PAT. Look, you've got fifty percent, I'm sitting down and I'm talking but I don't get in at night and I'm not Helen.

ROSE. Why have you got on Helen's ring if you're not Helen?

PAT. Helen died! You gave it to me!

ROSE. I did not!

***

ROSE. (*Partly to the ghost, in the third person*) She comes over here in the evening. Just about when I'm fixin' to go to bed and I don't know how she gets in 'cause she don't have a key. She wears dresses of an evening. She don't wear nothing but old pants durin' the day. And I hate it 'cause I don't think she stays the night. And she don't ever put her car in the driveway at night like she does durin' the day. I don't know where she leaves it. Helen, where do you put your car?

***

ROSE. Helen?

PAT. I'm Pat.

ROSE. Pat's here of a night like she ought to be. I know Pat.

PAT. Do you?

ROSE. I know you too.

***

ROSE. (*Speaks to the ghost of Helen again, easier now*) Well, it's about time. You want a cookie? I got some of that old stick candy Irene brings me. Somebody's got to eat it. You want a ham sandwich? Well, I ain't got that. (*A joke*) You want to look at the jewelry? You used to like to. What do you come here for if you won't eat nothin'? You could do them dishes. (*Another joke*) You could get you a mess of them beans, I ain't goin' to eat 'em. (*She will, but it is how she makes the invitation real, something beyond polite*) You want a mess of beans? You want five dollars? I'll see you get five dollars! You're gonna get ever'thing I got!

***

ROSE. Helen!

PAT. Pat.

ROSE. Olivia! Viola! Helen! I don't care who you think you are! I know who you are if you don't!

***

If the choice in a production is for the performers to switch roles, this is the sequence that device should be used.

ROSE. Helen?

REE. Helen is dead.

ROSE. She is not.

REE. You want Olivia.

ROSE. Olivia's dead.

REE. She drove.

ROSE. Who are you?

REE. Irene.

ROSE. Irene's dead.

REE. She's not.

PAT. Where on earth is Pat?

REE. Pat who?

ROSE. She's dead too. Ever'body but me and I still don't get to die. It's my punishment for wanting too much.

***

N. Pat speaks to the ghost of Helen.

PAT. Helen? This is the new Helen and you've turned into Pat. You know why don't you? She wanted me to live with her and you seem to have moved in. I know she's deluded. She hits at little woolly brown things with a broom. But you don't act like a delusion, you don't chase her. And you do act like a ghost, don't eat, won't sit, never speak. And she is glad to see you. And you've been here every night for what, two years now? Helen, could I know sometime?

***

N. There is a second dream.

PAT. We are in bed together. That is part of how I know it is a dream. We would never be in bed together, being in the same car is hard enough. But there we are. They are asleep. I am not asleep, I can't sleep. I know why I am in bed with them. I am in the middle. I got into the middle. There is no room in the middle and it is too warm as I knew it would be. I know what I am going to do. And I do it. I take my pillow and lay it over Rose and rest myself on top of it. Ree sees me. She wakes up. All she would have to do is say stop. I would stop. I would be glad to stop. I would like to stop. I would like for her to be my mother. She should say what I'm doing is wrong, that I deserve to be punished and she should send me out into the night to cut my own switches. But she doesn't. We smile at one another. And she lies back down and pretends to sleep herself. I move my pillow and I rest on top of Ree. I was invited. When it is done, I sit in the bed, in the half dark of city nights, of bedrooms when someone is confused or ill and the bathroom light stays on, the half dark of dreams, and I hold their hands and I cry because I loved them and they are gone.

***

N. She fell.

PAT. She tells us about falling . . .

ROSE. It was a hole deep enough to a buried me in and it was right in the middle of the kitchen.

PAT. But sometimes I know she falls. She'll have a scrape or a bruise.

ROSE. Sometimes I'll lay half a day before I can get up.

N. This time, it was public. She fell in her driveway next to Ida Cole's tree while she was taking out the trash. A man who was driving by saw her fall. He stopped to help but he was a man and a stranger.

ROSE. He could of done anything he wanted. He could have stabbed me, Helen.

N. Her neighbors heard her calling. When they found her, the stranger was with her, she stopped yelling. The stranger and the neighbors decided to call the rescue squad because she was acting funny and she wouldn't let anybody touch her. The rescue squad were also men and strangers . . .

ROSE. Hit was awful where they put their hands.

N. They found that her heart beat was very erratic and they wanted to take her to the hospital just in case.

ROSE. In case I wasn't dyin', they was goin' to see to it.

PAT. Her neighbor called me.

N. (*As the neighbor*) "I like to never got in here to the phone book. Your grandmother has three locks on ever' door and all of 'em locked, I like to a never got in here and I can't find your mother's number."

PAT. Of course, Margaret, tell them to take her if you think she needs to go.

N. Margaret Goodman is not a woman to take chances with old neighbors' lives.

PAT. I called across town.

N. Price with Ree in one car and me from my house in my car, left all the suppers sitting and drove the twenty miles. I took a change of clothes so I could stay the night if I needed to and I took my dog because she'd get out more if she went with me than if she stayed and I like her company. When we got to the hospital, Grandmother was laid out in one of the gowns with an open back in the air conditioned emergency room.

PAT. Hello.

ROSE. You ain't never where I need you.

N. Ree insisted she be allowed to stay with her.

REE. She's my mother . . .

PAT. How do you feel?

ROSE. I'm cold.

PAT. I found a blanket.

N. The nurse who gave it to me said only one visitor per patient was allowed in the emergency room.

PAT. One of us will leave in a minute.

ROSE. My head feels so quare. I never felt like this before.

N. Ree packed the blanket around the part that felt quare.

ROSE. You're a smotherin' me!

N. I took the blanket . . .

REE. She's my mother . . .

N. . . . and spread it across Grandmother.

PAT. What happened?

ROSE. I fell.

PAT. I heard.

ROSE. I was takin' out the trash.

REE. Mother, you don't have to do that . . .

ROSE. Who do you think'll do it if I don't?

REE. I would but Price won't let me, that other man tells him not to let me have a car ...

PAT. Ree ...

REE. He won't let me have a car and he tells Price ...

ROSE. What?

PAT. Ree! I'm going to take you to the waiting room.

ROSE. You don't take nobody nowhere. I'm a dyin' and you're gonna to stand here and watch.

REE. Is something wrong with Mother?

ROSE. There's things the dyin' get to say to the livin' and the livin' don't get to talk back.

PAT. Are you OK?

ROSE. Everybody talks back to old women. I ain't said a word for years but one of you said something on top of it ...

REE. I better get Price, she listens to Price ...

ROSE. Put a lid on that pot!

PAT. Ree ...

ROSE. People don't like old women, they don't want old women. You don't want me.

REE. Price'll know what to do.

ROSE. I asked you to make her hush!

REE. I come over here every Saturday.

PAT. Ree, please ...

REE. Price knows. He drives me. I used to drive. We buy food and I buy a ham.

PAT. Ree, hush ...

REE. You don't tell me what to do. Everybody tries to tell me what to do. This is my mother. You're not kin to anybody, you go home.

ROSE. Helen!

PAT. Ree, buddy ...

REE. Olivia!

ROSE. You have never loved me like I loved you. I would never of left you alone and you left me. Everybody I loved best left me. I have been alone ...

PAT. You have not ...

ROSE. Irene's always a flutterin' around somewhere.

PAT. Do you have to be so stinking mean?

ROSE. And you, princess, you had a duty and you didn't do it and the Lord may forgive you but I don't.

N. She lay like death had seized her. For a moment, I thought she had managed a parting shot and gotten away.

PAT. I hope the Lord lets you in.

N. The nurse who wanted one of us out of the emergency room stuck her head through a corner of the curtain that hung around the bed.

REE. My mother is dead.

N. The nurse flew into action. Emergency room machines.

PAT. No! She wants to die . . .

N. (*As the nurse*) "Then why did you bring her here?" (*As Pat*) The nurse began shaking her, throwing aside bed clothes, attaching electrodes . . .

ROSE. Make it stop . . .

N. It was a distant voice.

PAT. Please . . .

N. (*As the nurse*) "Talk to the doctor."

ROSE. Oh, Lord, don't let 'em keep me.

N. She lay there trying to will her soul and her body apart but she didn't seem to be making much progress. The nurse switched on the machine and her heartbeat appeared on a graph. It was very fast but it slowed as we stood watching. "She was excited," said the nurse. The emergency room doctor pushed aside a corner of the curtain. "Mrs. Catron," he sounded like he had a public address system built in, "What you've got is an ear infection, it's affecting your balance and it makes your head feel funny."

ROSE. Who is he?

N. "An ear infection," he said again, "it's why you're having trouble standing up."

ROSE. Nothin' is wrong with my ears except I can't hear out of 'em.

N. "Well, you have an infection. Now, I'd keep you but I have an emergency-only situation here at the hospital so I'm going to have to send you home." He looked at me. "She does have someone with her?"

PAT. She will tonight.

N. (*As the doctor*) "She should have someone with her all the time."

PAT. Sherlock.

N. (*As the doctor*) "She needs to be kept in bed. She shouldn't be walking around with this infection. She could fall again."

ROSE. What does he want, Helen?

N. He said it again. "An ear infection." And he said, "You have to get up and get ready to go now. We need this bed."

ROSE. I'm trying to die.

N. (*As the doctor*) "I'm going to give you a shot for pain."

PAT. For pain?

N. "She fell," he said. A second nurse rolled her over and administered a shot that evidently hurt.

ROSE. They're not gonna let me die.

N. "We don't like patients to talk like that in the emergency room," said the nurse. She was trying to be cheerful. She pulled the electrodes off Grandmother's chest and moved the machine beyond the curtain. She promised to send an orderly with a wheelchair.

REE. Is Mother going somewhere?

N. The orderly was there, impatient, long before we were ready for him. We had to put on shoes.

PAT. Grandmother, you have to get up. You have to open your eyes and sit up.

ROSE. Lord. Lord. Lord.

N. It was an unwelcome resurrection, embarrassing after you have announced your intention to leave the world and spoken your last words.

REE. I should tell Price. He'll worry.

PAT. Stay where you are ...

REE. I can tell.

PAT. Ree!

REE. Nobody lets me do anything.

***

N. She did not have an ear infection. Her doctor hunted the next week. Her doctor did find erratic fluctuations in her blood pressure, the sort of thing that could make a person feel quare in the head and lead into the valley of the shadow of death, no joke. Her doctor thinks she had a stroke. She may have had a second, she may have been very close to dying. I don't know what kept her from it.

ROSE. I don't get to die till everything I love is gone.

N. And I don't know why the emergency room doctor said what he did. I don't understand why, if he thought she had an ear infection, he didn't treat her for it, begin antibiotics, something ...

PAT. Unless he lied.

ROSE. He decided me layin' in his fancy bed would be a waste of the bed.

PAT. He told me

N. (*As the doctor*) "You have to take her home"

PAT. and take her home, I did.

ROSE. You mean you took me back to jail.

N. Price and Ree came by. Price is obliged to search her house to make sure there are no robbers or other strangers before she will go in.

PAT. I bought a six-pack of beer on the way from the hospital. There were no robbers. Price took Ree on home. The dog and I prepared to stay the night.

ROSE. Are you movin' in?

PAT. No.

ROSE. Then don't bother me. Where you gonna sleep.

PAT. On the sofa.

ROSE. You could sleep with me in the bed.

PAT. I wouldn't sleep, Grandmother.

ROSE. Well I might if you did.

N. I gave the dog a bowl of water.

ROSE. She's gonna mess the house.

N. I left her to get ready for bed and drank a beer while I walked the dog.

ROSE. She lets that dog sleep in the room with her.

N. I washed her dirty dishes. She was still getting ready.

ROSE. I been doin' this longer than you have.

N. I saw her to bed, tucked her in.

PAT. The doctor said you need to stay in bed.

ROSE. What?

PAT. Stay in bed. Now, sleep tight.

N. I say sleep tight to Ree when I tuck her in. She said it to me.

PAT. I made myself a bed on Helen's sofa.

N. It was too short; I bent my knees to stay there anyway. I could have gone upstairs but it was closed in the summer heat, the windows nailed shut. Even the downstairs was hot and close. The dog found a place on the floor and panted like slow bellows.

PAT. I wasn't sleepy.

N. I was going to read, maybe drink a second beer in hopes of going to sleep at all. But there she was, up again. The dog saw her first and beat her tail against the floor. Whop, whop, whop, whop . . . (*The sound should be suggested*)

PAT. You're supposed to stay in bed.

ROSE. Well, you're out here and you're a sittin' down this time. Do ye' talk?

PAT. Grandmother, I talk.

ROSE. Most nights you don't.

PAT. I just don't say what you want.

ROSE. You want a bite of jelly?

PAT. No.

ROSE. You don't never eat nothin'.

PAT. I do. Just not jelly and not right now.

ROSE. You do not eat.

PAT. We'll eat in the morning.

ROSE. You won't be here.

PAT. You're not supposed to be up.

ROSE. I come to look at you.

PAT. Got your eyeful yet?

ROSE. Well, it's your sofa. Put a sheet on it.

N. I put her back to bed. But not for long. The dog was the warning. She'd hear Grandmother get up and begin wagging her tail without bothering to stand up. It became a signal. Whop, whop, whop . . .

ROSE. That door ain't locked.

N. So she tested the door that was locked twice over.

ROSE. You gonna come in my room?

PAT. No. Go back to bed.

N. And we went.

PAT. Stay this time.

N. Whop, whop, whop, whop . . .

ROSE. Somebody's tryin' to get in, there's a car in the driveway.

PAT. It's mine!

N. Whop, whop, whop, whop ...

ROSE. There's a light on, Helen.

PAT. Grandmother, I'm reading! And you're making me mad!

ROSE. You're not patient like you're supposed to be.

PAT. Get in the bed and stay in it! I won't stay here if you don't!

N. So she went, shuffling and unbalanced, back to her room.

PAT. I helped her into bed again. I pulled her covers up. I turned her lights out. I shut her door.

N. I do this for my mother too, when I stay with her. Every two or three hours all night long. I tell my mother,

PAT. Price likes for you to get your beauty sleep.

N. I said to Grandmother,

PAT. The doctor said to stay in bed.

N. I call the names of their authorities.

PAT. I lay back down to read. (*After a moment Rose approaches Pat from behind with a pistol in her hand. She points the gun at Pat's head*)

N. The dog came to her feet this time, her back hairs stood up in patches and she began to growl. I grabbed her, held her but I was afraid to look.

PAT. Helen?

N. I wanted the ghost, I wanted Grandmother to be seeing something besides a delusion. I wanted her to be more than just old and crazy. And she was. She was old and crazy and armed and dangerous. (*Pat looks at Rose. The gun stays pointed at Pat*)

ROSE. The man from Ida Cole's tree ... (*Rose pulls the trigger*)

N. She pulled the trigger, but the safety was on.

PAT. Give me that! (*Pat gets the gun and turns it on Rose, angry, frightened*)

ROSE. You're a killin' me! (*Pat lowers the gun*)

N. I realized the dog was not frightened of Grandmother. She was still barking at something in the bedroom.

PAT. Helen.

N. Pat speaks to the ghost of Helen.

PAT. Have you stayed in this world dead or did you come

back again out of duty? Or love? Whose life is this, Helen? You keep your mother (*Pat releases the safety on the gun*) I keep mine. (*Pat turns the gun on Ree*) Can death be a gift?

N. I locked grandmother in. If she fell, then she fell. I took the gun (*Narrator can take the gun from Pat*) and the dog and went to the car which was shaded from the moon by Ida Cole's big tree and I slept, folded across a back seat that was no more comfortable than Helen's sofa but there was air outside and the dog did not pant in the heat.

***

PAT. It is the third dream of murder.

N. As I think about them, they are the ancient elements that made up life before the periodic chart: water, air, fire. This one is fire. There is no earth dream. Maybe earth is left for the real dying.

PAT. Or maybe, tonight, I bury them. Invite them into their graves and shovel on the dirt.

N. In this dream, we are at Grandmother's house. Ree and Rose sit in the chairs in the bedroom.

PAT. I am there but I do not sit.

N. Grandmother is talking about bringing in her geraniums.

ROSE. This is the last year, I hope it is the last year. You'll have to do it, Irene.

N. And Ree is talking too.

IRENE. One of these days, we're just going to get in the car and go somewhere. We won't tell anybody where we're going, we'll just do it.

N. They do not hear each other. Besides, Ree doesn't care about geraniums and Rose doesn't want to go anywhere. I listen to them both.

PAT. I don't want to listen anymore.

N. We are there half the afternoon and they say the same thing over and over but they do not talk with one another.

ROSE. Flowers are so much trouble.

IRENE. I want to get in the car and go.

N. I want to get in the car and go. The difference is that I have a place in mind. Home. I have on my coat. I've had it on for hours but Ree will not get up.

PAT. Ree!

N. I beg another time.

IRENE. Mother and I are talking.

N. Oh, you are?

PAT. I'm going to light a fire under you if you don't get a move on.

IRENE. Why don't you? Get rid of the geraniums.

ROSE. Light one under me too and we'll all go.

PAT. If you want.

N. I wad up newspaper and stuff it under their chairs. I go out to the garage and get the lawn mower gasoline. I pour it over the newspaper.

PAT. I'm gonna do it.

IRENE. Do it. (*Pat lights a wooden match and keeps it burning*)

N. So I light the fire.

PAT. Is it hot yet?

ROSE. Not yet.

N. The room is filling up with smoke.

PAT. When it's hot you'll come outside . . .

ROSE. We will.

IRENE. When it gets hot.

PAT. It is hot.

IRENE. Then you go outside.

PAT. And I do. (*Extinguishes the match*)

N. I get in my car without waiting for them and I drive home.

PAT. In the dream, I am convinced I know where home is.

(*Blackout*)

samuel l. kelley

PILL

hill

author's introduction

Chicago was my Uncle John's passion. "The greatest city in the world," he proclaimed with boundless enthusiasm as he drove guests on tour around the Windy City. He was a self-appointed spokesman, goodwill ambassador, and cheerleader to visiting guests, many of whom were "less fortunate" relatives from the South.

Uncle John's tour included stops at the controversial Picasso sculpture in Daley Plaza; Johnson Publishing Company on downtown Michigan Avenue, Chicago's monument to black progress; and the Enrico Fermi lab at the University of Chicago. "That's where they split the atom!"

But the highlight of the Windy City tour was the trip to Pill Hill, the legendary black upper-class neighborhood on Chicago's South side, home of the "pill-pitching doctors and wheeling and dealing lawyers," that had come to epitomize the pinnacle of black achievement. The race had potential and the proof was on the Hill. African Americans who didn't live there claimed to know somebody who did, or "knew somebody who knew somebody who knew somebody on the Hill." If one's own socioeconomic lot didn't live up to the expectations of southern kinfolk lured North by Cadillacs, Lincoln Continentals, and Bonnevilles, a trip to the Hill was the correct antidote.

During the thirties, after two years of college, Uncle John had settled down in Coahoma County, Mississippi, to teach African American school children. His English was "proper," as African Americans called it. His dress was fit for a man out of *Esquire* magazine, except a black man sporting fine clothes and speaking the Queen's English in Mississippi was out of place. A white landowner left word with Uncle John's brother, "Tell that nigger he had better not come back through here again [on his way to that school house]."

Uncle John caught the train to Chicago, joining the

139

hundreds of thousands of African Americans who made their way North in search of the Promised Land. Many — as had my Uncle Albert — had packed their bags and left under the cover of darkness to escape a penury system of perpetual indebtedness that consigned them to obscene poverty in the midst of a thriving white aristocracy.

In Chicago, Uncle John studied typing and shorthand and took an office job, but hostility and jealousy from white coworkers forced him to leave. He went to work in the mill, for almost thirty years he did. If the mill was liberation from the racial oppression he left behind in the deep South, in the North it was a self-imposed exile from the harsh world awaiting African Americans who sought to fulfill their professional aspirations.

Mill wages made for a comfortable middle-class existence. When blacks began moving into Southside residences, he purchased a modest two-flat home, almost too modest for the stately French Provincial furnishings that adorned the living and dining rooms, and the fine china on which special guests dined.

Like most working-class African Americans, Uncle John espoused the Puritan work ethic and was a diehard believer that hard work kept food on the table, even if it didn't triumph over racism. He became a fundamentalist Christian. He didn't smoke, didn't consume alcoholic beverages. Mayor Richard Daly was his hero. Much to my astonishment, the fuss over marijuana puzzled him — he had tried it once and didn't get high. Each day he dressed in a suit and tie and went off to the mill. Once there, he changed into his overalls and worked all day. At the end of his shift, he showered and put on his suit and tie and departed, his head held high, his spirit unbowed.

The self-appointed family historian, he traced our roots to North Carolina and across the ocean to Madagascar. He saved his money and with his family toured West Africa in the early sixties when many of those nations were gaining independence. Films and slides of his tour formed the basis of his African lecture, which he eagerly presented to anyone who stopped by. He hosted Africans in his home and sent money, to help farm projects, back to the mother-land. Yet, at home in Chicago, he scorned as superficial and shallow the youth of the sixties and seventies who wore long Afros and dashikis.

Eternally optimistic, he had recovered from a stroke, which he suffered after he retired, was a widower for two years, then married a member of his church. He would live until the year 2000, to see the arrival of the twenty-first century before leaving this "earthly sojourn," he told me. Nineteen-eighty was to be the beginning of a new journey, a revival of the spiritual connection to the diaspora, to renew the ties that bind. The trip would be extensive, first to visit relatives in the deep South, on to North Carolina to retrace the family roots, then across the ocean to Africa. He sold his home, moved, temporarily, into a second-floor apartment in the home of his step-son-in-law. A few days later he was dead. Heart attack. Age seventy-five.

"I loved my work at the mill," Uncle John would say with great pride. And he had every reason to. The mill had been good to him. Yet I sensed the winds of change racing across the horizon the winter of 1977 when he entered the house and announced with characteristic resolve that he was voting for Jane Byrne for Mayor of Chicago. The Daly machine, now headed by Mayor Michael Bilandic, was in for a traumatic overhaul. The political landscape of America, indeed the world, would never be the same.

The mill was anything but a liberation for the postwar baby-boom generation of the sixties and seventies. For them, the mill was a dead-end street, a painful reminder of opportunities missed and denied, of personal stagnation. Job security was becoming a myth, layoffs the reality. The civil rights explosion opened up doors through which the unskilled were unable to enter. On their southward drive to the mill they met the newly emerging professional black middle class headed downtown to Michigan Avenue in their navy blue suits, wing-tipped Florshiems, and silk ties, attaché cases in hand.

A source of much both pride and envy was the arrival

from the South of a new breed of African Americans. They came armed with degrees in business, education, and sociology earned at black colleges in the South. Many were the "less fortunate" relatives who had spent their summers in the North earning college tuition. Their sights were set on the major corporations that lined Michigan Avenue, on starting their own business, on cashing in their teaching credentials at the Board of Education.

Trapped in a changing world, the mill became a temporary waiting station until the workers found the "right job," or "something better." The longer they stayed, the greater the desperation to quit.

The truth is, *Pill Hill* is not about black men at the Chicago steel mill — and it never was meant to be. It is about human beings struggling to find their niche in a rapidly accelerating and increasingly volatile world. Joe is a grim reminder to all of us that hanging onto a job we hate wreaks mental, psychic, and eventually physical havoc. But quitting is hard to do when the check coming in pays the bills. Barring a traumatic experience that compels us to act in haste, we hang on in fear. Facing the unknown generates cognitive dissonance and gnaws away at the conscience, creating unbearable agony. Like Hamlet, we are propelled into action by our inaction.

The ten-year period covered in *Pill Hill*, from 1973 to 1983, with the men gathering at Joe's for a party every five years, reflects a dramatic and revolutionary era in American life. It begins with the bell-bottoms and floral shirts of the early seventies, which always drew shouts of recognition from the audiences when the play debuted at the Yale Repertory, and ends in the early eighties, with the Reagan-era obsession with materialistic excesses. The yuppie images in Act 3 drew howls of recognition at every performance. The eighties, after all, was a time when we defined success by the Mercedes or SAAB we drove to work, the price and location of our home, and the name on our designer clothes.

In the eighties keeping up with the Joneses was in, social responsibility passé. The homeless and mentally ill were turned out onto the streets. They stumbled in our paths in the subways and train stations, camped at the footsteps of our work places, in the alleys of and bowels beneath our largest cities, while the seductive stroking of an Actor-President beguiled us into thinking it was an illusion. When we couldn't walk by them with a clear conscience, we smiled, dropped coins in their cups, and, behind their backs, complained to City Hall for not cleaning the "trash" off the street.

"Nigger" and "kike" crept back into the vocabulary but we turned a deaf ear. We winked in approval and secretly applauded Saddam Hussein for containing the Iranian threat with poisonous gasses. Cocky with confidence, Wall Street became the heartbeat of America. The stock market was invincible, or at least we thought so. Corporate raiders rode high on junk bonds. Even Yale, that bastion and guardian of the liberal arts, succumbed to defining itself by the number of Yalies earning top dollars on Wall Street.

The price of assimilation rose even higher for African Americans chasing the pot of gold at the end of the rainbow. They looked askance at pressing social issues. They thought the sky was the limit as they headed up the corporate ladder, but they soon discovered that joining the "good old boys' network" comes with an exorbitant price tag, mostly at the expense of their own cultural identity. And even then being "in" didn't guarantee one entry into the private all-white clubs.

Success estranges friends. Being a "Farrells Man" places one on a pedestal, a statue at which we gawk in envious admiration. Reticence, for fear of destroying the myth, is taken for arrogance, being "uppity." Jealousy and misunderstanding are the by-products; alienation and loneliness the inevitable consequences. Still these "striders" are heroes to friends and relatives in the old neighborhood and role models to a generation of African American men sinking to the lower depths. And so they wear the mask, comouflaging their pain beneath the Brooks Brothers suit and behind Dale Carnegie smiles.

I had the urge to write before I became a playwright. I

began formulating ideas for what became *Pill Hill* just before leaving the University of Michigan in the summer of 1976, initially setting the play in an auto factory, but only because the inspiration had come from people I knew who had worked there. My first classes in creative writing were fiction and poetry at the University of Michigan.

Later, living in Chicago with my Uncle John, and while teaching at Chicago State and the University of Illinois at Chicago, I switched the setting to the mill. Uncle John, his son Eddie, and my Uncle George had close to a hundred years between them at the mill. I met young men who wanted to get away from the mill and similar unskilled jobs. Some had quit and gone on to college full time. Others worked by day and attended school at night.

Seeing a production of Ntozake Shange's *for colored girls who have considered suicide/when the rainbow is enuf* inspired me to focus on black men, but it would be several years before I began writing in earnest. My Ph.D. dissertation at Michigan took precedence.

It was at the State University of New York at Cortland that I staged a modest production, using students with no theatre experience. The response from black men was phenomenal. A colleague in the English department, Joel Shatzky, saw the production and invited me to join his playwriting workshop. Even though my playwriting career had begun in earnest, I put *Pill Hill* aside until I began my playwriting studies at the Yale School of Drama. There, with encouragement from Dennis Scott and Leon Katz, I took it up again. By chance, I submitted it with two other plays to the Heritage Theatre at the Yale Afro American Center. Caroline Jackson, the director, selected it for a staged reading.

It played to captive audiences who paid to see undergraduates put on a staged reading for the three-day run. Parents, many from the South, up for Parents Weekend praised the play and discussed at length its significance for them and their children. Inspired, I developed the play for a workshop production the following spring at the Yale School of Drama. It generated a phenomenal response, this time from a predominantly white audience. I continued developing the script through the summer. In September, Lloyd Richards, Artistic Director of the Yale Repertory, selected the play for the 1990 WinterFest series. Again it succeeded, reaching the old and young, across racial and gender lines. The recent performances at the Philadelphia Theatre Company, directed by Oz Scott, and at Penumbra in St. Paul, Minnesota, have all touched a universal chord.

I wish to thank those who have lent their support to the development of my career, and this play in particular: Joel Shatzky, Jim McKee, Crystal Williams, and the Black Student Union at SUNY Cortland; the Yale Afro American Heritage Theatre and Caroline Jackson; my Yale School of Drama family; and Lloyd Richards for selecting *Pill Hill* for its professional debut at the Yale Repertory Theatre. Finally, I am grateful for the outstanding work of the cast and production crew who helped to bring *Pill Hill* to life at the Yale Repertory Theatre.

setting

The play takes place in Joc's basement apartment in a low-income tenement area on Chicago's South side.

characters

JOE: Age 22−32, steel mill worker.

ED: Age 22−32, student and former steel mill worker, lawyer.

CHARLIE: Age 42−52 steel mill worker for twenty years.

AL: Age 23−33, former steel mill worker. Real estate salesman.

SCOTT: Age 23−33, steel mill worker and college dropout.

TONY: Age 21−31, steel mill worker, salesman.

act 1

1973. Late summer. Chicago's Southside housing projects. Joe's basement apartment. 10:00 P.M.

The stage has two main acting areas, the living room at stage right and the dining room at stage left. Further upstage left is the kitchen, also a part of the playing area. These areas are used throughout the play, with the dining area getting most attention during the card games. There is an atmosphere of optimistic transition about the apartment. It is a bit too small for the highly energetic men who inhabit it, too small for their large ambitions, their physical prowess, their dreams.

The one window to the outside is covered with bars. Through the window, when the curtains are parted, one can look up onto the street and across to other apartments. A bedroom and a bath are off stage. The inexpensive furnishings are showing signs of wear and tear. A dinette table doubles as a recreation place. At least one of the four chairs doesn't match. The sofa is worn, but has character. Against the right wall is an inexpensive stereo. There is also a simple end table and a lamp. A set of new, unopened encyclopedia is highly visible. A used cabinet and buffet round out the dining room. A television is there but not in use. Snacks and beer cans are about, but this is not the kind of festive atmosphere that characterizes a celebration. It is more characteristic of an intense rap session, underscored by bittersweet reflection, the frustration and anxiety that come with the urgency about career changes and the uncertainty of life ahead. And there is the raunchy humor and jive — the life of the party — not to mention the vibrant energy exuded by men approaching the peak of their physical lives.

Charlie is about forty-two, in good physical condition, seasoned and toughened, yet seared by the harsh hand life has dealt black men of his generation. He has escaped a life of penury in the Mississippi cotton patch and is proud of the life the mill has enabled him to live, but he is sympathetic to the frustrations and anger of the younger men who no longer find in the mill the financial security and personal gratification their parents and grandparents found.

Joe is getting a beer from the cooler. He has a deck of cards in his hands, or somewhere close by. He is tall, somewhat lithe, and

walks with a funky strut, reminiscent of the hip, street youngsters.
He was the kid-prankster in high school, popular, but not highly
disciplined. You might say his life peaked in high school. His
costume is more flamboyant, including the high-heel shoes and the
bell-bottoms that characterized the fashions of the early seventies.
He indulges heartily in frivolity, but wants to be taken seriously
about his talk of leaving the mill.

Underneath Ed's generally cool visage is a man of purpose, of
complexity; an angry man, defiantly competitive, driven by the need
to achieve, haunted by his father's ghost. Ed prods Joe about leaving
the mill.

On the surface, Scott is super cool. Underneath the flair, the cars,
the dress is the rage at his own failure, at being exploited by a
college that needed his body to win football games. When he and Ed
meet, the sparks fly.

Al's image of the outside world, as is the case of the others, is
romantic. The mill is not providing the opportunities for the life he
wants to lead, or that his wife wants. The world is changing
around him, but he does not anticipate that the world outside the
mill in white-collar America is another jungle, one in which only the
fit survive.

Tony finds his lot in life, selling. His boyish charm, his
determination to win approval and status from his financial success
and to compensate for his lack of a college degree drive him.
Silently, he enjoys making a business move every time Ed makes one
step up the ladder.

JOE. History and poli sci? You got a double major!

ED. I couldn't decide which one so I majored in both.

JOE. I'm majoring in history. I aced U.S. history with Mrs.
Johnson. I got an A minus. You got a B plus.

ED. I beat you in Illinois state history.

JOE. Illinois history! What's the state motto?

ED. State motto—State ...

JOE. (*Taking answer from Ed*) State sovereignty, national union!
State flower?

ED. What—ah ...

JOE. Violet! The state bird?

ED. Ah ...

JOE. Cardinal! State song?

ED. Illinois!

JOE. You couldn't miss that! State animal?

ED. Animal?

JOE. White tail deer! State tree!

ED. Ah ...

JOE. It's one in your back yard, dummy!

ED. White oak!

JOE. State mineral!

ED. I can't remember all that crap!

JOE. Fluorite! Talking 'bout you beat me in Illinois history. Only thing you know is the "Land of Lincoln." And you wouldn't know that if it wasn't printed on your license plate! Capital of Nebraska?

ED. Lincoln!

JOE. Michigan?

ED. Lansing! Pennsylvania?

JOE. Philadelphia!

ED. Harrisburg! Ha, ha! Delaware?

JOE. Ah ...

ED. Dover!

JOE. Ecuador?

ED. What!

JOE. Quito! Gotcha! You got your math together?

ED. Got me a tutor!

JOE. Tutor! What you need with a tutor? You should a asked me!

ED. Got to keep a high GPA for law school.

JOE. How much he charging you?

ED. *She* doesn't charge ...

JOE. Wait a minute. What you mean "She doesn't charge."

ED. I tutor her in history and she tutors me in math.

JOE. You sly fox.

ED. Not what you think. It's purely academic ...

JOE. Her place or your place?

ED. Sometimes we meet at her place, sometimes mine.

JOE. Yeah, I get it. You Northwestern studs call it "tu-tor-ing!" I know I'm going to college now!

ED. Ah, quit lying!

JOE. I ain't lying!

ED. You'll be at the mill until your ass is pushing up daisies.

JOE. I'm walking into personnel and I'm telling them sapsuckers to put my check in the mail—just like you did.

ED. Pour piss on my head and tell me it's raining.

JOE. Seriously, Ed, I'm telling them what they can do with that humping job soon as I get my next two or three paychecks. I got sense enough to know the mill is a dead-end street.

ED. Right, Joe. A dead-end street.

JOE. And I ain't working my ass off for the rest of my life just for the chance to choose my own plot in Silent City.

ED. Joe, instead of going to the union, you should have thanked Shep for firing you and sent him a farewell bouquet telling him what he can do with his job.

JOE. Wait a minute now, I got a right to work at the mill. (*Upon seeing Charlie enter*) Ain't I Charlie?

CHARLIE. Yeah, Joe, you got a right to work at the mill. (*Good-natured humor*) But if you ask me, you ought to stay until you get Shep's job, then you can tell them what to do with that job.

JOE. Shep damn near wet his pants when I got my last promotion. Say, Ed, when I get Shep's job you can come on back to the mill.

CHARLIE. You gonna look out for your boys, Joe?

JOE. The cream of the crop ought to rise to the top!

CHARLIE. Sounds like every day is gonna be a holiday when Joe takes over!

ED. Going back to the mill Monday sounds like a real picnic.

JOE. We never should have gone to the mill in the first place!

ED. We had no choice in the first place.

CHARLIE. You had a choice.

ED. What kind?

JOE. 'Kinda choice, Charlie?

CHARLIE. Choice between the steel mill and chopping cotton for twenty cents an hour in Smithville, Mississippi.

JOE. Helluva choice, Charlie . . .

CHARLIE. (*With unbridled pride*) That's what I's doing the summer Cousin Wesley came down from Chicago in a spanking new red and white Oldsmobile—raving about the steel mill riches. (*With abandonment*) Man! I dropped my hoe! Borrowed Mama's suitcase and I was on my way to the Promise Land! I thanked God for Liberty Steel when I got up for breakfast and when I went to bed at night. I did cousin Wesley one better. I got me a Cadillac!

JOE. Naw!

ED. You had a Cadillac, Charlie?

CHARLIE. Sho nuff did . . .

JOE. Get out of here!

CHARLIE. I had to out do Cousin Wesley. Shoot, man, I cruised back to Mississippi in my spanking brand new Cadillac—white-wall tires, gold-filled cavities, and my wife and two kids by my side!

JOE. Charlie in a Cadillac!

CHARLIE. Told everybody to come on up to Chicago and make some of that good steel mill money! I wasn't the only one shouting the news around the cotton patch. So many of "us" up here from "down there" till we call Chicago "Upper Mississippi."

JOE. You see, Charlie, mill work was the only decent thing you Mississippi Negroes could get.

CHARLIE. You say you leaving the mill?

JOE. Sure as shit stinks.

CHARLIE. Where you headed, Joe?

JOE. (*Boastfully*) I'm headed to college, law school, then I'm getting on at Farrells! Baddest law firm in the Windy City!

CHARLIE. Be for real, Joe!

JOE. Why the hell can't I make it to Farrells if I want to?

CHARLIE. Okay, you're right, Joe.

ED. What we have here, Joe, is a contradiction—you say you're headed downtown to Farrells while celebrating your return to the mill. I don't get it.

JOE. Listen, Eddie, buddy, I'll be on Pill Hill before you or any other uppity Negro I know get there.

CHARLIE. Pill Hill! (*Recalling with excitement*) When we started moving in them fine homes on the Hill everybody and his mama swore before Goose Creek, they had kinfolk on the Hill!

JOE. Or swore be damn they knew somebody who knew somebody who knew somebody on the Hill! Remember how
Mr. Willie used to drive us over to the Hill and show us
them fine homes?

CHARLIE. I did Willie one better, I made my boys promise
"Daddy" they'd own a piece of the Hill one day.

ED. You want a piece of the Hill, Joe?

JOE. My pad is gonna be right on the Hill with the pill-
pitching doctors and wheeling and dealing lawyers.

ED. Now you talking, Joe!

JOE. Hell yeah, I'm sending Shep my farewell bouquet!

ED. (*Holding up beer in salute*) Joe!

JOE. (*Sudden burst of excitement, holding up can in form of a toast*)
Ed!

CHARLIE. You ain't going to work Monday, Joe?

JOE. Yeah, I'm going.

ED. What!

JOE. Till I get my first two or three paychecks.

ED. Come on, Joe ...

JOE. I got six more payments left on that Mercury Cougar ...

CHARLIE. Six months!

JOE. And four left on my stereo ...

CHARLIE. I don't know, Joe ...

ED. That Cougar ain't got six months of life left in it.

CHARLIE. I'm telling ya ...

ED. Better make your move tonight, Joe, if you're going to
beat Al out.

JOE. Al! Pam ain't gonna let Al quit the mill ...

ED. Don't bet on it ...

JOE. Not as long as he's keeping her in that red Camaro.

ED. Scott wants out, too ...

JOE. (*Spurt of loud laughter*) Scott! I know you lying now!

ED. That's why he goes ape shit whenever somebody talks
about leaving.

JOE. Scott will be at the mill long as his sorry ass looks down
towards the ground. (*Mimicking Scott with much amusement*)

CHARLIE. Scott was down at Southern University for a year or
so wasn't he?

ED. For two and half years ...

JOE. And he never did find the classrooms. (*Mimicking Scott*) "Hey man, I'm supposed to be playing big time pro ball with the Pittsburgh Steelers." Every time that bird brain sees a touchdown on TV he gets sick for the pros.

ED. He got kicked out on academic probation.

JOE. Second time they kicked him out his old man told him to take his behind to the mill or pack his bags and hit the road. Like Ed's Mama told him to do.

ED. Get the lie straight if you're going to tell it.

JOE. "Eddie Lee, you been 'round this house nearbout the whole summer—ain't found no work yet."

ED. "I'm thinking about going to college."

JOE. "If you was going to college you'd a done did like Scott, got yourself a scholarship."

ED. "Scott has a football Scholarship!"

JOE. "I don't care what kind a scholarship he got. That boy done got hisself in college. Did you forget you got a high school education?"

ED. (*With air of sassy teenager*) "Thanks for the reminder, but I do 'recall' attending my own graduation."

JOE. "You better 'recall' whose table your behind eating at, Mr. Smart Mouth, and get your mannish behind over to the mill. I know they'll find something for you to do."

ED. So off to the mill my black behind went! And they had the nerve to give me my old man's job.

JOE. (*With much amusement, as if acting out heart attack*) I can see Mr. Willie now—rolling over in his grave, "Don't take that job, Eddie, unless you want the *big one* at forty-five!"

ED. Their offer sounded okay to me for a quick minute.

CHARLIE. Sounds damn good when you broke, hungry, and out of work!

ED. Two weeks later I knew I'd landed my parachute in the wrong camp!

JOE. (*Cracking on Ed*) 'Cept it took four years for you to get the nerve to walk away.

ED. (*Retorting*) And that's a hell of a lot faster than some folk I know.

JOE. Damn you, Ed. Get the game going.

ED. Forget the game, Joe.

JOE. Pull up a chair, Charlie.

CHARLIE. I don't know, Joe . . .

JOE. You'll catch on in a couple of hands.

CHARLIE. I'm rusty at this game . . .

JOE. Just watch me.

ED. Get in a couple of summer sessions and you'll be caught up with me.

JOE. Ed, stop procrastinating — sit down and get your hand.

ED. I brought that application for college you asked me to bring.

JOE. We deal with the application after the game.

ED. We deal with it now, Joe!

JOE. Anybody for another beer?

CHARLIE. Yeah — I'll take one.

JOE. (*Going after beer*) Check these out if you doubt my plans for college. (*Referring to encyclopedia*) Encyclopedia Britannica! Best encyclopedia in the world. Bought um from Tony.

ED. Tony!

JOE. Last week.

ED. Come on, Joe! I know Tony quitting the mill too if he keeps finding suckers to buy books they'll never read.

JOE. I'll be a heavy ass mother hubbard by the time I'm done reading all that.

ED. We'll go for Northwestern.

JOE. Northwestern! Michigan, man. Northwestern's football team sucks.

ED. We won't be playing football.

JOE. Get your hand, Ed.

ED. (*Resisting*) Takes four to play whist.

JOE. I ain't had accounting 101. (*Doorbell rings*) Da da! And I don't think I'm going to need it tonight! (*Crossing to door*) Brace yourself for a schooling at the card table. (*Joe opens door. Al enters, still reeling from a knock-down-drag-out domestic quarrel*)

AL. (*Entering in a huff, looking haggard and tense*) Hi, Joe, Ed, Charlie.

JOE. Look at you. You come through a hurricane on the way over?

AL. Yeah — had a knock-down-drag-out fight with my old lady.
She tells me she's got to have a four-bedroom house and a
brand new Firebird. "Four bedrooms, baby! We got me
and you and two kids. What we need with four bedrooms?"
"We got to have an extra bedroom for the visiting kinfolk."

CHARLIE. Time for somebody to start moonlighting!

AL. I told her if she wants all that I got to be more than a
two-bit inspector at the mill and she's gonna be doing
something else beside standing behind a cosmetic counter
in a downtown department store pushing perfume bottles
under people's noses and smearing war paint on their
faces.

JOE. It's makeup, Al.

AL. It's horse manure and I'm tired of rubbing my nose in it!
(*Reaches in coat pocket and pulls out handfull of cut-up credit
cards*) Look at this! (*And flings them around room*) Goddamn
credit cards! I told her I was tearing up every one of these
damn credit cards. "I know your black ass lying now!"
"Yes I am. The hell if you charging my ass into the
grave!" "Nigger, get you black hands out of my purse
before I break um off!" (*To others*) I'm not owing my soul
to these department stores any longer. Takes damn near a
whole year to pay off the Christmas bills. "We got big
families to buy presents for Christmas." "Let them eat
turkey and sweet potato pie." (*Pulling more cards from his
pocket*) I ask her, "Where the hell did you think we were
going when we got married, woman?" "We got married
because I was five months pregnant and we were trying to
make it to the alter before my daddy lynched your ass."
"Okay, okay," I told her, "but it's gonna be a cold day in
hell when number three get here." (*Shaking head in astonishment*) Whew! Then she scared the shit out of my ass. "It
might be on the way now for all you know." "YOU BETTER
STOP IT IF HE IS!" We are both bright and intelligent
people. Four, maybe five years from now, we could be
through college. I told her that. She looks at me. "You
might find yourself marching down that aisle *solo*!" (*With
measured, provocative tone*) I told her: "That ain't no big deal,
baby, 'cause I'm MARCHING DOWN THAT AISLE BY MYSELF,

OR WITH SOMEBODY ELSE IF I HAVE TO."

JOE. That's when the pots and pans started coming after your ass.

AL. (*Amused relief*) She went for the frying pans, I left for the party!

JOE. (*Getting beer for Al*) Cool yourself off with a beer.

AL. Make it champagne. I sent Shep my farewell bouquet today.

ED. What I tell you, Joe?

JOE. Quit lying, Al.

AL. I'm for real, Joe.

JOE. You ain't quitting the mill.

AL. My Cousin Phil just finished up his degree in Business Administration.

ED. Already?

JOE. Time be flying by like crazy . . .

AL. He hasn't been up here two weeks and has landed a job in management training with IBM.

JOE. Well blow my ass down!

AL. On his way to the executive suite!

CHARLIE. Alright for Cousin Phil!

AL. He was one of our "less fortunate" Mississippi kinfolk we were helping out.

ED. You can't be jealous, Al.

AL. I'm not jealous, not the least goddamn bit! My first cousin, comes up here, freeloads off my parents, earns his tuition, finishes college and brings his ass back up here on my turf and lands a job at a place where I thought I could only dream about working.

CHARLIE. Ain't you proud of Cousin Phil?

AL. I'm proud as hell of the son of a bitch! Damn near half that Mississippi Negro's graduating class up here getting the white-collar jobs and we were born in this city!

CHARLIE. Al, I hate to throw it up in your face, but Phil doesn't have a wife and two kids to look after.

AL. My old lady threw that in my face along with the pots and the pans tonight. You see her daddy's life begins and ends at the mill, and he's got in his thirty years. Now he's telling her I ought to spend my life at the mill.

CHARLIE. The mill has been mighty good to her daddy.

AL. Charlie . . .

CHARLIE. He retired with a house and two cars in the garage.

AL. Charlie, you got ten years to retirement, I got twenty-six. My honeymoon with the mill is over!

JOE. What makes you think a college degree gonna make you better off than you are now?

ED. Didn't you hear what he said about Phil?

JOE. A college degree like a still born baby if you don't do nothing with it.

AL. I don't intend to use it for toilet paper.

JOE. Do what I'm doing . . .

ED. What the hell you doing?

JOE. Go back to the mill till you get five or six paychecks under your belt.

AL. That's like a stupid horse going back into a burning barn.

ED. And everybody but the horse knows his ass is in for a scorching.

JOE. I ain't cutting my nose off to spite my face. Tell them Charlie.

CHARLIE. Quitting when you got a paycheck coming in is like a warm bed in winter, easy to get into and hard to get out.

JOE. You'll be at the mill when I get there Monday morning. Here you go, Al. Check out my application for college if you don't think I'm serious about quitting.

ED. You're too chicken.

JOE. (*Going for card table*) What—I ain't taking this crap from a college boy. Get the game going. (*There is no real interest in the card game*)

ED. Going back is a game of chicken, Joe.

JOE. It's security, bird brain. You should have learned that in one of those books you be pushing around the library. Pull up a chair, Charlie. You be my partner.

CHARLIE. (*Hedging*) Told ya—I ain't gonna be much help to you.

JOE. (*Trying to be humorous*) See, the reason I'm going back Monday is cause Charlie needs somebody to keep him company.

CHARLIE. Don't come back to keep me company. I got in

twenty years.

JOE. Twenty years, Charlie. You damn near old as Methuselah.

CHARLIE. I feel like it when I'm going to work on the graveyard shift.

JOE. Come on over, Al . . .

AL. Naw, naw, I don't have much time, Joe.

JOE. (*Spurt of loud laughter*) Time is all you got till your old lady cools off enough to let you back into the house. Get your hand, Ed.

ED. I'm not playing, Joe.

JOE. Don't rain on my parade, Ed.

ED. (*Going to phone and dialing*) Call Shep and tell him you're not coming in Monday morning because you're quitting.

JOE. Shep isn't on the evening shift.

ED. (*Dialing*) We'll see about that . . .

CHARLIE. He's on the evening shift tonight, Joe.

JOE. I'll tell him Monday morning.

AL. Monday morning — tell him now . . .

CHARLIE. You going to work to tell the man you quitting?

ED. (*Ed dials number and speaks*) Shep? Yeah. Ed. Ed Williams. No, no, no. I'm not coming back. I got somebody here who wants to talk to you about coming in Monday. (*Covering mouthpiece and beckoning Joe*) Joe! Shep is here. He's waiting for your answer. (*Joe hedges, but Ed speaks as if Joe is there*) He's coming — here he is, Shep. (*Others wait in anticipation. Joe takes phone as if about to speak, then after a moment hangs up*)

JOE. (*Realizes Ed has pulled a joke on him*) The next time you pull that number you better have your B.A. and your law degree to back it up.

AL. You have to let go, Joe.

JOE. Not until I know where my ass is landing. I got to have something to latch on to.

ED. Joe . . .

JOE. Can't just up and walk off the job.

ED. What will you have to latch on to the next time they kick you out?

JOE. I'm paying the union to protect me from bastards like Shep. Pull up a chair, Al.

AL. Joe, what do you see beyond the mill?

JOE. What?

ED. Yeah, Joe ...

AL. When you let go, what do you see?

JOE. (*Fearfully*) What if I ...

ED. Slip and fall?

AL. You won't ...

ED. Tell him, Charlie, he'll land on his feet ...

AL. Yeah, Charlie ...

ED. Didn't you land on your feet when you left the cotton patch?

AL. Charlie!

CHARLIE. (*With anxiety*) I can't speak for Joe!

JOE. Get the game going!

ED. Charlie! (*Doorbell rings and Joe rushes to answer it*)

JOE. I got it! (*Joe opens door. Scott and Tony are there. Scott is handsome, flamboyantly stylish in clothes that accentuate his athletic physique. Tony is dressed in a sports jacket and tie, more typical of the part-time encyclopedia and Bible salesman he has become, and the more sophisticated salesman he hopes to become*)

JOE. Welcome to my return-to-the-mill party.

SCOTT. Till Shep kicks your ass out again. (*Grabs a handful of munchies and strikes a pose by the door, waving to others*) What it is, good people. (*Others speak to Scott variously. He blushes and turns to window, looking outside with great pride*)

JOE. (*Noticing how Tony's dressed*) Tony—

TONY. Joe ...

JOE. Dressed like you here to con somebody into buying a Bible.

TONY. (*Blushing, but with pride*) Practice makes perfect.

SCOTT. (*To window, beckoning to Joe*) Joe, over to the window.

TONY. (*Going to window*) Got him a brand new hog.

JOE. (*To window, then outside*) What? Naw! Let me go get a look at Scott's new ride. (*Scott and Joe exit. Tony turns to others*)

TONY. (*Pulling out card*) Evening, Mr. Charlie. In need of a Bible?

CHARLIE. Salvation is free!

TONY. You got the money, I'll put a price tag on it.

CHARLIE. Not on mine you won't.

TONY. (*Passing card to Ed*) Ed.

ED. Save it, Tony.

TONY. You need a complete set of the World's Great Books and Encyclopedia Britannica to go along with that degree?

ED. They free as long as I'm working in the library.

AL. You got a quick lesson on how to make a killing in real estate?

TONY. Pam looking for a house?

AL. Might as well learn the real estate business while I'm shopping for a house. (*Scott and Joe enter*)

JOE. Burgundy with white interior!

TONY. Matches his outfit.

JOE. (*With much amusement, teasing*) Who's ragged ass VW is that out there?

SCOTT. Ain't my shit —

JOE. Somebody call a tow truck to haul that trash to the junk yard.

SCOTT. Whoever he is he can't be looking for any broads in a contraption like that.

JOE. You say that trash heap will scare the women off?

ED. I'll bet the owner isn't sleeping in his VW.

SCOTT. (*Faking surprise*) Ah! EXCUUUUUSE me, Eddie brother! Didn't know that was your ride.

ED. I'm sure you'll get over it, Scott.

SCOTT. I'm sooooo sorry!

ED. (*With stinging sarcastic irony*) Tell me something I don't know.

CHARLIE. Al's quitting the mill, Scott ...

JOE. He's not quitting the mill.

ED. The hell if he ain't quitting.

SCOTT. What's that?

ED. He's coming to his senses. (*Other dialogue intersticed between Scott's and Ed's speeches, though spoken with the awareness of the growing tensions between the two men*)

JOE. Say, ah, Scott, Tony ...

SCOTT. Something wrong with the mill?

JOE. I'll get you guys a beer ...

ED. The mill is fine with me.

SCOTT. Lay off the mill, chump.

ED. Even if some bird brains can't see a dead-end street staring them in the face.

JOE. Kind a beer you guys want?

SCOTT. Stuff it Ed!

ED. Suck an egg, Scottie.

JOE. (*From refrigerator*) Bud for you, Scott?

SCOTT. (*Overlapping*) Scott! My name's *Scott*, Eddie boy.

JOE. Kind you want, Tony?

TONY. Take what you got.

SCOTT. Mill my bread and butter.

JOE. Charlie?

CHARLIE. (*Deliberately humorous, uneasily*) All of it taste the same
   to me ...

ED. Man can't live by bread alone.

SCOTT. Mill was your bread and butter, too ...

JOE. Speak for yourself, Charlie ...

SCOTT. Your *bread* and your *butter* before you started pushing
   books 'round the library for peanuts and ice cream wages.

AL. (*With annoyance*) Chill out, Scott ...

ED. It's your life, Scott.

SCOTT. Eat shit, dog face!

ED. After you, moose breath!

SCOTT. Listen, cat litter breath ...

ED. I don't have to, roach turd!

SCOTT. Damn if you don't, camel breath!

ED. I'm not going to, camel fart!

SCOTT. Camel snot, camel ass, camel toe jam!

ED. (*After a quick beat*) Camel cum.

CHARLIE. Gentlemen! Give that camel a break!

SCOTT. (*Furious*) I don't like the idea of this snob talking 'bout
   the mill like he's some big shot.

ED. The mill is a great place to work, Scott.

SCOTT. You see, Charlie! I know what the punk is doing.

ED. The mill comes highly recommended.

SCOTT. I have a great urge to leave my footprints on somebody's
   rear end for bad-mouthing the mill.

ED. Face it, Scott, it's your old man's ass you want to kick.

SCOTT. Listen, punk, just because your goddamn old man
   kicked the bucket at the mill doesn't mean everybody else
   is gonna fucking drop dead on the job!

JOE. Chill out, Scott ...

AL. Scott! (*Fearful anticipation for a tense moment*)

CHARLIE. Sorry, Ed —

ED. Don't — apologize, Charlie!

SCOTT. (*To Joe, anxiously*) I need a light, Joe.

JOE. (*Whispering*) You bring it? (*To others with much amusement*) Remember how Mr. Willie dressed up for the mill?

SCOTT. (*To Joe*) Yeah, I brought it.

CHARLIE. (*With great admiration*) Yeah ...

JOE. (*To Scott*) Kind you got?

CHARLIE. Navy blue suit ...

SCOTT. (*Low, to Joe*) Mexican red.

CHARLIE. Every day ...

JOE. (*To Scott*) Great shit!

TONY. Don't forget his Stacy Adams.

JOE. Boy, Mr. Willie be coming in to work sharp as a needle dick dog.

ED. Strutting to the car with his head up, chest out, shoulders back. Heading downtown to be in the "business folks' rush hour."

JOE. He be putting the dudes to shame on Michigan Avenue.

ED. "Boy, bring me my attaché case."

JOE. How come he didn't wear wing tips?

ED. Made his feet look too damn big.

JOE. "Eddie son, your old man's gonna drive down here ten years from now and wave to you and Joe crossing Michigan Avenue with the business folk. You boys better wave back, you hear."

ED. (*Bitterly*) I still see his face all twisted in pain the day that stroke cut him down like he was a piece of firewood! Ripe old age of forty-five! Every day I walked into that place I saw his face.

JOE. That was Mr. Willie's ghost chasing your ass. "Eddie son. Told ya. Wanna see you downtown." (*Deliberately comical*) Without them wide ass wing tips. (*Enjoys his joke tremendously, others laugh at the unexpected relief*)

SCOTT. (*Quiet desperation*) Joe!

JOE. Hold on!

CHARLIE. I got that sinking feeling in the pit of my stomach when Willie came in — hurt me to see him changing into his filthy inspection overalls. But when I saw him leaving decked out in his three-piece navy blue suit (*With much admiration and pride*) straightening up his shoulders and sticking out his chest, stuck my chest out and straightened my shoulders, too!

SCOTT. (*Impatiently*) Joe — got to get that light!

JOE. Hold your horses!

AL. So how come you didn't quit, Charlie?

CHARLIE. Who the hell said I want to quit?

JOE. Charlie knows where that Cadillac and them gold-plated teeth came from.

SCOTT. (*Satirical amusement*) Nothing like driving back down home to Mississippi in a spanking brand new Cadillac.

CHARLIE. You guys lay off my Cadillac.

SCOTT. (*Restless*) Meet me in the bedroom, Joe. (*Scott goes into bedroom*)

JOE. Come on in for a quick smoke guys — Tony ...

TONY. Catch you in a minute.

JOE. Al, Ed ...

AL. You can smoke mine tonight, Joe.

JOE. What's the deal, Ed?

ED. Don't want to teach Sunday School on a high.

JOE. I keep forgetting you lawyers into ... (*Joe exits to bedroom, gesturing as if snorting coke*)

TONY. Gentlemen, I'd like a few moments of your time to speak to you about the gift of knowledge.

ED. The gift of knowledge ... (*Ed and Al listen with a mixture of amusement and mild annoyance, becoming increasingly impatient*)

TONY. The gift of knowledge is our key to success, the gateway to a world of opportunities. Knowledge endows us with the self-confidence we need to get ahead and stay ahead in the game of life. For the more you know, the greater your chances for climbing the ladder of success. Knowledge deepens our understanding of the past, helps us comprehend the complex world in which we live, and prepares us for an uncertain future. Knowledge enriches our impoverished lives in the fine arts and humanities and strengthens our sense of cultural awareness! Knowledge opens our eyes to the wonders of nature, and the beauty of our blessed planet! Knowledge can save us many needless trips to the library!

ED. Wait a minute, Tony!

AL. Get to the point ...

TONY. Encyclopedia Britannica comes recommended by the greatest educators ...

AL. How much Tony?

TONY. For just a few dollars a month.

AL. How few?

TONY. You can own this famous edition ...

ED. Tony!

AL. How few?

TONY. For just thirty-five dollars a month ...

ED. (*Nodding toward bedroom*) Tony—get that crap out of here!

AL. Go smoke a joint! (*Joe opens door and sticks head out*)

JOE. Say, listen, ah, Tony. Scott wants to buy a set of encyclopedia ...

TONY. Yeah?

JOE. Uh uh, I knew that would get him in here. We ain't got but a few hits left.

TONY. (*Grabs briefcase and heads into bedroom*) I also have the Great Books, every thing you wanted to know about the great philosophers but was afraid to ask.

CHARLIE. So what's it gonna be with you and the mill, Al?

AL. Phil made it, so I know damn well I can make it.

CHARLIE. You'll fall flat on your ass doing it because Phil did it.

AL. I'm doing it because I have to, dammit!

CHARLIE. That's right! "Because I have to, dammit!" Just what I told Mama when I borrowed her suitcase to get the hell out of Mississippi.

AL. (*To himself*) I'm not falling into a goddamn rut at the mill for the rest of my life!

CHARLIE. "I ain't busting my ass in the MAN's cotton patch for twenty-five cents an hour to retire on welfare cheese and powdered milk—NOOOOO LAWD!"

AL. If I'm busting my ass for a living—damn well better be for something I want to do.

CHARLIE. "I'm taking my black behind to Chicago and making me some of that good steel mill money."

AL. If they close down the mill, only thing I'm trained to do is hang out at the unemployment office.

ED. (*Picking up on Al's line*) Until they send you over to the welfare line.

AL. That'll be a cold day in hell.

CHARLIE. "I'm gonna have myself a home and two cars in the garage."

ED. Your mother try to stop you from leaving Mississippi?

CHARLIE. You ever heard tell of a colored person saying no to the Promise Land? More money I made, more she got for herself. She wanted to ride in my Cadillac too.

AL. I'm not making sense to you, man. You've been at the mill too goddamn long!

CHARLIE. You make a helluva lot of sense to me. Man's a damn fool to stay on a job he hates.

AL. You saying I ought to quit?

CHARLIE. I haven't said anything.

AL. Yeah you did!

CHARLIE. Wait a minute — don't go putting words in my mouth!

ED. I thought that question was settled when you walked in baptizing the place with cut-up credit cards.

AL. Charlie?

ED. Charlie can't make up your mind for you!

AL. Butt out, Ed! You don't have a wife and two kids to look after. Charlie?

CHARLIE. Don't look at me.

AL. You got twenty years at the mill, man!

CHARLIE. Don't care if I been there a hundred years I'm not telling you nothing about quitting.

AL. I'm asking your advice, Charlie!

CHARLIE. Your wife got the last word on that.

ED. Looks like you guys will be seeing each other Monday morning.

AL. Butt out, EDWARD! Charlie?

CHARLIE. Even before I left the Mississippi cotton patch, I had the image of the Cadillac I was driving back home in. Long black one, with fins — kind that make you feel like you were floating on air — like it would just up and fly any minute. Shame they don't make them like that any more. (*Joe, Tony, and Scott have entered*)

JOE. I can see Charlie heading back down to Mississippi in his brand new El Dorado, drinking Kool Aid and eating homemade ice cream on the back porch with the home folk and bragging about his steel mill riches!

SCOTT. My man, Charlie, driving down home in a brand new hog — thank God for GM.

JOE. Charlie, tell Tony and Scott about that Cadillac.

CHARLIE. (*Resisting, anxiously*) You guys don't want to know about that Cadillac.

TONY. Yeah we do Charlie!

CHARLIE. No you don't!

JOE. How many speeding tickets you get?

TONY. Speeding tickets ...

SCOTT. Naw, man, he can outrun the cops in a Cadillac ...

TONY. Me and Scott missed the Cadillac story ...

SCOTT. You owe us one, Charlie ...

JOE. Come on, Charlie ...

CHARLIE. (*Uneasy laughter*) Figured all I had to do was put on my Stepin Fechit mask when I got to Cairo, Illinois and I'd be home free. (*Others are amused*) See, I didn't worry about the people sitting in, marching through water hoses, police dogs, getting shot, murdered while they sat in church shouting and praising the Lord. I had my Cadillac — hell I had Cadillac immunity! Pulled up in front of my kinfolks' house — whole lot of um scrambling to "RIDE IN COUSIN CHARLIE'S CADILLAC!" They wanted to come back to Chicago. Bet you I cruised to the grocery store a dozen times before noonday — showing off my Cadillac. I got my wife and two boys and headed over to Smithville so Mama and Daddy could show the neighbors how fine their boy from up North was doing — 'twas near 'bout sundown. The MAN pulled up beside me — lights flashing! "Pull off the highway behind me at this here next road, boy." Wasn't speeding. Hell, I's cruising! Pulled off behind them. Flashed my gold teeth. Far as I's concerned I had Cadillac immunity. (*Spurt of painful and bitter laughter. Proceeding with painful difficulty*) They got out—walked back to my car. "Boy, where you get this here car?" "Bough it." "Whatcha buy it wid?" "My money." "Got us a smart nigger from up North on our hands. Been running all over town in this here car, boy." "Beg your pardon?" "Nigger, my partner said ya been running your black ass all over town in this here goddamn car!" "Down here to stir up trouble?" "Nope, won't be no trouble from me if . . ." "Boy, did I hear you say 'NO SIR?'" "I don't remember." "Get your ass out the car nigger! "Gonna refresh your MEMORY." "Get your ass out the car, nigger!" "Over in front of this police car." "On your knees, boy!" (*Struggling, painfully*) Got down on my . . . . They stepped up—one on each side—stuck both pistols behind my ears. Cocked the pistols! "Clean off them headlights." "Touch um wid ya hands and I'll splatter ya colored brains from here to Chicago." I started licking— grime, grit, bugs. Licked um clean. "You forgot the other side, BOY!" "Start licking, nigger!" I licked them—clean. (*With unbearable difficulty*) Bertha hid my sons' faces in her bosom. "Stand your black ass up." "Drop your pants." I hedged. One of um's foot knocked my ass out of kilter. Dropped my pants. Tall lanky one pulled out a hunting knife. "Drop your goddamn drawers." "HUH?" "Your drawers, NIGGER! YOUR GODDAMN DRAWERS!" Dropped my underwear. He stepped up behind me. "Grab your toes." "Your toes, NIGGER!" I . . . I . . . gra . . . grabbed my toes . . . fe . . . felt his knife against my balls. "Cough nigger!" (*Coughs delicately, as though knife is against his balls*) "Louder!" (*Louder, but delicately*) "Louder, nigger!" (*Again, delicately*) "This ain't gonna do." "Make the nigger sneeze." "Take a deep breath, boy." "DEEP BREATH BOY!" "Now—gimme a gut-busting sneeze, boy!" "GUT-BUSTING SNEEZE, NIGGER!" (*At the point of sneezing Charlie gives a loud spurt of angry, bitter laughter*) Broke down crying. Bastards had me where they wanted me. Took my money, threw my wallet at me. "Boy, don't let sunup catch your black ass in this town." "Hear what the man said, NIGGER!" "YESSIR!" (*With much relief*) Next morning—saw that Chicago skyline rising to meet me. Parked that Cadillac. Washed it. Waxed it. Pulled it up in

the garage. Jacked it up on four blocks. To hell with that
Cadillac! Looking out for my family and getting them a home
and making sure my boys would never see me on my knees
licking the MAN's headlights was the most important thing
in my life! I got me a second job — moonlighting janitor —
fifteen years I did. (*With affection*) Bertha, she went to
work ... we cooked that old Irish potato more ways than
the good Lord counted days in the month. "What's for
dinner honey?" "Chicken pot pie, baby!" "I'm into my
second helping — ain't found a piece of chicken, sweetheart
...." (*To others, with amusement*) Helluva lot of ways to
cook beans and corn bread ...

JOE. Corn bread and buttermilk ...

ED. Corn bread and collard greens ...

SCOTT. Corn dogs, I eat corn dogs ...

AL. Corn muffins for me, man ...

ED. I can get down on some hush puppies and collard greens ...

TONY. I like corn waffles myself ...

AL. (*Unguarded moment of pride*) My old lady makes me
muffins!

SCOTT. You got to try corn dogs, man!

AL. She makes my muffins with whole kernel corn!

JOE. Grandma Bee made me corn bread and molasses.

CHARLIE. Cornbread and molasses! Staff of life for my people.
(*Shaking head in amazement*) Can't believe it — twenty years
at the mill.

JOE. Long ass time, Charlie.

CHARLIE. Don't seem like it — every time I look around my
wife telling me what she wants for Christmas.

JOE. Years be flying by like months these days.

AL. Look at how fast them four years at the mill have gone by.

JOE. You ain't lying.

CHARLIE. All you need is a strong back to do what we do.

JOE. Four years of college will fly by before you know what's
happening.

CHARLIE. I've thought about it, prayed over it for a long time.
(*With resolve*) I'm gonna operate that machine. You guys
hear me? I'm gonna operate that machine! What you guys
gonna do?

JOE. (*After a moment, resolutely*) Tell you what? Don't you guys look for me at the mill Monday morning.

AL. I'm right behind you, Joe ... (*Lights out*)

act 2

Five years later. Late evening. Joe's apartment. The temporary look that characterized Joe's apartment five years ago has settled into a state of permanence. Al and Joe huddle for a joke by Joe that's just gotten through the punch line as scene opens.

AL. Sold my first house to Cousin Phil.

ED. Pill Hill?

AL. Oak Park.

ED. (*Rising from chair and holding up beer can in form of toast*) To Chicago's next real estate success story!

AL. And to your success in Northwestern law school. (*Ed and Al slap cans together in cheerful toast. Joe joins in awkwardly*)

JOE. (*Impotently*) Yeah — to you guys. (*Eagerly, to Al*) I'm gonna be your first Pill Hill customer.

ED. Don't make him starve to death, Joe.

JOE. I'm serious as a heart attack. Last Monday, I decked myself out in a three-piece pinstripe suit, and my wing tips, my attaché case in my hand and I strutted into Farrells ...

AL. Come on, Joe ...

JOE. I ain't jiving — brother sees me coming in, props himself on his mop, winks and gives me a high five!

ED. Got something for you Joe. (*Slapping application into Joe's hand*) An application to college.

JOE. Good — I'll get on it first thing next week.

ED. All you got to do is sign it.

JOE. (*Looking over application*) You filled some of it out already.

ED. Getting myself in some legal practice. You got to get your letters of recommendation.

JOE. Kennedy-King is a two-year junior college. You went to Northwestern.

ED. Get a great GPA at Kennedy-King then transfer to Northwestern.

AL. Why did they demote you back down to testman's helper?

JOE. Somebody ruined the measurements on a carload of steel and Shep blamed it on me. How the hell can one man ruin a whole carload of steel? He jumps up in my face. "Boy, you calling me a liar?" Man, I knocked his ass to the floor. And the union backed me up!

ED. So who ruined that steel?

JOE. The hell if I know. Charlie too scared to talk 'cause he's up for promotion and Scott got his tail tucked between his legs 'cause he's scared he'll get bumped if he spills the beans. You know I'm the only one in the gang who had the courage to stand up to Shep and tell the bastard he was wrong.

ED. You won your case, you got your job back ...

AL. You've proved your point ...

ED. So get the hell out!

JOE. Naw, naw, man ...

ED. What!

JOE. I got to go in Monday ...

AL. Joe!

JOE. I can't wait to see Shep wipe the egg off his face Monday morning when I walk in.

ED. Listen, man, the mill is going to run, with or without you and Shep.

JOE. I won't be there no longer than it takes me to get my next two or three paychecks.

ED. I heard that tired ass song five years ago.

JOE. It ain't no tired ass song! Soon as I save up a few months ahead on my Great Books.

ED. Your what?

JOE. Here, let me show ya. Keeping um in the plastic covers so they won't collect dust. The Great Books!

ED. Come on, Joe ...

JOE. Getting ready for college and law school.

ED. Tony still running his game on you.

JOE. (*Taking himself seriously*) See, the way I figure it, every college graduate ought to have a working knowledge of the great minds.

AL. Most profound, Joe ...

JOE. I can sit at my desk and converse with the great minds.

AL. Most profound ...

JOE. (*Over at books, pompous, serious air*) Look at all this—Aristotle, Euripides, Sophocles, Cervantes, Dantee ...

ED. Dante man! Dante!

JOE. Dante. Be a heavy ass mother hubbard by the time I'm done reading all this shit. (*The men are placing party banner up: "Congratulations Charlie"*)

AL. What time is Charlie getting here?

JOE. He'll be here after his shift.

AL. Charlie said he was gonna do it. "I'm gonna operate that machine. YOU GUYS HEAR ME?"

JOE. And he did it—he's a big dog now.

ED. (*Pulling application out for Joe*) I need your signature on that application, Joe.

JOE. Give me time to check it out.

ED. Free service for tonight only.

AL. (*Pulling stamped, addressed envelope from pocket*) I just happen to have a stamped envelope, already made out to the admissions office.

ED. Come on, Joe.

JOE. I don't know about this.

ED. My fee goes up to one hundred per hour after midnight.

AL. OUCH!

JOE. (*Al on one side and Ed on the other*) Don't get too close—can't tell what else you got up your sleeve.

ED. Joe—come on!

JOE. All right, all right!

AL. (*Holding up envelope*) Sign it and drop it in, Joe.

JOE. I haven't read it yet!

ED. Trust me, Joe. (*Doorbell rings*)

JOE. I got to get the door.

ED. Joe! (*Overlapping*)

JOE. They here! (*Overlapping*)

AL. We got to have your John Hancock on this application, Joe.

JOE. (*Signing application*) All right, dammit! (*Joe crosses to door, excited*)

ED. Well done, Joe ...

JOE. (*Opens door and Scott and Tony enter*) Lawd today!

TONY. Joe, congratulations.

SCOTT. For what? Shep sent his ass back to the front door and made him crawl his way back to first base.

JOE. That suppose to be a joke?

SCOTT. I'm kidding, Joe ... (*To Ed and Al*) Steel mill alumni!

ED. Your world, Scott. I'm just thankful to be here ...

SCOTT. (*Taking Ed's line, with good-natured humor*) ... "thankful to be here!" Yeah — I bet you are ...

AL. What you driving?

TONY. Cadillac!

SCOTT. (*Pulling out champagne*) Something for Charlie — celebrating his promotion to chip machine operator. So, Mr. Real Estate, sold your first pad on the Hill?

AL. Saving my first Pill Hill house for Joe.

SCOTT. You'll be saving it till the Hill turns into a ghetto.

JOE. Piss off, Scott.

TONY. (*Pulling bottle of champagne from bag*) Joe, look what I brought.

JOE. You didn't have to do this.

SCOTT. It's in honor of himself.

TONY. (*With much delight*) My new job selling home insulation supplies.

JOE. Cashing in on the winter freeze?

SCOTT. Right in your back yard ...

TONY. (*Proudly*) Figure the folk over here gonna need some insulation this winter.

SCOTT. Wake up on a cold January morning in a dump like this — reach down and you'll feel icicles — *hanging off your ass*!

JOE. (*To himself, Tony's excitement*) I could use a gig like that.

AL. Who's the company?

SCOTT. Windy City ass warmers!

TONY. (*Blushing*) Lansing Home Insulating Company.

JOE. How you pull that off?

TONY. I showed the MAN my outstanding sales volumes in Bibles and encyclopedia and his eyes lit up Christmas trees. Only thing that matters is whether or not I can make a buck. I'm marketable because they need me to sell home insulation to brothers and sisters in this part of town.

SCOTT. The MAN shows his face in this neighborhood, he may not get out. (*Crossing to refrigerator*) Where your beer, Joe?

JOE. I hope you ain't forgot what a refrigerator looks like.

SCOTT. Where's your lite, Joe? (*Looking through beer*) You know this regular beer ain't good for my waistline.

JOE. Hit the floor and do fifty push-ups.

SCOTT. Bull—now I got to find some broad and work off these calories.

TONY. I'll give you a few bucks to tip me off to some good neighborhood leads, Joe.

SCOTT. You can start with this dump.

JOE. You won't sell the time of day to these people 'round here.

TONY. Joe, I'm a salesman! Get my foot inside the door, run my sales pitch and crack the toughest nuts.

JOE. (*Mainly to himself, while Tony carries on*) I tried selling Bibles once.

TONY. (*With much excitement*) Gentlemen!

JOE. (*Speaking with amusement*) My ass damn near starved to death ...

TONY. This is a country of buying and selling!

JOE. Sold one Bible the whole week ...

TONY. All you have to do is make your customer believe in you and you can close a sale *right now*!

JOE. (*Through laughter*) Got laid more times than I sold Bibles!

TONY. (*Picking up on Joe*) Joe, you got to make your customer believe he's purchasing eternal life! A man sells peace of mind, not Bibles. In your hands is the key to his happiness. You know you hot when you can sell a dope addict a gold-plated Bible.

SCOTT. (*With much amusement*) I ought to be selling Bibles on the side.

TONY. My biggest problem is getting black folk to buy from their own people. You should see the look on their faces when I walk in, and I'm in my three-piece suit — three-piece, mind you!

AL. Scared you gonna rob um . . .

ED. You know "we" steal everything we get our hands on.

TONY. Last week, one of "our" families made me answer every humping question in the sales book. Know what they told me after that?

SCOTT. WRONG COLOR, BROTHER!

TONY. "Need more time, young man." Next day I show up with my white buddy Steve and he closes the deal without so much as a question from the Negroes. Had to split my bonus with that white boy. Don't like bringing the MAN along to legitimatize my game, but I'll bring him along to make my sale if I have to.

ED. Don't you feel like a pimp ripping off poor black folk?

TONY. I'm providing a service — KEEPING COLORED FOLKS WARM!

ED. You brainwashed, Tony.

TONY. For thirty grand a year, I'll be brainwashed!

JOE. Thirty grand!

SCOTT. (*Repeating*) Thirty grand — you college boys hear that?

JOE. Great day in the morning. (*Going for glasses, while Scott opens bottle*) Let's drink a toast to this rich ass colored boy.

SCOTT. I'll pop the cork.

JOE. Don't spill a drop of that crap on my luscious carpet.

SCOTT. This brew too rich for this roach motel.

JOE. (*Breathless*) Thirty grand! (*To Al and Ed*) And he ain't set foot inside of a college.

TONY. (*Blushing with deliberate modesty*) Oh no, no. I'm not "college material."

ED. Don't be humble, Tony. It doesn't become your profession.

TONY. (*Deliberately, lightheartedly*) So Al — got any decent homes for me to look at? Something to match my thirty grand.

AL. Sure Tony . . .

TONY. (*Humble but triumphant*) Forget it — think I'll stay put.

AL. You jerking me around?

TONY. No, no, no — had an instant change of heart.

AL. (*Holding up champagne to light*) Where you buy this champagne Tony?

ED. (*Smelling champagne*) Yeah — this stuff has a pedestrian aroma. Thank God for Boone's Farm.

AL. You saying it smells like cow piss?

ED. Tony?

TONY. I wouldn't know. I've never been that close to a cow's behind.

AL. (*Reading from label, deliberately*) Alabama Valley Sparkling Champagne! With a French accent!

ED. Damn, Tony, never heard of them.

SCOTT. (*Angrily*) Hey, if you snobbish punks don't like this, bring your own champagne next time!

JOE. Chill out, Scott. To Tony! (*They hold up their glasses and drink with cheers*) Tony, you the first steel mill dropout success story!

ED. Where you get that "first success story" from, Joe?

JOE. Call me when you get your first case under your belt. And you buzz me when you sell your first pad on Pill Hill.

SCOTT. Could be a long ass wait . . .

ED. You gonna need a first-rate lawyer the next time Shep gives you your walking papers. One problem, Joe.

JOE. What's that, attorney?

ED. I won't be around to help.

SCOTT. In other words, Mr. Big Time Lawyer can't blemish his whiter-than-snow record on two-bit steel mill workers.

JOE. That's the last straw. Get the game going. Take my hand, Tony.

TONY. I don't have time, Joe . . .

JOE. Come on, one quick hand . . .

SCOTT. Don't be chicken, Tony. I'm in the mood to humble a few cocky people myself.

JOE. Guess Ed don't mind a mill worker giving him a licking.

TONY. I'm on!

AL. Who's my partner, Joe?

JOE. Take your ass kicking with Ed.

AL. My what?

SCOTT. You afraid of an ass kicking from a couple of steel mill workers?

ED. Keep the faith, partner.

JOE. Don't start praying on us Ed. See, all a Sunday school teacher like Ed need is the faith of a mustard seed — he can move mountains.

SCOTT. (*Teasing*) No shit — kinda mountains you move, Eddie, brother?

ED. (*A deliberate sting*) Kind that take brains, not brawn.

SCOTT. I take that to mean you college boys done got soft in the crotch. (*Tony and Ed compete to win, but the attention gradually shifts primarily to the card game*)

AL. Time is it?

JOE. Forget the time. You stuck here till your old lady picks you up. Pam has this wimp cooking and washing dishes.

SCOTT. Cooking and washing dishes!

AL. It's part of the going back to school package.

JOE. She got him baby-sitting, too.

SCOTT. You learn how to boil beans yet?

AL. Beans get tender, turn the heat down to simmer, add chopped green peppers, pimentos, onions, hint of garlic, and dine on a poor man's gourmet dinner.

SCOTT. "Oh dear me."

JOE. I think you losing your balls.

ED. Al is changing with the times.

JOE. Keep quiet before I put your business in the street.

TONY. Five.

ED. My business?

AL. Pass.

JOE. Sunday school teacher shacking up with his old lady.

SCOTT. What you call that, Ed? (*Knock on table, "pass"*)

ED. Changing with the times!

TONY. Hearts.

JOE. (*Looking over Scott's shoulder, unable to restrain himself*) Helluva hand, Scott.

SCOTT. (*Annoyed with Joe*) Damn, git your ass in the kitchen and wash the dishes.

AL. (*Passing dish to Joe*) You can start with this one.

SCOTT. Too bad you ain't got no broad here to do the dishes.

JOE. Her mother is sick.

SCOTT. (*Ignoring Al*) If my old lady ask me to wash a dish when I get hitched, I'm suing her for divorce and collecting the alimony ...

ED. You won't collect if I'm her lawyer ...

SCOTT. I'm collecting.

JOE. My old lady will be back next week.

SCOTT. Next week! Take you that long to make a hit? (*Gets up and starts to telephone, pretending to be in a hurry*)

TONY. (*Annoyed with Scott's antics*) Watch your hand, Scott!

SCOTT. (*Crosses to phone, but Joe restrains him before he dials and leads him back to his chair*) Give me ten minutes and I'll have fresh meat walking through that door for everybody.

JOE. (*Restraining Scott*) Hold your rod, Scott. We know you a noted cocksman. Ed's the only virgin around here. Take that back. He did have one piece — the day he was born. (*Scott and Tony do a Johnny Carson crowd: "Hooooo ooooh"*)

SCOTT. Ed wouldn't recognized a piece if it walked up to him and tapped him on his rod. Ed, your rod is like a muscle. You have to exercise it. If you don't, it gets flabby, out of shape, shrinks up like a dried out prune.

ED. Kind of like the brain. (*Al and Tony do a Johnny Carson crowd: "Hooooo ooooooh"*)

JOE. Let's see if you got enough brains to win this game, attorney ...

SCOTT. (*Curious, but amused*) Seriously, Ed — 'bout time you and Carol tied the knot. Two years under the same roof is a long time.

JOE. Try explaining that to us, Sunday school teacher ...

SCOTT. I'm on Ed's side. Sunday school teacher got a right to unload his balls once in a while like everybody else.

TONY. (*Increasingly annoyed at Scott's frivolity*) Watch your hand, Scott.

SCOTT. It's a card game, Tony.

ED. So, Al, which one of your boys going to be the lawyer in the family?

JOE. Your boys might want to work at the mill.

AL. They might want an ass kicking.

JOE. A doctor is what I was supposed to be in the family —

missed my calling.

SCOTT. Your ass missed by a long shot.

JOE. (*Stung, retorting*) By about as far as you missed making the Chicago Bears.

TONY. Make one of them a crackerjack salesman!

AL. We aren't having but three kids.

SCOTT. You gonna stop screwing?

AL. Getting my tubes tied — (*Scott and Joe grimace, reaching for their crotches*)

JOE. OOOOOOOOOOUCH!

SCOTT. You crazy, Al!

TONY. What if something happens to your kids.

AL. We'll adopt.

JOE. Don't make sense adopting when you can make your own. Right Sunday school teacher?

ED. I'm for zero population growth.

TONY. Have one so people won't be suspicious of you.

SCOTT. You saying my man might have a little sugar on him?

TONY. Nooooo — wouldn't do that.

JOE. I know you ain't calling my man a CANDY ASS.

TONY. Watch your hand, Scott.

SCOTT. Keep your cool, Tony. I know how to run this show.

AL. (*With delight*) Thank the Lord my plans working out on time.

JOE. Pam won't need your change when she gets her degree.

AL. It's not the money that binds us.

SCOTT. O dear me, another love story.

ED. Did I hear somebody say Ed was gonna get his ass kicked? (*Ed collects books. Slaps winning card on table ecstatic, he claps hand with Al*) Put it there, partner!

TONY. (*Angry, jealous outburst at losing to Ed*) Dammit, Scott, we had their asses up shit creek!

ED. (*With great relief*) Whew!

TONY. But you threw the game away ...

AL. Man — I thought my ass was grass ...

TONY. You threw it away. You weren't concentrating on the board.

SCOTT. It's a second-rate card game and it ain't costing you a penny to play it (*to Ed*) even if some college punks around here don't see it that way.

ED. I'm packing my bags and moving to the backwoods, making my home in a hollow log, and drinking muddy water the day you candy ass steel mill wimps school me at the card table. Can I get a witness?

JOE. (*Deliberately provocative*) Praise the Lord, Reverend Eddie. Think you can convert me?

ED. JESUS SAVES!

JOE. S AND H GREEN STAMPS!

ED. One ailing woman touched the hem of His garment and He made her whole!

JOE. (*Deliberately signifying*) Sounds like that sweet little old mama of yours . . .

ED. Joe! Don't start signifying on me. (*Others stand astonished— in fearful anticipation*)

JOE. (*Shrugging shoulders, provocatively*) I just said some sweet little old lady I know.

ED. (*Reprimandingly*) Hey, man, we're too old to play that signifying game.

JOE. I don't play it—cause I don't know how. Just so happens this little old lady I know . . .

ED. (*Calm, calculatingly slow*) Joe! You gonna make me mad.

JOE. What you gonna do? Sue me, attorney?

ED. I'm gonna tell you how many children your mama had.

JOE. (*Stunned*) What you—(*Halting*)

ED. She didn't have one, she didn't have two, she had ninety-nine ugly motherfuckers just like you.

JOE. (*Going after Ed, but others quickly intervene*) Damn you. I'll kill that son of a bitch—talking 'bout my mama!

AL. Come on . . .

TONY. Cool out, Joe.

JOE. (*Calming down*) Damn Sunday school teacher talking 'bout my mama!

SCOTT. Where did you learn that kind of language, Sunday school teacher?

ED. The Lord revealed it to me! (*There is a knock at the back door*)

JOE. (*Crossing to door*) Bet I know who that is. (*Opens door and Charlie is there in sharp suit. He's got gift-wrapped champagne in bag*) Charlie!

CHARLIE. Gentlemen!

JOE. (*Noticing clothes*) Look at you, dressed like you on your way to the executive suite. What they do, make you president?! (*Laughter*)

SCOTT. (*Passing bottle of champagne to Charlie with card attached. Others congratulate him variously*) For you, Charlie — the best bottle in the store.

CHARLIE. You guys didn't have to do this.

SCOTT. Yeah we had to, Charlie ...

TONY. Speech ...

CHARLIE. You shouldn't have ...

TONY. Speech, speech ...

JOE. You can go back to Mississippi in another Cadillac.

THE MEN. Speech, speech ...

CHARLIE. It's no big deal ...

THE MEN. SPEECH, SPEECH ...

CHARLIE. It's no big deal ...

SCOTT. No big deal!

AL. What you mean no big deal?

CHARLIE. Doesn't take brains to operate that machine.

JOE. You hear that, Ed?

CHARLIE. Any one of you guys can run that contraption ...

TONY. Come on, Charlie ...

SCOTT. It's taken you twenty-five years.

ED. How does it feel, Charlie?

CHARLIE. I wouldn't know.

AL. You wouldn't know?

CHARLIE. I wouldn't know ...

ED. Charlie ...

SCOTT. What you mean — what — they can't do that!

CHARLIE. They say I'm not good enough to drive that truck.

ED. Charlie ...

SCOTT. Bull!

AL. Not good enough ...

SCOTT. Charlie, you can run the goddamn mill!

CHARLIE. They been telling me for six months I was in line for operating that machine, now they say I got to be outstanding on my evaluations ...

TONY. You are outstanding, Charlie ...

CHARLIE. It's not in writing ...

ED. What are you saying?

CHARLIE. They pat you on the back and tell you "outstanding" to your face, then they write you up "average" on your evaluation.

ED. Charlie ...

SCOTT. Average ...

TONY. Average, Charlie ...

JOE. Damn, Charlie!

CHARLIE. Twenty-five years and not a day out of work and not one outstanding on my record.

ED. Not one Charlie?

CHARLIE. Not one.

SCOTT. That's fucked!

ED. Charlie, do you have proof of discrimination on your evaluations?

SCOTT. What the hell you talking that proof noise for? The man standing here bleeding and your ass talking about proof. How much proof your butt need?

JOE. Chill out, Scott ...

ED. If you want it to stand up in court, you need evidence ...

SCOTT. Shut up talking that courtroom crap.

CHARLIE. Don't make a big deal of it, you guys ...

SCOTT. This damn ATTORNEY done got on my last nerve.

CHARLIE. Everybody can't operate that machine! (*Passing champagne to Joe*) Congratulations on your return to the mill, Joe. I can't stay—need to rest up for my next shift.

ED. Your next shift?

JOE. Come on, Charlie, to hell with the mill. Take the day off ...

SCOTT. Call in sick ...

CHARLIE. Can't do that.

TONY. They won't miss you, Charlie ...

JOE. They owe you one day off ...

CHARLIE. No, Joe. Them folk don't owe me a penny. I'm going in Monday like I been going for twenty-five years.

JOE. Drop dead on the job Charlie and the mill will go on running without you ...

ED. It's not to late to walk away ...

SCOTT. Don't be telling him nothing 'bout quitting.

CHARLIE. Can any one of you guys boast of a perfect attendance record at the mill? I got that! They ain't gonna take it away, so don't be telling me not to go in. I can still count my blessings.

AL. Yeah, you can count your blessings, Charlie ...

CHARLIE. The Lord's been mighty good to me. Every day I pray and ask for the strength to get up and get to the mill, and as long as I'm in sound mind and body I'm going in. I still got time to operate that truck. Scott, old buddy, guess we'll be seeing each other Monday morning. I better be on my way.

TONY. It's all right, Charlie ...

AL. We know you outstanding ...

ED. Outstanding, Charlie ...

JOE. Damn right! I'll walk you to the car ...

CHARLIE. No, no, I'm fine ...

AL. Drop me off at home, Charlie ...

CHARLIE. I'm not going home ...

AL. Drop me off, anyway ...

CHARLIE. I'M NOT GOING HOME! (*After a moment*) I'm sorry. I can't go home to my family. I can't let Bertha and the boy's see me like this.

AL. You have to go home, Charlie.

CHARLIE. No, no, I can't. Bertha has been busy all day preparing a dinner of thanksgiving for us tomorrow. I can't ... can't tell her ...

SCOTT. It's no big deal ...

CHARLIE. IT'S MY LIFE! Operating that machine is the only thing I got left to look forward to at the mill! It's my life! My life. I have to ... to go ...

AL. I'll drive you ...

JOE. (*To the others*) You guys hold down the fort ...

SCOTT. See you Monday, Charlie ...

CHARLIE. You bet you will ... (*Al, Joe, and Charlie exit*)

TONY. (*Noticing wine for Charlie*) Charlie forgot his wine. You guys take it easy. (*Tony exits. Scott and Ed do not speak, as if both are afraid to break the silence. The tension is unbearably thick.*

Scott grabs his coat and starts to door)

SCOTT. I'm gone—tell Joe I'm meeting some broad across town.

ED. Tell him yourself ...

SCOTT. (*Angrily, commandingly*) *You* tell him!

ED. He'll be back any minute ...

SCOTT. Damn that. I got enough of Joe's scrappy ass party and the crap about quitting the mill. Tell him I'm gone— gone somewhere to meet some broad ...

ED. I'll tell him that "meeting some broad" lie, but what's the real reason you sneaking out behind your old buddy's back?

SCOTT. (*Stunned, offended*) What you—look at this sorry excuse for a party celebrating his return to the mill. Joe's been fired twice. Demoted to the basement, and he's gonna spend his life in the basement long as he keeps screwing up.

ED. You and I both know one person doesn't ruin a car load of steel. You mean somebody had to take the blame.

SCOTT. Okay, ATTORNEY, somebody had to take the blame!

ED. And you didn't have the spine to speak up for your buddy.

SCOTT. Listen, I'm staying cozy with Shep's two-faced cheese-eating ass so he'll never have a chance to write me up a shitty evaluation.

ED. So stay cozy with Shep for twenty-five years and then what do you get—a chance to be a machine operator. I wouldn't count on it.

SCOTT. What you ...

ED. (*With air of courtroom lawyer*) YOU GOT TO BE OUTSTANDING, SCOTT!

SCOTT. (*Incensed*) You got no right to say that to me.

ED. (*Provocatively cool, with bitter edge*) Charlie can't walk away, but if Joe had left the mill five years ago, he wouldn't be crawling back Monday to be in the company of his so called "buddies," who show up at his return to the mill party then bad mouth him behind his back.

SCOTT. (*Seething*) KISS MY ASS!

ED. (*Calmly*) After you, my man, after—

SCOTT. (*Exploding in a rage, lunging after Ed, snatching him up from chair by collar*) Say it again and I'll chill the shit in your ass! (*Pushing Ed back in chair after a second*) It's snobs like you who make my ass ache. (*Furious*) You gonna hang your law degree in the welfare office and go to the ghetto where everybody can say "He's one of ours"? Hell no. You'll be on Pill Hill looking down your nose with a no-thank-you attitude toward the folk who made it all possible for you to get there and who'll keep you there. You'll still be a second-rate, second-class nigger—just like your boys in Cabrini Green and Robert Taylor Projects, 'cause you still black. Who do you think lived on Pill Hill before the uppity ass niggers started spilling over into the "white" folks' neighborhood, while they flew to the suburbs like the plague was coming after their asses? That's right—J.Q. HONKEY was on Pill Hill first. So your shit is still second class, don't care where you get your uppity ass law degree! Least you forget the mill saved a whole generation of snobs like you and your kinfolk from starving to death.

ED. (*Exploding in bitter anger*) MILL DIDN'T SAVE MY OLD MAN!

SCOTT. MAYBE YOUR OLD MAN'S NUMBER WAS UP! (*After a moment of painful silence, Scott speaks, contritely*) I'm sorry.

ED. (*Listlessly*) Don't apologize . . .

SCOTT. No—I mean it.

ED. Maybe his number was up.

SCOTT. Don't say that about Mr. Willie! (*Spurt of painful laughter, struggling on, starts uneasily towards door, stops, then begins talking to himself*) Dammit! Man! Seems like yesterday—had more college football scholarships than I could count. (*Turning to Ed*) Remember?

ED. Yeah?

SCOTT. Fastest running back in the Windy City! (*Wide-eyed with excitement*) You see my pictures plastered all over the sports pages?

ED. Yeah?

SCOTT. Recruiters lined up at my doorstep. (*Flexing muscles, ecstatically*) Hell, I still got the touch! Look at that! Still solid as a brick shit house! Hundred fifty push-ups a day! (*Contemplatively*) Had my life mapped out—all the way to the Super Bowl! (*Increasingly excited*) The number one

American high school star signs on with a big time university. Sports announcer rattling off my stats. Heisman Trophy! Cover of *Sports Illustrated*. Number one draft choice—on my way to the Super Bowl with the Pittsburgh Steelers. Off seasons I'd be making television commercials chasing cars through airports—bitches wetting their panties chasing after me: Scottie! Scottie! Scottie, Baby! (*Taut with intensity*) One day on that field—one day—I'd take that ball and run it into eternity! (*Breaks wildly and catches imaginary ball and dashes forward weaving around opponents with slow-motion ballet-like perfection*) LISTEN TO THE CROWD! HEAR UM! Everything looked great till I twisted my ankle, and then I busted my kneecap two weeks into the season. Sidelined—for the rest of my life! Everybody forgot my name. Hated going to class—*went to college to run that football!* End of the year—my grades were lower than a snake's belly. Kicked out the back door without so much as a "thank you Scottie, boy," My old man told me to get my ass to the mill—or pack my bags. (*Venomously*) I prayed every day for that son-of-a-bitch to drop dead at the mill, just so I could prove him wrong! (*Painful laughter*) Bastards don't tell you only one in a million black dudes ever become big enough football stars to chase cars through airports. They make it look so goddamn easy on TV! (*With venom*) If I come back into this world a nigger in my next life, I'm going to curse God and die! (*Bitterly*) You know what I hope. I hope the mill closes. That way I won't have to go back to that place with all them Mississippi niggers!

ED. You can quit, you know ...

SCOTT. Don't tell me what I can do! If I walk off, I'll have to fight my old man, so don't tell me I can just up and quit, because you don't know shit from bread about what I have to do!

ED. Hey, man, I'm sorry.

SCOTT. Listen, I ... I ... applied for a job at the Transportation Authority. (*Looking to Ed for support*) You think I can make it?

ED. You'll make it, Scott.

SCOTT. Yeah. Hell yeah! Meet lots of fine women driving that
bus. Give Joe my regrets! (*Stops at exit, and turns around to
face Ed*) Ed, I'll be looking for you on Michigan Avenue.

ED. Yeah ...

SCOTT. But look out, I'm gonna be on your heels.

ED. Yeah—so long, Scott. (*Scott exits. Ed goes to window and
looks out. After a moment or two, he becomes restless. Is
about to go when Joe enters*)

JOE. (*Looking around, with trepidation*) God, man. Charlie kept
saying he didn't want to let us down. Where is Scott?

ED. Scott's gone. He isn't going in Monday.

JOE. Quit lying ...

ED. He's applied for a job at the CTA.

JOE. I got sense enough to know he didn't wanna be here in
the first place.

ED. (*Uneasily*) I'm going home, Joe.

JOE. (*Upset, restraining Ed*) Hold up! Stay awhile—the night
still young—we can play a couple of hands ...

ED. (*Getting up to go*) The game is over, Joe! So what's it gonna
be Joe?

JOE. You know, Ed, I thought we'd be rich by now, living
in a house on Pill Hill ...

ED. That some kind of fantasy, too?

JOE. Hell naw! Check it out—five bedrooms. Carpet gonna be
so thick, your ass liable to drown in it. Fix up my basement
like a Vegas night spot, pinball, bar, cocktail lounge—home
entertainment center, decked out with the best speakers on
the market! You like it?

ED. Joe ...

JOE. What's that?

ED. Remember the story about Lot and his wife—at Sodom
and Gomorrah?

JOE. Oh God—Sunday school done started already. Yeah, I
remember—she turned to a pillow of salt.

ED. She didn't turn to a pillar of salt!

JOE. No shit.

ED. She *froze*, Joe.

JOE. That ain't what the Bible says!

ED. She froze in her old ways. Couldn't pull herself out of a decadent slump and start a new life for herself.

JOE. (*With deliberate indifference*) Like a lot of folk I know. Yeah — always talking about what they're going to do tomorrow.

ED. Tomorrow never comes! Today is all we got. It's now or never! No looking back, lest we freeze in fear and self-doubt.

JOE. Ain't gonna be freezing myself.

ED. Freeze, Joe, one more day, one more week, a year, a *lifetime*!

JOE. I get your drift!

ED. Proposition for you, Joe.

JOE. Lay it on me.

ED. I just found out there is a vacancy in my old job at the library.

JOE. There is, hey?

ED. Recommendation letter from me and the job is yours. (*Pauses for Joe's response, but Joe hedges*) No experience necessary. High school diploma is all you need. It's light work, Joe — checking out a few books ... some stacking, not a whole lot. I'll help train you if you want me to. I know the ropes. It's not a lot of money, but you can survive on it.

JOE. How much they paying?

ED. Enough for you to live on. (*Joe does not respond*) Joe, the job is yours. *Tonight*, Joe! I know the supervisor personally. (*Going to phone*) I'll call her right now if you want me to.

JOE. Hold up!

ED. Huh — what?

JOE. I ... I need a little time to think about it.

ED. (*In exasperation*) LIKE FUCKING TOMORROW!

JOE. I'm making pretty good at the mill!

ED. I'LL BE A SON OF A BITCH!

JOE. I can't just up and walk off my job — invested too goddamn much of my life!

ED. Invested what? Pain? Anger? Bitterness? And more of the goddamn same!

JOE. I got a check coming in! And the union behind me! I'm talking 'bout security.

ED. (*Spurt of Exasperated laughter*) God, man! I must be a fool —
asking you to give up your security at the mill to take a job
pushing books around the library.

JOE. I'm leaving no sooner than I get my first two or three
paychecks. (*Ed crosses and shakes Joe's hand*)

ED. Best wishes at the mill, Joe. (*Ed turns and goes to door and
exits. Joe turns and calls after him in panic. Ed stops*)

JOE. Don't mock me, man!

ED. Later for you!

JOE. Ed! It's got to be tonight!

ED. Tomorrow is time enough! Don't want you to give up your
security!

JOE. You're mocking me! Did you forget what it's like to drive
down Lake Shore Drive on a hot summer day, everybody
and his mama getting a sun tan. Us, too! Where am I
headed? To the hot, funky mill. Dragging in to work gets
to be a full time job! You walk in feeling like a keg of
dynamite. Shep comes in and starts his crap on top of my
crap. Ignites my fuse and I try my damnedest to plaster
his ass in the concrete! Just for that minute I don't give a
damn! Come to my senses and I'm out the door and
crawling back to the union on my knees and kissing ass to
get back on where I started the day I walked into that
humping place. Naw, man, never again! Ed, I'm sending
Shep my farewell bouquet. Know what Grandma Bee use
to say to me — God rest her soul. "Joe, if you make one
step, the Lord will make two!" I'm taking that first step,
tonight. Pull up a chair. Me and you mapping out the
road to Farrells.

ED. Farrells?

JOE. Farrells!

ED. Joe . . .

JOE. If you gonna fly, fly first class.

ED. There are no black lawyers at Farrells!

JOE. So what's that suppose to mean?

ED. You're talking out of your head.

JOE. Ed, we'd still be at the back of the bus if everybody had a
mind set like yours. Did you forget the time we sat in
Mrs. Smitherman's office and you said you had your sights

set on law school because it's what Mr. Willie wanted you to do and she looked at us and said "You boys ought to be realistic. Go to school and study refrigeration." You made her into a liar. You finishing up your law degree from Northwestern. And you don't think you're good enough for Farrells? You're outstanding, man, outstanding! The only thing standing between you and Farrells is yourself, man. Yourself! I say we make liars out of all those folk who say we can't make it! (*Ed hedges for a moment*) So what's it gonna be? (*They move towards table with eager anticipation. Lights out*)

act 3

Joe's apartment five years later. Winter. Even last-minute efforts to tidy up the apartment for the party don't camouflage the state of deterioration and dissolution that characterizes the atmosphere. Joe is more of a caricature of his earlier self. The hip, funky stride from Act 1 has taken on the appearance of a slightly burdensome deformity, even though he struggles hard to appear optimistic and hopeful. The initial moment with Ed is awkward, uneasy, filled with anxiety, as the two men struggle to get to know each other. A number of items — TV, stereo, Great Books — are missing. As scene opens, Joe is standing admiring Ed's Brooks Brothers suit.

ED. Brooks Brothers.

JOE. Brooks Brothers! Like tailor made ain't it?

ED. Yeah.

JOE. Tailor made Brooks Brothers suit! Company car?

ED. Mercedes.

JOE. Red! Betcha! (*Ed shakes head negatively*) Don't tell me — black, red interior!

ED. Champagne.

JOE. Blow my ass down! You tell Farrells they gonna have to get me an El Dorado with chrome fins and red velvet interior. Great to see you again!

ED. It's been a long time.

JOE. Too damn long! Never would a know'd them years was flying by if I hadn't looked in the mirror one morning and seen them crow's feet gathering under my eyes. ... (*Through nervous, desperate laughter*) Don't see none under your eyes. Farrells taking good care of you. Son of a gun! (*After an awkward moment, unable to resist, Joe reaches out and embraces Ed*) I'm proud to see you. Came by to see you, but the security guard wouldn't let me in. I told him me and you buddies from the mill. He talking 'bout he gonna arrest me for trespassing. I told him me and you buddies from the mill since we was knee high to a duck's ass. (*Nervous, self-conscious laughter*) I was scared you'd be walking in here with your ass on your shoulders too stuck up to come over and see your old mill buddy.

ED. Life is too short for that.

JOE. I didn't recognize your voice on that answering machine — You was sounding so prim and proper. Figured you's out with one of your clients taking care of business.

ED. Had a game of golf.

JOE. You playing golf?

ED. Comes with the territory.

JOE. Listen at you, "Comes with the territory!" (*Desperately, curiously*) Ed, I was wondering — you think there'll be room for me at Farrells — I mean when I get my act together?

ED. Sure, Joe.

JOE. Yeah?

ED. Yeah.

JOE. (*Reassured*) Man! I'm gonna be strutting around in my Brooks Brothers suit like you be doing. (*As if trying to resist an instinctive urge, but unable to do so, Joe goes for fifth of liquor, which is in a discreet place, and takes several swallows*) And you sho nuff looking good in it. Little something for my nerves. The celebration got me hyped up. I'm better already. No wonder they use this stuff for medicine. (*Replacing bottle*) I'm fine now — switching to beer soon as the gang gets here. You ought to get yourself a jerry curl to go with that Brooks Brothers suit.

ED. I don't think so.

JOE. I'll be standing tall soon as I'm in my Brooks Brothers rags. Turning over a new leaf this time! See—if you don't let people know you got your act together, they be talking behind your back. "Lazy nigger's ass ain't got a pot to piss in or a window to throw it out of." Ain't I right?

ED. Joe, you don't have to prove anything to me.

JOE. You can say that. You shit dollar bills. Oh—damn! I almost forgot, getting so absentminded. I got something for you. (*Goes behind sofa. Joe returns with picture, 11 by 17. It is a blown up newspaper article, front page with picture from the Tribune. Opulent frame*) Had it made especially for you. (*Holding up picture*) "FARRELLS HIRES FIRST SPOOK!"

ED. (*Embarrassed*) Joe I can't accept it.

JOE. I'm kidding. It says "First black on Farrells team." You the first one on right?

ED. Yeah ...

JOE. It's about time. Custom made frame.

ED. Joe, you didn't have to put out for a frame like this.

JOE. I don't fly second class.

ED. I should reimburse you.

JOE. Don't insult me!

ED. I'll put it away—in my car.

JOE. No, man, we have to put it on display for the party.

ED. No, no, you don't have to put it on display.

JOE. Yeah I do!

ED. It's the thought behind the gift that matters.

JOE. Now you don't believe that lie—see I know colored folks. They be saying it's the thought that counts, but if it's cheap, they hide that shit in the garage. It be hanging all right—above the lawn mower! (*Hanging picture on wall. It is a cheerful Ed, mocking the tension that gathers as the play progresses*) Look at you in that picture—grinning like a monkey in heat.

ED. Joe, could I ask you not to display it on your wall. I mean it's your party.

JOE. My party?

ED. Yeah, yeah ...

JOE. It's a reunion! What you drinking?

ED. What you serving?

JOE. (*Deliberately humorous*) Generic beer!

ED. Make it a "generic" lite.

JOE. "Make it a generic lite!" You ain't changed — still full of stuff as a Thanksgiving turkey. (*Joe takes swig from liquor bottle. Gets beer*) Two lites coming up — have one for myself. I like lite — fifty percent fewer calories. (*Passes Ed a beer*) You like lite?

ED. Yeah.

JOE. Me too . . . good for my waistline. Be like old times when the gang gets here — just like old times.

ED. Yeah.

JOE. Just like old times . . . (*For an anxious moment silence as each man sips beer*)

JOE. That's a silk tie ain't it?

ED. Yeah, yeah . . .

JOE. Silk comes from worms don't it?

ED. The silk worm.

JOE. Right the silk worm. Wonder how many worms in your tie? Helluva lot of them buggers going up in silk, cause everybody on Michigan Avenue be wearing silk ties. (*Afterthought*) I never see silk ties at the Salvation Army — except for the ones I wouldn't wear to a dog fight. How many silk ties you got?

ED. Seven.

JOE. One for every day of the week! (*Taking drink from liquor bottle*) A little dab will do for now.

ED. When is Al getting here?

JOE. He's supposed to be here. 'Bout closing a deal on a house. That son-of-a-gun making a killing in real estate. Never thought Pam would a stuck by his ass all this time. (*Ed notices new books*) Tony! Damn con artist sold me them books. I quit paying on them. Paying for shit you ain't using like paying rent on a dead relative!

ED. Tony coming tonight?

JOE. Tony shows up anywhere his nose sniffs out a sale for a Mercedes. You know he's gonna sell me my first Mercedes — to go with my pad on Pill Hill. (*Joe has pulled out cards, which have been visible all along*) How 'bout a quick warm-up hand before the gang arrives?

ED. (*Anxiously*) No, no — listen, I'm rusty.

JOE. Naw, naw, I ain't gonna be hearing no lame ass excuses 'cause you playing poker with the white folks. I'm taking you to the cleaners! Here. Check these out, Ed. (*Proudly pulling out books on cards*) *The Complete Card Player. A Short Treatise on the Game of Whist. How To Win at Bidding.* And this. *The Psychological Strategy in the Techniques of Winning at Cards.* Let's go for a quick hand.

ED. (*Anxiously*) Not right now, Joe. Maybe I'll take another beer.

JOE. (*Getting beer*) I'll let you off the hook for a few more minutes — till the party heats up. Been practicing my hand day and night. (*Passing beer to Ed*) I got a joke for you. What's got eight legs and races through the hall squealing "HOL DE DO! HOL DE DO! HOL DE DO! HOL DE DO! YO! DE DO! DE DO! DE DOOOO! Four West Indians trying to catch an elevator. (*Joe laughs boisterously*) Bet you ain't heard that one.

ED. I've heard it at work.

JOE. (*Through laughter*) What — they can't be taking our jokes! (*Ed reaches in container and cautiously gets single potato chip. Joe notices*)

JOE. Hungry?

ED. No, no — (*Overlapping*)

JOE. I am — (*Overlapping*)

ED. Just finished with dinner.

JOE. Ordered a large pizza. Get a chance to ride in that Mercedes.

ED. I'm in my VW.

JOE. Man! I wanted us to cruise over in your Mercedes and pick up the pizza. I get it — scared one of them ghetto rats gonna drive off in your Mercedes. (*Doorbell rings. Joe crosses to answer it on line*) I got it! (*Al enters, business suit. Joe offers soul shake*) What it is!

AL. (*Offering traditional handshake*) How are you, Joe?

JOE. What — I know you ain't forgot the soul shake.

AL. (*Responding with soul shake on his line*) Not much use for it in my line of business.

JOE. Now you talking!

AL. Congratulations, Joe. (*Pulling champagne bottle from bag and*

passing it to Joe) Don't crack the cork on this champagne
until you join Ed on the Farrells team. (*Turning to Ed*)
Attorney!

ED. Mr. Real Estate! (*Observing Al's attire, teasing*) I ought to
go home and get out of these rags I'm wearing.

AL. It's not the suit, it's the handsome gentleman in the suit.

JOE. Listen at you—ain't hardly got your butt inside the door
and already stroking yourself on the backside.

AL. Even walking like a Farrells man!

JOE. Got him one of them tight ass white boy walks!

ED. I own the patent to this walk!

AL. But you did fine tune it for the MAN. (*Checking out apartment*)
This it, Joe?

JOE. The darkest hour is just before dawn.

AL. I gather dawn is just around the corner. Joe, don't like
showing my face in this neighborhood after dark.

JOE. Got yourself on easy street, now you acting like you in a
war zone.

AL. There's no "Easy Street" in this business.

JOE. Pour piss on my head and tell me it's raining. What you
drinking?

AL. Scotch and water.

JOE. Scotch and what!

AL. Scotch and water.

JOE. Give you niggers five minutes with the white folk and you
start aping their asses.

AL. Joe, I'd appreciate it if you wouldn't use "nigger" in my
presence.

JOE. (*Getting beer*) Last time you had your Afro American pos-
terior over here you was drinking beer and damn glad to
get it. You driving a Mercedes, too?

AL. A SAAB.

JOE. A SAAB! Lawd today! What you done turned into, a
black yuppie?

AL. Just trying to pay the bills . . .

JOE. So, ah, you black Afro Americans make yourselves at
home while I get some Afro American music to enliven
this Afro American party.

AL. Where's the stereo?

JOE. I'll get my radio. (*Exits to get radio*)

ED. Somebody has been to the pawn shop.

AL. Lost a case yet?

ED. I'm a Farrells man!

AL. Say, I've got a real plum on the Hill. Doc Rogers' house — patio, olympic size pool, enclosed, five bedrooms, surveillance — let's go talk over cocktails.

ED. I've purchased a lakefront condo downtwon.

AL. A lakefront condo?

JOE. (*Entering with huge radio, blasting*) You guys got to hear this ... Gonna take you way back, now. Sho' nuff is ... Marvin Gaye and Tammy Terrell!

AL. Joe!

JOE. Yo!

AL. You got any Anita Baker?

JOE. Who? Naw — we gittin' into Marvin Gaye and Tammy Terrell ...

AL. Skip the music, Joe.

JOE. No sweat, I'll pop in George Benson to jazz things up. (*Setting up chairs for card game*) We'll get in a couple of hands to heat up the party.

ED. Joe, I told you, I'm rusty.

AL. I'm out of shape myself, Joe.

ED. No point in spoiling the party.

JOE. The game is the party! Pull up your chairs. (*Ed and Al make no move toward card table*) You guys gonna play or what?

ED. Takes four to play whist — I mean we can play, but it's not whist.

AL. Yeah, Joe — it won't be whist. (*There is a knock on the door*).

JOE. Well, looks like we'll be playing whist after all. (*Charlie is there. Looking much the same, except for a few more pounds. Jovial, making an extra effort to look younger than his fifty years*) Old man Charlie!

CHARLIE. (*Playfully boxing*) Old man! I don't know what you talking about. I'm good looking, as good as the day when I walked into the mill thirty years ago. (*Charlie pulls beer from bag and passes bag along to Joe*)

JOE. I'm getting my shit together this time, Charlie. (*Accepting bag, curiously*) Goodies for the party.

CHARLIE. (*In low voice*) Canned goods from the family to tide you over until you're on your feet again.

JOE. (*Heading to kitchen with package*) Yeah, yeah, gonna be some lean days ahead.

CHARLIE. (*To Ed*) I want the honor of carrying your briefcase through the front door of Farrells just once so I can say I've been inside the Big House! (*Embracing Ed, taking note of suit*) They teach you to dress like that in law school?

AL. It comes with the territory.

CHARLIE. Look who's talking.

AL. I don't get a hug?

CHARLIE. (*Embracing Al*) Hey, it comes with the territory!

JOE. Charlie! What! You pulled that Cadillac off the blocks!

CHARLIE. Going back to Mississippi in that Cadillac!

AL. Charlie . . .

ED. Come on . . .

JOE. Be for real, Charlie . . .

CHARLIE. Can' wait to get on that back porch with my lemonade. Cruising to the shopping mall as many times as I want!

JOE. I know you done gone a fool now.

CHARLIE. I'm driving up in the Sheriff's front yard, parking my Cadillac, getting out, grabbing the old boy and giving him a bear hug of a greeting! I'm sweeping his old lady up in my arms and giving the gal a hug and a tender peck on the cheek — can't do more than that with my wife looking on. Then I'm sitting down at his dining room table and enjoying myself a home cooked meal fresh from the garden served up on real china! After dinner, I'm putting the Sheriff and his old lady in my Cadillac and we taking a ride to you know where!

JOE. You don't deserve to get out of Mississippi with your balls if you that crazy.

CHARLIE. Sheriff Waters is my old high school running buddy. The times they are changing!

JOE. You got to find the SOBs who shaved your balls . . .

AL. Yeah, you got to, Charlie . . .

ED. Take them for a ride down memory lane . . .

JOE. Make the bastards get on they knees and crawl, Charlie!

CHARLIE. GENTLEMEN! (*Calmly, profound*) Let the dead bury the dead! Let's celebrate Joe's new beginning.

JOE. I ain't gonna be there no longer than it takes for me to get my next two or three paychecks.

AL. You headed back to the mill?

ED. Joe, you've struck out with the union.

JOE. Don't need the union—got the best lawyer in town on my case.

CHARLIE. Don't tell me you got Ed.

JOE. Hal Walker. Walker gonna kick ass till he gets me back on.

CHARLIE. How you get Walker?

JOE. Told Walker about how the bastards been putting the screws to me for the last ten years and before I finished my story he was smoking for their asses.

ED. Walker don't take nickel and dime cases, Joe.

JOE. You tell him that when he gets here tonight.

AL. Tonight?

CHARLIE. Walker coming here tonight?

JOE. That's what the celebration is about. You guys got to stay till Walker comes. Ed, I hope you don't mind 'bout me going to Walker.

ED. It's okay, Joe ...

JOE. I mean it ain't personal or nothing like that, cause I know you hot shot Farrells folk don't be wanting to fool with nickel and dime cases—it ain't personal ...

ED. Joe—it's okay!

JOE. Now don't take it personal—it ain't personal or nothing like that ...

ED. (*Piqued*) Joe—You got the best man for the job!

JOE. Hell yeah—Walker gonna kick ass till he gets me back on. Son of a bitch Shep. Felt like thirteen years of dead weight off my shoulders when his ass hit the floor! (*Drinks from liquor bottle*) Little something for my nerves. (*Arms outstretched*) Hey, Charlie! Where's my hug—don't I get a hug?

CHARLIE. (*Charlie embraces Joe*) Walker gonna take care of you, Joe.

JOE. Let's get on with the game — grab a chair, Charlie. You my partner. We playing whist.

CHARLIE. I don't know when I played whist last ...

JOE. I'm an expert at whist ...

CHARLIE. I don't know, Joe, I'm not gonna be much help to you ...

JOE. Relax Charlie, we'll beat the panties off these poker playing boys. Pull up your chair attorney. We gonna run these Michigan Avenue boys all the way back to Mississippi, Charlie. (*The phone rings and Joe rushes to answer it*) Hold your horses while I answer the phone.

CHARLIE. Ed, I want you to be the Men's Day speaker at my church. Come and tell us how you kicked ass on your way to becoming a Farrells man — now don't say "kick ass" in church ...

ED. (*Noticeable anxiety*) Charlie, I'd love to come, but I can't commit myself tonight.

CHARLIE. Our young men need to know what it's like to be a Farrells man. We'll pay you ...

ED. No, no, I couldn't take your money ...

CHARLIE. We pay two hundred and fifty to our Men's Day speaker ...

ED. It's not the money, Charlie ...

CHARLIE. What's your fee?

ED. Fifteen hundred ...

AL. Fifteen hundred?

CHARLIE. Maybe you can strike up a deal with your old mill buddy ...

ED. Charlie, I'd be honored. Here's my agent's number. Give her a call and let's see what we can work out.

CHARLIE. Agent?

AL. Your agent, he's got to contact your agent to get you to speak at his church?

ED. If I accepted every speaking engagement that came along, I'd spend the rest of my career telling people how I became a Farrells man.

AL. He's an old mill buddy ...

ED. All right, Charlie, I'll see what I can do for you ...

CHARLIE. (*Returning card*) No ...

ED. It's okay, Charlie ...

CHARLIE. You'd better check with your agent.

ED. I'll work it out ...

CHARLIE. Naw—don't want you to miss out on another Farrells client on my account.

JOE. Let's go get my pizza! Ed, you got headlight wipers on your Mercedes?

ED. Yeah.

JOE. I know I'm leaving the mill now!

CHARLIE. Let's get moving, Joe ...

JOE. You guys keep a look out for Walker.

CHARLIE. (*On exit, shaking head in amused disgust*) Headlight wipers ... (*Joe and Charlie exit*)

AL. Is it true?

ED. What?

AL. The headlight wipers.

ED. It's no big deal.

AL. I suppose I could have gotten headlight wipers on my SAAB if I'd wanted them ...

ED. No you couldn't.

AL. Oh yes I could!

ED. No you couldn't!

AL. You telling me I can't have headlight wipers on my SAAB if I want them?

ED. No, you can't.

AL. Why the hell can't I have headlight wipers on my SAAB if I want them?

ED. They don't have headlight wipers on SAABs.

AL. For fifteen hundred a speech, I'd speak every day, then I get custom made headlight wipers for my SAAB!

ED. You'd get a Mercedes with the headlight washers!

AL. No I wouldn't! I'd get a limo with headlight wipers! Damn! I took the wrong road in my life! What's it like?

ED. It's a Mercedes—German engineered ...

AL. Cut the Mercedes commercial! I want to know what it's like at Farrells. I bet you had them wetting their pants at the interview. You wear your Brooks Brothers suit?

ED. Tailor made. Navy blue. Silk tie. White and blue striped,

button-down-collar Hathaway shirt. Wing-tip Florshiems.
Brown leather Jomandi attaché case. Pierre Cardin designer
glasses. A Dale Carnegie smile. A John Wayne grip on the
handshake. My tight ass WASP walk!

AL. Hallelujah!

ED. (*Excited*) We're out to dinner — the five finalists. Steaks. I'M
A VEGETARIAN, BUT I EAT MEDIUM RARE COW CARCASS TO
IMPRESS THE FARRELLS TEAM! Desert. Chocolate ice cream
topped with silver. You can eat silver for desert, if you got
the money! The Farrells' rep rears back in his chair — cool,
calm, collected: "As you know, only one of you will make
the Farrells team." Everybody drooling at the mouth! "So
tell Farrells about yourselves." They brag about their trips
to Europe, the Middle East, South America, Far East,
Africa. Old man a doctor, judge, lawyer, banker. My old
man dropped dead at the mill. Hell, I haven't seen Disney
World! But I dropped my story from the law review on
him, and my New York and D. C. internships and the
bastard's ears perked up like satellite dishes! When he
asked what I could do for Farrells I promised the old boy
the world with a fence around it! You know that wonderful
sensation you get when you know the job is yours before
you leave the interview — and you don't have car fare
home?

AL. Aaahh! Yes!

ED. FARRELLS! FARRELLS! I WAS IN!

AL. Aaaaahhhh!

ED. I'm on my way to becoming a partner.

AL. (*With affection and admiration*) I envy your black ass!

ED. Al . . . they dropped the McClears case in my lap.

AL. What — hey man you win with McClears and you'll be a
superstar!

ED. Did you forget what McClears is about?

AL. What?

ED. Al, we're talking about eleven thousand five hundred and
sixty-nine black workers suing for denial of pay raises and
promotions that's going to cost the company at least fifty-
six million dollars in back pay.

AL. So take the money and lose the goddamn case!

ED. This isn't a joke! Do you know what happens when your supervisor pats you on the back and says "Outstanding job, boy!" to your face for thirty years while he's writing you up mediocre evaluations? It means you look around one day and all those people who came in with you and after you have moved up the ladder and you're still getting a slap on the back!

AL. You're not getting slapped on the back, you're getting fucked up the ass! So what else is new?

ED. Can't you see Farrells is putting me on the wrong side of the fence?

AL. The law isn't about right and wrong. It's about winning and losing!

ED. Don't tell me what my profession is about! You know why Farrells dropped the case in my lap before I'm slated to become a partner? Because McClears is forking over big bucks to Farrells for this nigger to take the company off the hook!

AL. Settle out of court.

ED. They won't—they're banking on it going all the way to the Supreme Court if they have to because they think it's conservative enough for things to go their way, and they need me on the team.

AL. Look at it this way—if you don't take the case, some Harvard spook will.

ED. Don't call me a spook!

AL. Come on, attorney par excellence! You didn't expect to become a bona fide member of the "good old boys' club" without passing a litmus test of loyalty to the gang. Blow off McClears and keep going to work in your champagne Mercedes!

ED. I've got a social commitment to those workers at McClears.

AL. Bull—your ass didn't have a commitment to the McClears workers until they dropped the case in your lap.

ED. Who do you think made it possible for your black ass to sell real estate on Pill Hill and flee to the suburbs so you'll be accepted in your Gammons office?

AL. I made it possible, because I walked away from the mill not knowing from where my next pay check was coming.

ED. You've got a short-ass memory if you've forgotten the people who marched through water hoses, police dogs and billy clubs, died for the day you could sell real estate.

AL. I'll tell you what I remember — I remember knocking on real estate doors for weeks on end and hearing "Sorry, no vacancies." Coming home and my old lady looking at me with fire in her eyes: "If you bring your black ass home tonight without a job, I'm gonna flush your degree down the toilet!" Let me tell you what happened to me a couple of weeks ago — I'm heading into my downtown office. This homeless woman is sitting there, her hand out for money. I reach in my pocket and throw her three quarters. She gathers them up and throws them back in my face. "You can do better than that!" That bitch sitting there in her feces and piss-soaked rags THREW MY CHARITY BACK IN MY FACE! I placed a five dollar bill in her hand. "That's more like it young man!" A part of me wanted to strangle her, but I saw my wife, my mother, my sister — I SAW MYSELF SITTING THERE MIRED IN MY OWN SHIT AND PISS! Now I have to eat and pay the bills, and keep people thinking that SAAB means I'm living well, because a hungry real estate salesman has "swindler" written all over his face!

ED. You in pain, Al . . .

AL. Goddamn right I'm in pain. You see, when we walked away from the security of the mill somebody should have told us it's the survival of the fittest in that downtown jungle. They should have told us there's no such thing as equal opportunity in this world. You latch on to the best opportunity you can get, or take when you have to dammit! And that means you work twice as hard if you have to because there are only twenty-four hours in the day, even when I need forty-eight, it's only twenty-four and I need my twenty-four to make sure I stay in the top ten percent of the sales at Gammons.

ED. Isn't the McClears case about making life fair?

AL. I don't need some gray ass judge to tell me I'm the last hired and the first fired!

ED. THE ME, MYSELF, AND I GENERATION HAS ARRIVED!

AL. Listen, brother. My Urban League dues are paid up. I'm

a lifetime member of the NAACP and I donate my check to Rev. Jessie Jackson's People United to Save Humanity every time his boys come calling at my door. My conscience is CLEAR!

ED. Al, you can send your kids off to Harvard in a Mercedes, but before you send them off, make sure you brand them with a PH on the forehead, so everybody will know they are not just some nigger from the Chicago ghetto. Because if you don't, somebody's gonna think they stole that Mercedes from some rich white kid.

AL. They're going in a SAAB! Listen, don't get self righteous on me. You can walk away from Farrells and join another big time firm.

ED. I can't walk away! If I turn down McClears, my career with a major law firm is washed up. If I stay — do you realize I could end up looking Thurgood Marshall in the face if this case ends up in the Supreme Court?

AL. (*Amused chuckle*) I'd love to be a fly on Justice Marshall's wall the day you show up in a chauffeured limo to argue on behalf of the McClears Corporation.

ED. You see Farrells has this colored section for me to fit into. I'm suppose to wash their dirty laundry!

AL. Affirmative action is alive and well at Farrells!

ED. Fuck affirmative action, fuck goals, fuck quotas! I never once identified myself by race on an application.

AL. You should have — would have saved the personnel manager extra paper work.

ED. Eat shit, Al!

AL. (*Spurt of laughter*) Ed, brother, I eat shit every day! We're singing the same song!

ED. I'm sorry. (*After a moment, Ed reaches up, removes picture, and places it behind sofa*)

AL. (*Putting picture back*) No, Ed. You can't destroy the dream. (*There is a knock at the door*)

ED. I'm going to tell them I'm quitting Farrells. Farrells. (*Ed goes for picture, but Al blocks him*)

AL. No!

ED. I have to . . .

AL. You'll ruin the party!

ED. Yes ...

AL. You may change your mind about leaving before Monday morning. Don't man! (*Opens door and is surprised to see Tony there, impeccably dressed. Champagne gift*) Tony!

TONY. (*Shaking hand*) Al! Ed! Guess what?

ED. What?

TONY. My Mercedes is longer than yours!

ED. You got wipers on the headlights?

TONY. I got every thing with it but the kitchen sink. Gentlemen. I am a married man.

AL. Tony ...

ED. You're married?

TONY. A Spelman girl!

ED. A Spelman woman ...

AL. Tony landed a Spelman lady ...

TONY. Teressa!

AL. I didn't get an invitation—you get an invitation, Ed? (*Ed shakes his head no*) We didn't get an invitation, Tony ...

TONY. The wedding was in Atlanta ...

AL. Atlanta ...

ED. Of course ...

TONY. I'm convinced beyond a doubt that most people never marry the person they truly love.

AL. You and Teressa had your first fight?

TONY. Fight?

AL. One of those things people in love do once in a while.

TONY. Teressa and I make love, not war! What the world needs is love! Love sweet love! It's the only thing there's just too little of!

AL. Love sweet love!

TONY. (*With lilt*) We don't need another mountain ...

AL. (*Interrupting*) Tony!

TONY. (*Proudly*) Teressa is an English professor—adjunct.

ED. An English professor.

AL. No point in going to college if you can have the professor.

TONY. Al—me and Teressa—I mean, Teressa and I—want to live on Pill Hill.

AL. Pill Hill ...

TONY. Doc Rogers' place.

AL. (*Taken aback*) You're talking two hundred and fifty thousand.

TONY. No sweat—it's for our wedding anniversary.

AL. Love sweet love! (*Going for brief case*) I just happen to have the floor plan and some pictures. I can think of no greater way of showing the depth and breath of your love than purchasing a home on Pill Hill for your lovely—Teressa! Give me a minute to set up next door. Ed—you don't mind if we conduct a little business?

ED. Go right ahead.

AL. (*Speaking on exit*) Tony on Pill Hill! Love sweet love!

TONY. Ed, Teressa and I are expecting. We'll name it Ed if it's a boy. If it's a girl, something with Ed in it—Edwina sound okay?

ED. No Edwina! Don't like the sound of Edwina.

TONY. Edna!

ED. No way! Sounds like that insurance company.

TONY. How does Edward Anthony Powell strike you?

ED. Sounds better than Edwina.

TONY. Edward Anthony Powell! I want you to be godfather to our firstborn.

ED. Godfather?

TONY. Will you honor us?

ED. (*Blushing*) Tony, I'm not sure what a godfather is supposed to do ...

TONY. Send little Eddie a savings bond for his birthday each year. Be there for his baptism. Baby-sit when his parents are away ...

ED. No baby-sitting!

TONY. I'm kidding, but you got to make his baptism.

ED. God, Tony, I don't know ... All right ... (*Unable to camouflage the swelling pride*) I'll be godfather to your firstborn.

TONY. (*Tony reaches out and embraces Ed in an emotionally charged embrace*) Thanks! Ed, do you think I'm overcompensating by marrying a college professor?

ED. Not if it's love sweet love.

TONY. Good, now I can fire my analyst. He tells me I'm overcompensating for not going to college by marrying a professor. I'm not paying that prick a hundred bucks an hour to screw up my marriage.

AL. (*Entering*) We're all set Tony.

TONY. Come take a look at my Pill Hill pad ...

ED. I'll join you in a minute ... (*Al and Tony enter bedroom. Ed rises and repeats, with pride, "Anthony Edward Powell!" There is a knock at the door. Ed crosses and answers door. Scott is there, dressed in suit, flashy ring and matching jewelry, shades and leather coat, which he wears caped over his shoulders. Beeper does not show*)

ED. Scott ...

SCOTT. Ed, old buddy!

ED. This is a surprise.

SCOTT. Joe didn't tell you I was coming? I wouldn't miss a reunion. You do know I'm working for the record company?

ED. The record company?

TONY. Sales and distribution — Southside record company? I see you left the Mercedes home and rode over in your ghetto bug. I can dig it. Got me a BMW.

ED. BMW?

TONY. Tired of flashy ass Cadillacs.

ED. The record business must be booming.

SCOTT. You only go around once in life. Yo — Joe here?

ED. Picking up a pizza.

SCOTT. Man I tell ya, I don't know what this world is coming to — white folks eating chicken wings, and colored folk eating pizza — somebody ought to wise up and start topping pizza with fried chicken and collard greens!

ED. Tony and Al are here.

SCOTT. (*Looking around room as if they are in room*) Where? Where, where?

ED. Next door.

SCOTT. Cool, cool. (*Relieved*) Yo — where's the rest room?

ED. Same place.

SCOTT. 'The hell is that — gotcha! Got to empty my bladder! (*Starts to bathroom, then stops*) You make it?

ED. Huh?

SCOTT. You make it — to — you know whatchamucallit?

ED. Yeah.

SCOTT. Yeah?

ED. Yeah.

SCOTT. MERCY ME! You big shit now ain't you? Dig it. I like
that. Yo—the restroom, where's the restroom? (*Ed points*)
Yeah, yeah. Check out my BMW!

ED. Yeah—I will.

SCOTT. Paid cash for that motha.

ED. Cash?

SCOTT. Yo—man, paying interest makes me feel like I'm being
pimped! (*Closes door and opens it again and steps back inside*)
Where you say they at—Al and Tony?

ED. Bedroom.

SCOTT. Bedroom? Doing what?

ED. Looking at a floor plan for a house on the market.

SCOTT. (*Relieved*) Oh yeah, yeah—Al doing real estate.
Bedroom—whew! Two brothers hanging out in the bedroom alone makes me nervous! (*Shouting to bedroom*) You
boys get your asses in here and say hello! Betcha that'll get
them! (*He starts to bathroom and his beeper goes off. Reaches for
his pocket and looks at Ed. Their eyes meet for an uncomfortable
moment*) It's my business box. Keeps me in touch with my
customers. You got it? (*Ed doesn't respond. Scott, almost unnerved,
reacts defensively*) Yo man—my business box!

ED. This time of night?

SCOTT. They call. I answer. On the dime. Twenty-four hours a
day. You got it?

ED. I got it, Scott.

SCOTT. Cool?

ED. Cool.

SCOTT. Cool! (*Scott goes to bathroom. Ed gets up and turns picture
around. Al enters*)

AL. That Spelman woman has my man's nose wide open.
(*Turning picture around*) So what's the verdict?

ED. Walker isn't coming . . .

AL. Farrells—I'm talking about Farrells. What's the verdict?

TONY. (*Enters from bedroom*) Ed, you got a Farrells card?

ED. What?

TONY. A Farrells card?

ED. Yeah . . .

TONY. Autograph it for me . . .

ED. I can't, Tony!

TONY. You got to!

AL. Ed, it's okay. (*Ed signs card*)

TONY. I got to have it to show to all those doubting Thomases at work who laugh behind my back when I tell them we old mill buddies. (*Ed passes signed card to Tony*)

TONY. Thanks.

SCOTT. (*Entering from bathroom*) Steel mill alumni! (*Tony and Al respond with greetings*) Long time no see! Stand back and let me have a look at all this successful black humanity. (*Pulling out a bottle of champagne*) I'm selling records, Tony selling Mercedeses, Al selling real estate. Pull out the champagne and let's drink a toast to all this success ... (*Door opens and Joe and Charlie enter with pizza*)

JOE. What I tell you Charlie?

SCOTT. Joe, Charlie ...

JOE. I knew when I saw that red BMW he was here ...

CHARLIE. BMW — moving on up in the world.

SCOTT. Changing with the times — get a glass and let's drink a toast to all these successful men of color.

EVERYBODY. CHEERS!

SCOTT. And to Charlie's retirement ...

JOE. And his return to Mississippi in that Cadillac!

EVERYBODY. Cheers!

AL. And for Tony's pad on Pill Hill.

JOE. Tony on Pill Hill?

CHARLIE. What's that!

JOE. The Hill ain't what it used to be. (*Good-natured laughter*)

SCOTT. And don't forget the man selling Tony his pad on the Hill.

AL. And to Scott's success in the record business.

SCOTT. Thanks guys ... (*Scott blushes, genuinely pleased at the accolades*) And to the man of the hour — to the first real man on the Farrells team!

EVERYBODY. (*Enthusiasm*) CHEERS! (*They drink*)

CHARLIE. (*Noticing Joe*) Hold on a second, you guys — and, and to Joe's new beginning ...

JOE. Yeah, yeah to my new beginning.

EVERYBODY. CHEERS! (*Greeting each other silently. Meanwhile, Joe goes for liquor bottle. Ed has moved downstage*)

JOE. Little something for my nerves. Well, on with the game! Grab your hand, Ed.

ED. Joe, let's hold off on the game ...

JOE. We got to finish the game ...

ED. Joe ...

JOE. Walker be here by the time we done with the game. Al, Charlie, pull up a chair, we finishing the game. Grab your chair, Ed ...

ED. (*To Tony*) Tony, want to take my hand?

TONY. No, no!

ED. You sure?

SCOTT. Tony ain't forgot his last game.

JOE. Come on, Ed — sit down and grab your hand.

ED. Scott — want to take my hand?

SCOTT. No, no, no, I want to be a spectator to this momentous occasion.

JOE. Don't tell me your old mill buddy is going to humiliate you at the card table. Get your hand and take your own ass kicking.

AL. It's okay partner ... (*Ed approaches table and sits. Joe grabs bottle and takes several swallows*)

JOE. Little something for my nerves. I'm cool now. On with the game! Bid, Ed.

ED. Pass ...

JOE. Never pass, Charlie!

CHARLIE. Three low ...

JOE. Damn, Charlie, you should a passed! Bid's on you, Al.

AL. Give me a minute.

JOE. Take your time, Al — we got all night and tomorrow. (*Al ponders*) Somebody wake me up when this nig — Afro American bids.

AL. Four low.

JOE. Damn!

CHARLIE. Make your bid, Joe.

AL. Take your time, Joe ...

ED. After midnight, Joe.

JOE. Five, dammit!

CHARLIE. (*Stunned*) Joe! (*Overlapping*)

TONY. Whew!

SCOTT. Somebody turn on the air!

AL. Lead out, Joe.

JOE. Hearts. Yall's ass is grass. (*Slaps card against Ed's forehead and onto table*) Handle that, attorney! (*Standing, slaps another card on table*) Better send up a prayer, Sunday school teacher. Collect my books, Charlie. (*Slapping card against Ed's forehead and standing*)

SCOTT. Ouch!

JOE. Everything you fellows wanted to know about bid whist but was afraid to ask. (*Slaps another card on table, but Ed cuts him out, as others look on in amusement*)

ED. Handle that, Joe.

JOE. Come on, Charlie.

AL. Somebody heard your prayer, partner.

JOE. Damn, Charlie!

AL. Play it again, Charlie!

JOE. You ain't got what the rooster left on the roosting pole, Charlie.

CHARLIE. I'm in good company.

AL. Don't start playing poker on us, Joe.

JOE. (*Slapping card against Al's head, then table*) I got your poker.

TONY. Aaahh!

SCOTT. Wheeew!

JOE. Don't let me down, Charlie.

SCOTT. Somebody better reach for his underwear.

TONY. Hanes or Fruit of the Loom?

SCOTT. Silk, man, silk ...

JOE. Come on, partner!

SCOTT. Strip down to your silk underwear ...

JOE. You 'bout as much help to me as Laurel is to Hardy.

SCOTT. ... and all the karate in the world won't keep the women away.

JOE. Wow!

ED. Damn, partner ...

TONY AND SCOTT. Ouch! (*Overlapping*)

JOE. Love ya madly, Charlie, baby! Come on. We can still make bid, Charlie. Wooah! Two more books, Charlie! (*Standing, and others follow*) Come on, Charlie. One more book, Charlie! (*Charlie throws out the winning card and Joe is wild with excitement. Embracing Charlie*) We made it, Charlie!

ED. Not so fast, Joe. Charlie cut my queen of clubs.

JOE. What!

ED. Charlie reneged, Joe.

JOE. (*Stunned, examining cards*) Reneged — what the hell — you got to show me the book!

ED. (*Ed reveals book*) We stopped their asses!!!

AL. No way you could make eleven books with that scrappy hand, Joe.

JOE. Damn, Charlie!

TONY. It's no big deal, Joe.

AL. Just a game, Joe ...

JOE. So how come you punks busting your asses to win? Damn, Charlie! You should have kept your eyes on the board. I lost, Charlie! The nigger beat me! (*Joe storms into bedroom and closes door in Scott's face*)

CHARLIE. Winning mean that much to you?

ED. I'm in no mood to get my ass kicked tonight, Charlie.

CHARLIE. For heaven's sake, it's a two bit card game!

ED. It's more than a card game to me, Charlie!

CHARLIE. I see what Farrells teaching you!

ED. That's funny, Charlie ...

CHARLIE. Ain't one damn thing funny about rubbing your heels in the wounds of an afflicted man!

ED. Ironic, I meant ironic!

CHARLIE. Ironic, nothing. You done got so high up you've forgot what it means to show a little compassion for a friend crying out for help. Hey, man, I don't care if you sit behind the biggest desk in the tallest building on Michigan Avenue, your shit stinks like everybody else's. Don't forget I knew you when you had the dirt under your nails and the buggers in your nose at the mill and they still there as far as I'm concerned, don't care if you are the first hot shot nigger at Farrells.

ED. Charlie ...

CHARLIE. The mill is closing! It's the only game Joe's got.

ED. Charlie ...

CHARLIE. You ain't got a damn thing to say to me!

AL. Charlie—Ed's got something to say.

ED. I'm quitting Farrells, Charlie!

TONY. What!

ED. (*Pulling out letter of resignation*) Here is my letter of resignation!

TONY. You hear that, Al?

AL. Quiet Tony!

ED. They dropped the McClears case in my hands and dared me to say no. I've got a chance to be a partner and earn a six figure bonus if I win this case. Charlie, my Farrells ID is my ticket into private clubs no black lawyer has ever networked before. Do you know what's going to happen if I don't come out of Farrells swimming for life?

CHARLIE. You standing there in your Brooks Brothers suit waiting for me to shed tears 'cause you gonna lose the headlight wipers on that Mercedes.

ED. God, Charlie, Don't you know why I can't stay? I did it for you.

CHARLIE. Naw, man, don't do it for me. I done pulled my Cadillac off the blocks and I'm on my way back to Mississippi to sit in the shade and drink Kool Aid.

ED. Charlie, the only thing I saw when they dropped that case in my lap was you, when you walked through that door the night you didn't get your promotion. And my father, working his ass off every day and dying right where he started. I knew I had to say no to the bastards—even when I felt like I was losing it all, because I knew you were with me!

CHARLIE. So what do you want me to do! Get on my knees and thank you? Not yet, man. Before I do that for your ass, you got to fall lower than a snake's belly, down with the grave diggers, all the way down on your knees and lick gnat shit from the MAN's headlights. Then I'm gonna reach down and give your sorry ass a hand.

ED. You telling me to send those McClears brothers down the sewer for thirty pieces of silver?

CHARLIE. I'm telling you what Mr. Willie would tell you, don't come driving over here in your VW with your tail tucked between your legs begging for sympathy. Dust your ass off, straighten up your shoulders and get back out there in that jungle because ain't nobody gonna give you a goddamn thing!

TONY. (*Panicky*) Don't hand in that resignation, Ed! Don't do it, man. You ain't changing the world by walking away from that Mercedes to scratch out a living in the dirt, because you gonna spend the rest of your life drowning in a shit load of bills. Tell him he can't walk away! Somebody tell this fool! Al, Charlie! (*Exploding*) SOMEBODY TELL THIS FOOL!

AL. TONY! (*Overlapping*)

SCOTT. TONY! YOU GONNA LIVE!

JOE. (*Oblivious to what has happened*) It's okay, guys ...

CHARLIE. No, Joe.

JOE. It's — just a card game.

CHARLIE. (*Struggling*) It's not okay, Joe!

JOE. (*Oblivious to Charlie's comment*) No sweat — we'll play it over ... (*Joe goes for the liquor bottle and gulps the remaining liquor*) Little something for my nerves. Better, much better! Somebody deal out another hand. (*The phone rings. Joe crosses to answer it*) Joe, here ... (*Pointing to phone. Covering mouthpiece with hand, to others*) It's Walker! What I tell ya! He 'bout in the neighborhood calling for directions. (*Back into phone*) Attorney Walker! Yeah, yeah, the celebration is in full swing. Waiting on you. I'm as good as back on with you on my case. What? Lay it on me now. Beg your pardon? Hey, if it's money, my word solid as the American dollar. Huh? (*Anxious, visibly shaken*) I'll pay up soon's I get my first two or three pay checks. What's that? (*In desperation*) Listen, Walker, you the best lawyer in Chicago — best in the whole country! You my only hope Walker. Walker! Walker. WALKER! (*Holding onto telephone as if it is a lifeline. He turns and faces men, all of whom stare in silence. He looks to Ed, beseeching*) Walker ain't coming. He ain't coming, Ed. I was wondering if you would — if you would (*faltering*) if you would take up my ...

ED. I'm sorry Walker isn't coming, Joe.

JOE. (*Drinks from empty bottle, trying to suck out a drop. Spurt of laughter*) It's finished! (*Throws bottle in garbage. It breaks.*

Looking around for sign of hope) You folk enjoy the party? (*The men struggle to give some affirmative, if impotent, gesture of approval*)

SCOTT. Everything's right on time, Joe — right on time ...

TONY. Great party, Joe ...

JOE. (*Looking around to others, hopeful*) Maybe we can plan to do this again next week ...

TONY. Yeah, yeah ...

SCOTT. Great idea ...

AL. Yeah, yeah, Joe ...

JOE. I'd host it here, but I'm moving — down to the Homeless Mission Monday. (*The stricken men, unable to respond, avoid looking at each other. Joe speaks reassuringly*) Hey, everything is cool. (*Joe throws up a hand, as if the group is about to take up a collection, which he would consider offensive*) Don't even think about it. Breaks my heart to see them brothers at the Mission. Wouldn't be caught dead there — no longer than it takes me to get my next ... my next ... no longer than it takes me to get on my feet. (*Shaking head in disgust, fighting against the pain, though weakly*) Man! Them dudes at the Mission, they be like dead men. Washed up and ain't seen the prime of life! Be a cold day in hell before I let myself get trapped in that rut. (*Looking around at others, uneasily, frightened. Their discomfort is unbearable*) Say, I figure we can do this again next week at somebody else's pad.

TONY. I'm booked for the next month ... (*Overlapping*)

AL. Next week is out for me ... (*Overlapping*)

SCOTT. Full ass calendar myself, Joe ... (*Overlapping*)

CHARLIE. Next week is early, Joe ...

JOE. (*To Tony, hopeful*) Well, Tony, guess we'll have to wait for your house warming on Pill Hill. I'll be on the look out for my invitation.

TONY. (*Shaking hands with Joe*) Good luck, Joe. (*Scott's beeper goes off. He is taken aback, embarrassed, but defensively cool as others look on in embarrassed silence, somewhere between amused contempt and disgust*)

SCOTT. (*Looking around at others*) One of my customers at the record company paging me. Cool? (*No one responds*) They paging me for a delivery. Cool? (*No one responds*) They pay me big bucks to deliver this time of night! Cool? Hey, I'm providing a service! Nothing wrong with that! (*No one responds, the shunning unnerves, frightens and angers Scott. Until he explodes*) HEY, ANY ONE OF YOU SON-OF-A-BITCHES WITHOUT SIN, LET HIM THROW THE FIRST GODDAMN STONE!

AL. SCOTT! (*Overlapping*)

JOE. Ain't nobody naming names! You'd better be on your way. Don't want you to miss out on your delivery.

SCOTT. Later, gentlemen. (*Scott exits as beeper goes off again. Tony and Al follow. Joe goes to window and observes them. Charlie turns to Ed. Al says a silent farewell to Joe*)

TONY. (*Aside to Ed, as others exchange farewells, more visual than audible*) We'll have to hold off on that godfather invitation for now.

ED. (*Taken aback*) Tony — I want to be godfather to your first born.

TONY. We had better wait until we see which way things are going at Farrells.

ED. (*Crushed*) Tony! (*Tony heads out. Al comes forward*)

AL. (*To Ed*) Hang tough, Ed.

ED. I got to ... (*Al exits*)

CHARLIE. Ed — that Men's Day Invitation is still open. You got one helluva speech to give us ...

ED. Thanks, Charlie.

CHARLIE. (*Tapping Joe on back*) Joe ...

JOE. (*Struggling*) You deserting me, too — thanks for that care package.

CHARLIE. Any time, Joe, any time ... (*Exit. Ed and Joe turn away from each other, neither able to cross the gulf between them. Joe breaks the excruciatingly painful silence*)

JOE. Guess it's just me and you, like it was in the beginning. (*Ed doesn't respond*) Just me and you ... (*Ed does not speak*) Say — get a game going. (*Desperately goes for cards and shuffles nervously with them, dropping several to floor*) Game ain't over till I take you to the cleaners! (*Joe gives off spurt of desperate laughter, but Ed does not respond*) FORGOT! Takes four to play bid whist! (*Puts cards back. With excitement*) Be back on at the mill in no time at all ... (*Swelling anger, through desperate laughter, accentuated by Ed's silence*) Ed, if you ain't careful,

I'll beat your ass to Pill Hill yet. BEAT YOU YET, OLD BUDDY!

ED. (*Turned away*) Yeah ...

JOE. Soon's I get back on, getting me another job and quitting the mill and I be going off to college and law school—just like you did.

ED. Yeah ...

JOE. Say—think I can get your old job at the library?

ED. They filled it!

JOE. They did, hey.

ED. Five or six years ago!

JOE. No, sweat! You, you bring me a application?

ED. (*Flabbergasted, breathless*) What!

JOE. You know—one of them applications you suppose to fill out when you be going to college. You bring one wid you?

ED. (*Tersely*) No!

JOE. Uh?

ED. No, No, No!

JOE. No sweat—git me one first thing Monday morning. I be gitting on at Farrells—like you be doing.

ED. (*Ed clears his throat*) Uhhhh ...

JOE. Me and you be in a big high-rise downtown Michigan Avenue. (*Ed does not respond and Joe struggles on, taut with bitter anger. Joe pulls broken bottle from basket. Ed does not see it. He looks at bottle, contemplatively, as he talks on*) What you say about that? Hey?

ED. (*Barely audible tone*) Maybe ...

JOE. (*Bitterly*) HEY?

ED. (*Still turned away from joe*) Maybe we can ...

JOE. (*Exploding in rage, going after Ed with bottle*) Damn you, nigger!

ED. Joe!

JOE. Talking that dull ass "maybe we can" lie when you don't mean a damn word of it!

ED. You're wrong, Joe!

JOE. (*Swinging wildly, taunting, dangerously close*) Naw I ain't. You don't wanna be here with your old mill buddy. Done got too uppity for us low class niggers? I got your Farrells! Right here, attorney!

ED. I QUIT FARRELLS, JOE!

JOE. STOP LYING!

ED. QUIT, Joe!

JOE. STOP YOUR LIES! (*Ed catches Joe off balance and manhandles him to the floor, avoiding contact with broken bottle. He straddles Joe in an angry rage. For a quick moment it is as though Ed is going to break Joe's neck*)

ED. Damn you — I could break your neck and stuff your ragged ass remains in the garbage bin! Nobody would miss you, Joe! Nobody would give a damn! The people at Farrells would thank me for cleaning up the shit off the street!

JOE. Go ahead — you don't get no medal for wasting a dead man! (*Ed pushes Joe to floor and stands up. For a moment it is as though he wants to grind his foot in Joe's face. Joe struggles to get up. Ed extends his hand. Joe grabs it and Ed pulls him up. Ed throws bottle in basket*)

ED. THE MILL IS CLOSING JOE!

JOE. No . . .

ED. Closing . . .

JOE. They can't be closing the mill on me now!

ED. There's no going back!

JOE. I got to go back!

ED. The gates are barred, Joe!

JOE. No. I got to get my first two or three paychecks . . .

ED. JOE!

JOE. Then I'm gonna . . .

ED. You missed the boat, Joe. We were supposed to be partners, out there in that jungle kicking ass together! I need you out there in the fight with me, Joe, and you're rotting in this hole in the wall! Goddamn you!

JOE. (*After a moment*) What you gonna do without Farrells?

ED. I don't know. I might go back down to Eighty-seventh Street South . . .

JOE. Eighty-seventh Street South. That's damn near all the way back to Mississippi. You gonna end up chasing ambulances for nickels and dimes for the rest of your life!

ED. The sun is gonna rise tomorrow with or without Farrells.

JOE. Ed, you can't leave Farrells!

ED. Joe! (*Overlapping*)

JOE. (*Fearful*) Don't destroy the dream! (*Overlapping*)

ED. JOE! (*After a moment*) It's time to say goodbye.

JOE. (*Terrified*) Ed! ... ED—TAKE ME ... TAKE ME WHERE YOU BE GOING!

ED. Naw, man ...

JOE. ED ...

ED. I CAN'T TAKE YOU WHERE I'M GOING!

JOE. ED ... will you remember your old buddy?

ED. How can I forget you, man. (*After a moment, looking at Joe, through tears*) How about Monday if I come and give you a hand with your moving.

JOE. Yeah—sounds cool, to me. (*Ed exits. Joe goes and looks out window as lights fade in on him, shining through window*)

janet noble

away
alone

author's introduction

I often feel like an exile, but I suppose that's the way it is these days for most people pursuing a life in the arts, which are no longer considered an essential part of society. I was born in America thanks to some long-forgotten ancestors who were desperate and brave enough to cross the Atlantic. My father's family came here from Ireland in the mid-1800s in that great wave of immigration brought about by the potato blight and resulting famine of 1847. Perhaps they came from Donegal. I've been told that there's a graveyard full of Nobles in a village in Donegal.

Over the decades, there have been continuous waves of immigrants to these shores from all over the world but, because of my own family history, I am especially interested in the Irish. The 1980s brought another great influx, this one the result of Ireland's economic inability to provide enough jobs. The difference between the 1800s and now is that these new Irish immigrants are young and well educated. And there are quotas now so that many of them are in this country illegally. For them, the threat of deportation is a daily one. Some are away from their homes for the first time, facing Big City situations they never imagined in their wildest dreams. I was urged to write about the plight of these Irish men and women in New York City by Noel Comac, a young actor from County Tyrone who was in a production of my play *Kiss My Blarney Stone* in 1987.

Away Alone opened at The Irish Arts Center on December 1, 1989, the year that the number of young Irish in America peaked at 100,000. The response and support from the Irish community as well as the regular theatre-going audiences were wonderful, proving that the immigration experience is a shared one.

We were lucky to have Larry Kirwan and Black '47 (a band aptly named) to provide music which captured the spirit of life on "The Irish Mile" in The Bronx. Unfortunately, Comac was unable to return to America from

Ireland to be in the cast and share in the play's success. The title *Away Alone*, comes from the end of *Finnegan's Wake* by James Joyce, himself an Irish exile.

original production

Away Alone by Janet Noble, directed by Terence Lamude, setting by David Raphel, lighting by Harry Feiner, costumes by C. Jane Epperson, sound by Tom Gould, music by Larry Kirwan, and produced by Daniel Quinn, Andrew Sullivan, stage manager, and Marianne Delaney, assistant stage manager, opened on December 1, 1989, at The Irish Arts Center in New York City (Jim Sheridan, artistic director and Nye Heron, executive director), with the following cast:

LIAM	Michael Healy
MARIO	Paul Pillitteri
OWEN	Anto Nolan
PADDY	Barry O'Rourke
DESMOND	Don Creedon
MARY	Cora Murray
BREDA	Bronagh Murphy
YOUNG WOMAN	Joelle Martel

setting

The place is Bainbridge Avenue, The Bronx, New York. The time is The Present. Act 1 takes place from September to December, Act 2 from December through June.

characters

LIAM

MARIO

OWEN

PADDY

DESMOND

MARY

BREDA

YOUNG WOMAN

act 1

SCENE ONE

The Old Sod Bar, an ordinary, run-of-the mill local in The Bronx. Its history hangs behind the bar: the first $20 bill from opening day is framed along with the usual group photographs of various patrons on fishing trips and at political meetings, etc. There are dusty remnants of past St. Patrick's Days. At rise the lights come up on Mario behind the bar, setting up clean glasses. Liam enters, carrying a backpack. He moves tentatively up to the bar. Mario eyes him and goes on with his work. He sighs, then moves down the bar to Liam.

MARIO. You're Irish, right?

LIAM. Right, I'm ...

MARIO. Looking for a guy named Seamus, right?

LIAM. Right!

MARIO. Every guy from Ireland for the last three months been looking for Seamus. (*Silence*) You from Cork?

LIAM. Right. How ...?

MARIO. Seamus is from Cork.

LIAM. He's a little fella with red hair, wears specs?

MARIO. Right. You got him. You know him well?

LIAM. Actually, I don't know him at all. His mother's cousin is a friend of me auntie. She said I should look him up when I come over and she give me the address of this pub.

MARIO. Right.

LIAM. What times does he come on?

MARIO. He don't. Seamus don't work here no more.

LIAM. You don't mean he's gone entirely?

MARIO. Been three months now. You wanna find Seamus, try Seattle.

LIAM. Jaysus, where's that?!

MARIO. Out in Washington. State. On the blue Pacific.

LIAM. His mother's cousin told me auntie he was doing well here.

MARIO. He was. Until Immigration got wind of him. He did a fade to the west. Followed the sun. Told me he might head

for Hawaii. I guess he figures ... what the hell! If they
catch him, they'll pay his air fare home.

LIAM. Well. Fuck me. (*Lets his bags drop*) I thought Seamus
would put me up, ya know ... 'til I got myself sorted out.

MARIO. Don't worry about it. If you're homeless, you come to
the right place. New York City's the Homeless Capital of
America. (*Extends his hand over the bar to Liam*) The name's
Mario.

LIAM. Liam, here. (*They shake hands*)

MARIO. Well, now ... what'll it be? (*Liam doesn't understand*)
To drink.

LIAM. Oh.

MARIO. Guinness? It's on the house.

LIAM. On the house?

MARIO. Free. (*He sets a foaming glass down in front of Liam*)
Welcome to America, Liam.

LIAM. Thanks. (*He raises the glass to Mario and drinks*) Ah. I
guess I needed that. (*Silence*) I've got a job, anyway.

MARIO. Hey, you got a job ... you're ahead of the game!
Don't worry about a place to stay. Guys come in here
straight off the plane like you and they get fixed up easy.
So, what do you think of New York?

LIAM. I saw nothing. Come straight from Kennedy. (*Pause*) If
you told me a week ago I'd be in America today, I would
have called you crazy. I never planned to come. I was
happy staying where I was. Helped me da in the shop a
bit. Made posters for the youth council.

MARIO. What changed your mind?

LIAM. Peter Kelly come back from Brooklyn to fix his mother's
roof. They live at the end of the road. He fancied me
sister. One night, he asked her out for a Chinese dinner.
She didn't care to go out with him alone, so she asked me
would I go along. I told her no. I was only hanging about
the house, but jaysus ... I hate Chinese food! But then, at
the last minute, I changed me mind. (*Pause*) And possibly
me life.

MARIO. He gave you a job?

LIAM. Sure, I thought he meant on his mother's roof 'til he
handed me the money for the ticket. You could have

knocked me over. And here I am ... wherever I am.

MARIO. This is the Bronx.

LIAM. But where is that, exactly? Say, in relation to Brooklyn.

MARIO. North. So, when do you start the job?

LIAM. Monday. I hope I'm set up with a place by then.

MARIO. What sort of work?

LIAM. Construction. Peter's got his own firm. (*Mario moves back down the bar to serve another customer. The customer is unseen. Mario's greeting is to the audience*)

MARIO. Evening, Mr. Costelloe. (*He returns to Liam*)

MARIO. Mr. Costelloe. Wife died last year. How was the flight?

LIAM. My first time on an airplane. I sat next to a priest. I wasn't exactly looking forward to six hours of small talk with your man, but I figured it was a small price just to be on the safe side, you know? And didn't he take out the beads and start the rosary at lift-off. I could only hope he was praying for all of us. (*They both laugh and Liam takes another long drink. Someone puts money in the juke box and music plays. Bar noises pick up*) Is the weather always this hot?

MARIO. Heat wave. Dog days of September. Also known as Indian Summer. Don't ask me what the Indians got to do with it. They're always trying to pin something on the Indians.

LIAM. I feel so strange now.

MARIO. Jet lag. You'll be okay after a good sleep. You know anybody over here?

LIAM. No.

MARIO. I read in the paper that about 12,000 kids were here from Ireland this summer. And that was only in the New York City area. (*Silence*) Good for business.

LIAM. Yeah?

MARIO. Sure, It's quiet now but in about forty-five minutes, this place'll be packed. All Irish. Wall to wall. Before you guys started coming over, the neighborhood was a ghost town. They had signs all over the street: "Don't Move. Improve!" There was never anybody under sixty in here. Hell, I had a couple of regulars take heart attacks on me, right here at the bar. (*Pause*) Broke my heart when they carried those guys out. (*Silence*) You're lucky you speak English.

LIAM. Are you from Italy, Mario?

MARIO. Jersey City. That's across the Hudson River there.

LIAM. But you're Italian, right?

MARIO. Yeah. Polish and Irish. A little Dutch. It don't matter. I'm an American. Six months, you'll be one too. You won't know what hit you. All you'll need's the passport. (*He wipes the bar for a minute*) Yeah. You're lucky. You know that?

LIAM. How do you mean?

MARIO. You left home, you crossed an ocean. I left Jersey City for the Bronx. Whadda we got here? Nothing. A view of Manhattan. In Jersey City I had the sunrise. Here, I got a sunset. It's always Manhattan. (*Pause*) I never figured I'd end up here, on Bainbridge Avenue, pulling beers and pouring shots.

LIAM. I'd like to see Manhattan.

MARIO. Yeah. Everybody wants to see Manhattan. Everybody's got a dream. Used to be, that's all you needed. Take my advice and save your money, Liam. That's the first priority. New York ain't like it used to be. Today, you gotta have the cash first, up front. Dreams cost money, now. The dream's gotta wait. (*Owen enters and goes straight to the bar*) Hey, Owen.

OWEN. Give me a hit of Paddy's, Mario. Guy fell off the scaffold today. He was working right beside me. He was only after joking with me about the girls below. Fell four stories. It's a wonder he's not dead.

MARIO. Hurt bad?

OWEN. Broke both legs and there's some bad internal damage. Looks like he'll be going home.

MARIO. Tough. Well, meet Liam, here. He needs a place to stay.

OWEN. You need a job? There's an opening.

MARIO. He's got a job. He come in here looking for Seamus.

OWEN. You know Seamus?

LIAM. Not directly. He's a friend of the family.

OWEN. Where you from?

LIAM. Ballylickey.

OWEN. The back of beyond! Ever been here before?

LIAM. I'd never been to Dublin 'til I caught the plane.

OWEN. Well, you're on then ... if you don't mind sleeping
with me cousin. There are three of us. We've got two
rooms ... that includes the kitchen. The rent's $700 a
month. Your share of that'll be $175.

LIAM. Sounds grand to me.

OWEN. You'll also be expected to kick in $20 a week for meals.
To me. I do the cooking. (*Mario laughs*) I'm a very good
cook.

LIAM. Sold!

OWEN. Drink up, then. I want to stop off at the store for some
grub. (*They go out and Owen pays for the drinks*) I'm making
my specialty tonight, Mario.

MARIO. Oh yeah? What's that?

OWEN. (*Laughing*) Rice and beans. Come on, Liam. I'll show
you the Bronx. This place'll open your eyes. (*They exit.
Music. Lights out*)

SCENE TWO

*Lights up on the apartment. Only one large room is visible. Along
one wall is an old couch that folds out into a double bed. There are
piles of books and newspapers on the floor by the couch. Most of the
other furniture is makeshift and shabby. Clothes are strewn about
and there are posters on the walls announcing various musical
concerts. A faded carpet with a floral design covers the floor. The
right side of the room is taken up by a kitchen area. There's a table
made from a door that rests on saw horses. Otherwise, the kitchen is
neater than the rest of the room. It should be clear that someone
takes pride in the pots, knives, etc. To the left is the door to the only
other room, the bedroom. In the back wall is the door to the outside
hallway. Owen and Liam enter, carrying bags of groceries and
backpack.*

OWEN. Well, this is it. The Irish Embassy, we like to call it.

LIAM. It's grand.

OWEN. It's a bit of a squash but the landlord turns a blind

eye. We've had as many as six lads bunking here at one time. (*He puts groceries on the table and indicates the couch by the wall*) There's your bed. It folds out. Just put your gear over there and give me a hand here, will youse? Slice up this here onion. You'll find a knife in that drawer. And mince this here, too. We'll throw in some garlic.

LIAM. Mince?

OWEN. Yeah. Chop it fine. And mind your fingers ... I've seen enough blood for one day, thanks very much. Paddy and Des ought to be back soon. They're out looking for work. Paddy was on the job with me for a while, but he couldn't take the heights. Made him dizzy. Told me he used to fall out of trees back home. Though I don't know where he found them to fall out of ... he's from Connemara. Farmers, they are. Jeez, it was six months before we got the smell of cow shit off him.

LIAM. How long have you been over, Owen?

OWEN. Three years, on the fifth of next month. One year more and I'll have enough of the green saved to go back home and open a nice little restaurant. I think Dublin's ready for gourmet food. Toss that all in the pot here while I open the beer. (*Owen puts beer and other groceries in the refrigerator. He removes two bottles of beer, opens them both and puts one down for Liam*)

LIAM. That Mario is a real friendly fella. He was telling me about Seamus going to Seattle.

OWEN. You want to watch out with the small talk.

LIAM. What do you mean, Owen?

OWEN. Sit down 'til I tell you. No time like the present. Listen, now. We used to hang out with Mario. He come over here a few times. Next thing, Immigration comes sniffing around Seamus. I'm not saying Mario had anything to do with it. Matter of fact, I'd say he didn't. Mario's no spook. But ... you don't know who Mario's friends are. You don't know who he talks to when he's not at the bar. Best not to give him any info he doesn't need, that he could pass along to the wrong person. Get my drift? The others think I'm being overly paranoid, but they're safe. I'm not. Since that fecking law was passed, the feds are on everybody's case. Coming around the site where I work, checking up. The foreman, Jimmy, gives the warning and I nick out the back. But there's always the odd time. The day Jimmy's sick. I'm just telling you, Liam. You're only just over. I've been worrying about Jimmy's health for three years. I've almost got what I came for and I won't tolerate any behavior that threatens that. Do you get me?

LIAM. I do, Owen. I'll watch meself.

OWEN. That's all right then. (*The door opens and in comes Paddy, with a big grin on his face. He puts a bag down on a chair and moves to the kitchen table*) Now, open a beer for Paddy, here.

PADDY. Have you found us a stray then. Ownie?

OWEN. Meet Liam. He's moving in with us. I found him sitting in The Old Sod, waiting for Seamus.

PADDY. How are ya, Liam? Well, mates ... take a good look. This is Paddy Reilly, the new assistant gardener on the J. P. Morrissey estate above in Larchmont, New York.

OWEN. You got the job! Good on ya, man! Tonight we celebrate!

PADDY. Ah, I'm in clover, Owen! You wouldn't believe this place. They've got horses up there! Not an hour outside the Bronx and I'm with the sweetest horses you ever saw. Not to mention a swimming pool big enough to hold a hundred head of cattle. Limo met me at the train. Yer man interviews me in a posh office above the stables. Introduces me to old Dan Devlin, the gardener. I gather he's not up to the job anymore ... bit long in the tooth and gone on the drink. He takes me out and shows me the grounds. Old Lady Morrissey is unhappy with her Japanese garden, it seems. Something about the Westchester Flower Show and her wanting to win first prize next year. I flung some words around. Never met the Morrisseys at all. Ah, mates, it's clover! Three hundred a week and all I have to do is weed the beds, move some rocks about and prune a bit. What I don't know, I'll learn from Devlin. He wants company. Des back yet?

OWEN. No.

PADDY. Listen. Owen ... go easy on him when he gets in.

You know, in case he wasn't lucky today. He's a bit sensitive.

OWEN. Well, maybe he should toughen up then. Between ourselves. I think he's too damned particular about work. It's not that hard to find a job. There's plenty a jobs out there. We've been carrying him for three months now.

PADDY. Wait now. He did that work with the moving company.

OWEN. And never got paid for it.

PADDY. How could he know they were bankrupt and he was helping them move out on their debts? Be easy on him tonight. I'm in no mood for a fight. It's a bit of luck we've got Liam here, to kick in on the rent. Where ya from, Liam?

LIAM. Ballylickey. (*Owen and Paddy exchange looks*)

PADDY. How do you like New York?

LIAM. I'm just off the plane.

PADDY. Ah, you'll be grand. Once you get the lay of the land. A mate of mine was coming home about five o'clock one night. Just off the job. As he was crossing the avenue, some bastard jumped out of a van, spit in his face and punched him around pretty bad.

OWEN. For no reason at all, mind.

PADDY. He made eye contact with him. That was it. There's a lot of crazy bastards out in the streets, Liam. Watch out for them.

OWEN. Don't be scaring him, Paddy.

PADDY. Look no one in the eye. They'll jump you on no provocation whatsoever. The same thing happened to another lad I know last week. The very same thing. Guy jumps out of a van and starts beating on him. With a lead pipe, mind. This one had a lead fecking pipe.

LIAM. Jaysus! In the Bronx??!

OWEN. You'd think you were in bleedin' Liverpool.

PADDY. It happens everywhere. Manhattan, Queens, Brooklyn . . .

LIAM. Brooklyn, too??!!

PADDY. Keep the old eyes open . . . but see nothing and you'll be grand, lad. Speaking of which . . . I saw the daughter.

OWEN. Who's the daughter?

PADDY. The one belongs on the Larchmont estate. A magnificent bit of flesh. She come galloping by while Devlin had me in the roses, checking for frips.

OWEN. You never miss a trick, Paddy.

PADDY. Ah, I see great possibilities there in Larchmont. (*He takes more beer from the paper bag on the chair and puts it in the refrigerator*) Well, what do you think of our wee home here, Liam?

LIAM. Looks like a bit of heaven to me right now.

PADDY. Ah, it's a kip ... but we're lucky there's only the four of us now.

OWEN. Most of the furniture was left here by the last lot. (*Owen gets busy at the stove, adding rice to the pot*)

PADDY. That carpet there, Ownie and me found that in the street. It's a perfectly good carpet. You'd be surprised at the stuff people throw away, Liam. Met a fella in a bar works for the sanitation department. He told me, on certain nights over there on Park Avenue, you can find a whole roomful of furniture. Perfectly good stuff.

LIAM. Wouldn't you be worried about fleas?

PADDY. Not at all, man. Them people over on Park Avenue live very clean. (*There is the sound of a key in the door*)

OWEN. That'll be Desmond.

PADDY. Mum's the word. (*Desmond enters*)

OWEN. Des! How are ya? We've got another mate here. Liam meet me cousin, Desmond.

LIAM. Hello, Desmond.

DESMOND. Yeah. How are ya? Just over?

LIAM. Flew in today.

DESMOND. Welcome to hard times.

PADDY. No luck, Des?

DESMOND. Fuckin' bitch wanted me to walk her dogs, man. Six of the nastiest looking little mongrels you ever saw.

OWEN. What's the matter with that? I don't see the harm in ...

DESMOND. Ah, hold on there, Owen ... hear the whole story. I'd have to dress them first.

PADDY. Dress them?!

DESMOND. Little wee boots and coats on six wee nervous little dogs.

OWEN. Four boots apiece . . . Christ, what's that make, Paddy?

DESMOND. Twenty-four fuckin' little wee boots! *After* their coats are on and they're mad as hell and crazy to get out in the park for a piss. Just this morning an old man come up to me in the street without shoes, for fuck's sake! Take my advice and take the next plane back, Liam. This country's full of nutters.

OWEN. I thought the advert said she wanted a chauffeur?

DESMOND. Oh, she did, she did. *After* I walked the dogs. And you shoulda seen what she fed the little beasts.

PADDY. Speaking of which . . . I'm half-starved. What's that muck you're stirrin' up there, Owen?

OWEN. Lovely rice and beans.

DESMOND. Not again?!

PADDY. Ah, jeez, Owen, can't you give us a fry now and again? My tongue's hanging out for a sausage.

OWEN. This is nutritious stuff here, lads. Complex proteins.

PADDY. Rice and beans! What do you think we are here . . . Aztecs?! I want a fry!

OWEN. The eggs in this country are contaminated.

PADDY. We give you our money . . .

OWEN. You give me your money, yes. And I refuse to poison you. If you want to destroy your bellies with fast food and commercial additives, do it on your own time. You put me in charge of the cooker and I won't have that on me conscience.

DESMOND. (*Sitting at table*) I tell you, Paddy, them dogs ate better than we do.

MARY. (*Enters. She carries a chic-looking shopping bag which she puts on the table*) Eat hearty, lads! I worked a food festival at the Javits Center today. What a scene! Give me a chair. I'm knackered!

DESMOND. (*Looking in bag*) What's this, then?

LIAM. A food festival?

MARY. To introduce the public to the very latest in designer food.

PADDY. (*Eating*) What's this here?

MARY. Chocolate cheese.

PADDY. I've never heard of that.

OWEN. (*Coming over from stove*) Let's have a look.

MARY. I was at the chocolate booth. Everything was covered in chocolate. There was even chocolate soda bread. A fast-selling item ... there was none left to bring back.

PADDY. Chocolate soda bread?

DESMOND. Ah, they go too far.

MARY. I'm exhausted. Picture this: great crowds of people, all fat, bearing down on you with their hands out. Mind you, these are not hungry people. Dressed to the teeth, they were. At the end, the sight was horrific. Didn't they come 'round to the booths for the leftovers? I had to fight tooth and nail to keep this for youse. What they couldn't stuff in their faces, they stuffed in their bags and up their jumpers. Not an experience I'd care to repeat! (*Liam's presence suddenly registers with Mary*) Hello, who's the mighty stranger?

OWEN. Liam's just over from Cork. He's moved in.

MARY. Where in Cork?

LIAM. (*Yawning*) Ballylickey.

MARY. Oh, you must meet Breda. Her brother's in Ballylickey. (*Paddy laughs*) Stop your laughing, Paddy. Breda's a bit strange, is all. (*There's more laughter and muttering about Breda*) Just for that, I'm bringing her over. (*She exits while the others groan*)

PADDY. Ah, hold off on Breda 'til we eat. She'll spoil me appetite.

DESMOND. We're in for it now. (*He goes to drawer in the press, gets out a nude centerfold and puts it on the refrigerator door*)

PADDY. (*Yelling*) Bring some more grub back with ya!

OWEN. Wait'll you see her, Liam. I swear, if it wasn't for the others, I'd put a lock on the door.

PADDY. For fuck's sake, watch your language around her. Bloody hell breaks loose if there's so much as a bejesus out of ya.

OWEN. She goes all purple in the face. It's fuckin' gruesome. (*Laughter comes from the hallway*)

PADDY. Here they come! Watch out for yourselves! (*Into the apartment with Mary comes Breda*)

MARY. Liam, meet Breda. There's also Rose, Eileen, Paula, Brenda and Joan. They're still at work.

DESMOND. (*Darkly*) You'll meet the lot of them soon enough, Liam.

BREDA. There's seven of us. We spill over a bit.

PADDY. (*Sitting on the couch*) You'll want to watch your back. They're always in here.

MARY. Oh, Paddy, you'd be lonely without us. Admit it. (*She sits beside Paddy*)

PADDY. If your mothers knew what youse were up to here. Where's that Joan one now?

MARY. Gone to her cousin's in Oregon.

BREDA. What do you care where Joan's gone to?

PADDY. Don't be starting in on me, Breda ...

OWEN. Help yourself to the drink there, Breda. We're having a party.

BREDA. Is there any soda?

OWEN. In the fridge. (*Breda goes to the refrigerator. The others laugh when she reacts to the centerfold*)

BREDA. (*Recovering her composure*) Mary tells me that you're from Ballylickey. (*Sits at the table next to Liam and starts eating*)

PADDY. I'll tell you, Liam ... greenhorns and narrowbacks, that's the only lingo you want to learn.

MARY. You're the greenhorn.

OWEN. And the local boyos are the narrowbacks. Some of them think we're taking their jobs from them. (*Owen takes food away from Breda and puts it in the refrigerator*)

DESMOND. Which, as it happens, we are.

OWEN. Are we, now? Well, Des, I haven't noticed any inclination on your part to take anything ...

PADDY. Watch your back, Liam. Donkey hunting, they call it. You'll be grand if you watch out where you drink.

OWEN. Yeah. Stick with us.

MARY. You'll get to know your way around soon enough. We'll show you where to get the papers from home. And Mario's grand at The Old Sod. He'll cash your checks for you.

LIAM. That there bar seemed sound enough. How's the crack?

PADDY. Oh, jaysus, lad ... that's a word you're never to use!

OWEN. Crack over here is a different thing entirely.

MARY. It's a form of cocaine they sell in the streets. You've never heard of crack? Where've you been, Liam?

BREDA. There's none of that in Ballylickey ...

PADDY. Don't be throwing that word around. First thing, they'll have your money off you, the crack'll be up your nose and your life a living hell from here out.

OWEN. Six blocks in any direction here and the scene gets pretty rough.

PADDY. Best not to leave the neighborhood.

LIAM. How'll I get to Brooklyn?

BREDA. What do you want to go to Brooklyn for?

LIAM. Me job!

DESMOND. You have a job?!

MARY. Take the subway. It's just at the end of the block.

OWEN. No problem on the subway.

MARY. Just don't be traveling alone late at night.

OWEN. The important thing to remember is ... keep your mouth shut around strangers.

PADDY. The immigration's everywhere. You heard about Seamus, did you?

BREDA. I have a Donnelly visa.

DESMOND. (*Sitting on the arm of the couch*) Ah, it's not as bad as they're making it out, Liam. Sure, you'd think we were all prisoners here.

MARY. We have some great times, really. We go to concerts and things.

BREDA. (*Aside*) Where were you last night, Dessie?

DESMOND. That's my business.

MARY. Tell him about the night you lost your shoes, Paddy.

PADDY. I thought I was a goner that night!

MARY. We really do have some great times, Liam.

PADDY. I was with Owen and Des here ...

MARY. Some girls I work with threw a party out in Brighton Beach. Paula, Joan and I went out together. We left directions for them ...

DESMOND. We got lost.

OWEN. Jeez, we didn't know where the hell we were.

BREDA. There's no need to swear, Owen.

MARY. Breda!

PADDY. We ended up in Coney Island.

OWEN. We stopped for a few jars just to get our bearings. They told us we only had to walk east a bit.

DESMOND. So, out we go to the beach, to take an orientation from the sun.

PADDY. They've got an amusement park out there, Liam, with a bloody big rollycoaster.

DESMOND. Paddy wasn't up for the rides so Ownie and I left him there.

OWEN. With strict orders not to move.

PADDY. I fell asleep. Sure, we'd been traveling for hours!

OWEN. Next thing, we're back and there he is ...

DESMOND. Starkers and the skin burnt off him.

LIAM. Did they steal the clothes off ya?!!

OWEN. We thought he had sunstroke for sure.

DESMOND. The Great Red Whale.

LIAM. Your clothes, Paddy, did they ...?

PADDY. Never lay out in the sun with a drop taken, Liam. It'll do queer things to you.

OWEN. We got him up and dressed and then, off we went to the east.

MARY. My friends sent out a search party and eventually they were found ...

DESMOND. And none too soon.

OWEN. Ah, it was a great party though.

PADDY. Great gas!

MARY. Swimming and dancing ... there was a band. Oh, ... do you remember the one guy dressed up like Dolly Parton? He was mad! Jumped in the pool he did, and his breasts swelled out to here.

BREDA. You never told me that!

MARY. We can't be telling you everything, Breda. We want to spare you. It was brilliant!

PADDY. 'Til we come home.

OWEN. Paddy got separated from us. Strayed off down the platform when we weren't looking ...

PADDY. I took a cab home. The driver spoke no English.

DESMOND. About half-three, here comes Paddy . . . in through
the door, on all fours.

PADDY. I was dog tired! I think he had me out in New Jersey!
I remember a tunnel. I still don't know how I lost me
shoes.

BREDA. Do you like the beach, Liam?

MARY. We'll have to take you to the beach sometime, Liam.
We'll have a picnic.

DESMOND. What do you think of New York so far, Liam?

LIAM. Well (*Yawning*) . . . when that there train from the airport
come up out of the ground, that was pretty spectacular. I
mean to say . . . it's no place like home.

MARY. I feel like dancing. Let's take Liam dancing!

BREDA. (*Edging close to him*) My brother lives in Ballylickey.

LIAM. (*Innocently*)So does mine. (*Music. Lights out*)

SCENE THREE

*Lights up on The Old Sod Bar. Liam is sitting at the table. It's a
month later and he's much more relaxed. He's wearing a bandana.
Mario enters with a tray of bar glasses.*

MARIO. Liam! How's it going?

LIAM. It's going great, Mario.

MARIO. What are you drinking?

LIAM. I'll have a beer. What do you think of me new watch?

MARIO. Very nice!

LIAM. I met this black guy . . .

MARIO. Tyrone?

LIAM. Right! Sure, he give me a good price on it. Have a look.
It's no ordinary watch. See this here little gizmo? It comes
out, see?

MARIO. And then what?

LIAM. Look. See there? It's a compass.

MARIO. You get lost much, Liam?

LIAM. Yeah . . . but what happened this morning was nothing
to do with me. I was on the right train this time. Jeez . . .
you know, it's bad enough when the local goes express on
ya. But the one this morning jumped the tracks! I swear to

you ... it went from the west side to the east side on us.
The train was packed. We were all sitting there, waiting
for Times Square and here comes Grand Central Station.
People panicked. We all jumped off. Nobody knew what
happened. They give us no warning.

MARIO. The Train From Hell. You never know when you'll get
on one of those. How's the job?

LIAM. Ah, the job's fine. Renovations, mostly. You know, there's
a row of houses out there in Brooklyn reminds me of
home.

MARIO. Yeah?

LIAM. This one house we're working on ... we're gutting it
completely. The new owner wants everything out. He's got
some kind of designer he comes 'round with now and
again, to check on the progress. Seems a shame. All the
rooms have this plaster work 'round the ceilings ... oak
leaves and acorns and such ... but your man wants none
of it. So, out it goes. Why would a man buy a sound house
and destroy it?

MARIO. That's taste, Liam. There's no accounting for taste.

LIAM. Peter Kelly showed me what it's to look like when we're
finished. There's to be a wee elevator, and there's only the
four stories.

MARIO. The rich don't walk.

LIAM. And no windows, Mario!

MARIO. They don't need to see nothing, either.

LIAM. Well, if my da could see me ripping the place apart it
would break his heart.

MARIO. The man's got the money and you got the job.

LIAM. Yeah, I guess so.

MARIO. You ok where you're living?

LIAM. Yeah, thanks, Mario. The set-up's perfect.

MARIO. I figured you'd be ok. Those are good guys. I been to
some Knick games with Owen and Des. How are you
getting along with the women?

LIAM. (*At first, Liam doesn't understand*)Oh. You mean Mary and
them?

MARIO. Yeah.

LIAM. Oh. Fine. But, to tell you the truth, Mario, I see a bit too much of them for my taste. I mean to say, they're nice and all but ... they're always stopping by. You can't blame them, living all together the way they do. Still and all, I wouldn't mind a bit more privacy. Des and me sleep in the room there, on the couch, and you never know when they'll be dropping in on ya.

MARIO. I wouldn't mind some of them dropping in on me. (*He moves away to the other end of the bar*) You want to go easy there, Mr. Costelloe. It's early yet. (*He returns to Liam*)

LIAM. (*Lowering his voice*) Heard anything from Seamus? (*Mario smiles broadly and beckons Liam over to the bar. He reaches over behind some bottles and brings out a postcard which he passes to Liam*) Honolulu! Jeez, Mario, he's actually in Honolulu! Fair dues to him.

MARIO. Look at that beach. Huh? Not bad. I could live in Honolulu easy. They got no winters there. All you'd need is a couple a pairs a shorts. Look at them girls there.

LIAM. They must have a rainy season, though, Mario. Hawaii's a tropical place.

MARIO. You get yourself an umbrella. Or sit in the bar 'til it blows over. No problem.

LIAM. Barring the odd typhoon.

MARIO. Typhoon? Yeah, they got typhoons, I guess. But how many could they have? Typhoons are seasonal. One or two typhoons a year ain't bad. I wouldn't let that stop me.

LIAM. There must be all kinds of work out there, with all them tourists. Maybe Des should try Hawaii.

MARIO. He was in here last night until I closed up. Been hitting it pretty heavy lately.

LIAM. He's been out of work a good while now.

MARIO. I hate to see that happen to a guy. It's tough. But ... the guy don't have a drinking problem. Not yet, anyway. You know what I think?

LIAM. What?

MARIO. The guy's in limbo. He don't know where he is. I seen it happen. It's like shock. He'll be all right once he finds out where he is.

LIAM. You think so?

MARIO. Sure. Depression. I read in the paper there's a lot of it in Ireland. They figure maybe 20,000 people got depression over there.

LIAM. You read that?!

MARIO. I'll tell you something else.

LIAM. What?

MARIO. I think what you got with Des is ... I think maybe you got a poet.

LIAM. You do?

MARIO. Sure. I never knew a poet personally. But you listen to him talk? He's in here some nights, he's got the whole bar listening to him. These guys only listen if you're talking horses or ball games. You ever listen to him when he talks?

LIAM. He does read a lot.

MARIO. Nothing wrong with that. Yeah. Old Des is a very intelligent guy. (*Liam finishes up his beer. Mary enters the bar*)

MARY. Hi, Liam! (*She takes a check from her bag*) Could you cash this for me, Mario?

MARIO. Can do. (*He goes to the cash register*)

LIAM. What are you working at this week, Mary?

MARY. I'm back doing private duty nursing. I've a lovely patient this time. A rich old man. Too weak to try anything. Nice watch. Met Tyrone, have you? (*Mario puts her money on the bar and gives her a beer*) Thanks much, Mario. (*She joins Liam at the table*)

LIAM. What do you mean, try anything? You mean they ...

MARY. Of course, it's nothing like what poor Rose has to contend with. Those interns in that hospital where she works are another sort of problem entirely. Always grabbing and groping at her, they are. Last week, she had one come at her during surgery.

LIAM. While a patient was on the table?

MARY. A routine appendectomy, I think she said. She nicked him with a scalpel. (*She takes a drink of beer*) Did you hear Breda on Sunday morning?

LIAM. Hear Breda?

MARY. Yeah. Did you not hear her screeching like a banshee at about half-six?

LIAM. No. I heard nothing. What happened to her?

MARY. It was Paula brought it on. That Paula! She'll stop at nothing ... I shouldn't be talking to you at all like this but then, how'll you ever learn, right?

LIAM. Learn what?

MARY. Well ... there's a lad works in The Roaring Twenties that Paula fancies. She's been staying out 'til dawn for weeks, now. And Breda complains when she gets in late and wakes her. Paula's not a light foot, by any means. She wakes us all but sure, she's happy. It's only Breda complains. So ... Saturday night, Paula's on her way out to meet Kevin and Breda starts in on her. She's not to stay out 'til dawn, tomorrow's Sunday, like that. Well, Paula, as cool as you please, says she wouldn't dream of it. And she sailed very grandly out the door. True to her word, none of us heard her come in. Now, Breda's usually up for early mass on Sunday, with never a sound out of her. 'Til yesterday, when half-six rolls 'round and she's screaming bloody hell and scaring us all out of our wits.

MARIO. What the hell was it?

MARY. Your man, Kevin. Tucked up there on the couch, between her and Paula. Just as snug as you please. I tell you, war was waged over him and he never stirred. Just smiling and snoring away. I can't believe you heard nothing, Liam. When that one raises her voice, it goes right through you.

LIAM. That there Kevin must be a deaf mute.

MARY. He's very nice. After Breda went off to mass to pray for us all, we had breakfast with him. He's an actor. From Pittsburgh. Ah, that Breda. She doesn't know what to make of Paula. Or me either, for that matter. Do you know ... Breda thinks I fancy Des! Who knows what put that into her head.

LIAM. Have you traveled much since you've been to the states, Mary?

MARY. Traveled. You mean like ... far?

LIAM. Yeah. I'm thinking I'd like to see the country a bit, you know? Chicago, San Francisco. The Grand Canyon, maybe.

MARY. The Grand Canyon?

LIAM. Yeah. I like the sound of that. Have you been anywhere else since you've been over?

MARY. I was in Boston with Owen for a weekend. That was a gas. And I've been to Trenton. That's in New Jersey.

MARIO. You been to Trenton?

LIAM. Trenton? What was Trenton like?

MARY. The Bronx.

LIAM. Abilene. I'd like to go there.

MARY. Where's that?

LIAM. Out west somewhere. Yeah. I might like to go there. Stop off in Cheyenne, maybe. And Tombstone. Las Cruces.

MARIO. Don't forget Las Vegas, Liam.

LIAM. Why not? I'll get me one a them sightseer tickets. Go everywhere out there. Fargo, Yosemite, Albuquerque ...

MARIO. Piscataway. You like exotic names, Piscataway's right across the river.

MARY. Honestly, Liam! Here ya are, dreaming of the wild west and you haven't even seen Manhattan yet. Tell you what! Owen and I will take you to Manhattan at the weekend. Would you like that?

LIAM. I would, yeah.

MARY. Right then. We'll start you off at Broadway and Forty-Second Street. Well, I'm headed home. Are ya coming?

LIAM. I am. I only have to pick up some mushrooms for Owen.

MARIO. What's he cooking?

LIAM. Jeez ... I don't know, but he needs them mushrooms he said. Three pounds a them.

MARIO. That's a lot of mushrooms.

MARY. Whatever he's cooking ... I'm half-starved. Let's go, if we're going. (*Liam puts money on the bar as they head for the door*)

LIAM. See you, Mario.

MARIO. Anytime.

LIAM. (*To Mary, on the way out the door*) I could even see Seattle, maybe ... (*Music. Lights out*)

SCENE FOUR

A few months later in the apartment. Paddy has his suitcase dragged out and clothes scattered all around. Owen comes in with groceries and mail.

OWEN. What's all this?

PADDY. (*Trying on a jacket*) What do you think, Owen? How's the fit?

OWEN. That's new. Nice stuff. What's up then?

PADDY. There's a big blow-out up in Larchmont this weekend. The Yanks have something called Thanksgiving Day. Deirdre says it's her mother's favorite holiday. So, I bought this here jacket. I'll need a bit of flash up there with the nobs.

OWEN. Hold on there, Paddy. You mean you're going up to the party?

PADDY. (*Shyly*) Yeah.

OWEN. You don't mean as a guest?

PADDY. Yeah. I'll stay in the big house and all.

OWEN. This Mrs. Morrissey sounds all right. (*He puts a letter on top of the chest of drawers*)

PADDY. Oh, she didn't invite me. Deirdre did. She figured it would be a good time to tell the parents about her and me. (*The door to the bedroom slams*) Des is reading.

OWEN. That'll pay the rent!

PADDY. What do you think I should take up there, Owen?

OWEN. (*Shouting at the door to the bedroom*) You could at least do the washing up now and again!

PADDY. Ah, leave it, Owen. Help me here. I'm nervous of this. Supposing they find out I work for them?

OWEN. You mean, they don't know that yet? (*He goes behind the counter and starts putting groceries away*)

PADDY. Nah. They never walk 'round the place.

OWEN. Well, they're gonna want to know how you two met.

PADDY. Deirdre figures we'll just say we met at a concert. I'm a friend of some friend.

OWEN. Mmmm. Come over here and chop this onion for me, will you?

PADDY. I can't get that smell on me now. Deirdre's picking me up in an hour. I've got to get packed. (*He returns to his suitcase*)

LIAM. (*Enters, carrying a big box. He's changed in the last month ...
gone native. He wears a black leather cap, sunglasses that flip up.
He's very excited*) Wait'll you see this here, Owen!

OWEN. What've you got this time?

LIAM. I was down at the pub ...

OWEN. Bar.

LIAM. Right ... and this here black guy I know, Tyrone, came
in and ...

OWEN. Is that where you've been getting all your gadgets?

LIAM. Yeah ... well, anyway, this here Tyrone ... (*He is busy
putting the box on the table and opening it*)

OWEN. Jaysus, Liam. You want to be careful. That stuff's
probably hot.

LIAM. Only when it's plugged in. Look at this, Owen. Isn't it a
beaut?!

PADDY. What the hell is it, a TV? We've got a TV.

LIAM. It's a microwave.

OWEN. (*Whistling*) What'd that cost ya?

LIAM. Only $50.

OWEN. That there was stolen, Liam.

PADDY. What's a microwave?

LIAM. What do you mean, it's stolen, Owen? It fell off a truck.

OWEN. Tyrone said this?

LIAM. Yeah.

OWEN. Well, if it fell off a truck, it's also broken.

LIAM. No. The truck was parked at the time.

OWEN. Oh, grow up, Liam! You are the most naive, the
dumbest paddy ... all this time you've been bringing this
stuff home here. We're liable to be raided! Didn't I warn
ya to stay away from the blacks?!

LIAM. I don't see why ...!

OWEN. I swear to jaysus, you are a receiver of stolen goods!

PADDY. Lend me a white shirt, will ya, Liam?

LIAM. I thought you'd be happy to have this, Owen. It's a real
time-saver. Look here at the instruction booklet. You can
make a whole roasted chicken in fifteen minutes! And you
can do it on a paper plate.

PADDY. Roasted chicken?

LIAM. Yeah. Bakes a potato in five. See, it kind of nukes it with these waves of rays ...

PADDY. X rays?! Christ, Owen's perfectly capable of poisoning us all with a regular cooker ... he needs no help from the rays.

OWEN. Let me see that booklet. (*Liam passes him the instructions*)

PADDY. Come on now, Liam. Lend us a shirt.

LIAM. (*Noticing Paddy and his suitcase for the first time*) Where are you off to?

OWEN. He's going to Larchmont to eat turkey.

PADDY. Lend me a white shirt. I only have the one. (*Liam goes to the chest of drawers*)

OWEN. I wouldn't, Liam. He'll only dribble caviar on it.

PADDY. I could do with another pair of socks too, if you can spare it.

LIAM. You're lucky I just did my laundry. (*He gives Paddy a shirt and socks, then crosses to Owen at counter*)

PADDY. What do you think of the jacket, Gizmo?

LIAM. Nice stuff. Will you be needing a monkey suit?

PADDY. Jeez ... I never thought!

LIAM. Well, what do you think, Owen?

OWEN. You're right enough. This could be a handy little item.

LIAM. Let's plug her in and see what she can do. (*They get busy arranging a place for the microwave oven*)

PADDY. Will I be needing a monkey suit, do you think? Owen?

OWEN. Let's nuke some of last night's lasagna.

PADDY. (*Exasperated*) Hold on a minute, lads! What about me tux??!!

LIAM. Easy, Paddy. I'll get Mary over here. She'll know. She's always working those posh parties. (*He goes out into the hall and shouts for Mary*)

PADDY. A tux. Owen?

OWEN. Don't be bothering me, now, Paddy. Can't you see I'm on the verge of a culinary breakthrough? (*Liam returns with Mary*)

MARY. (*Posing elegantly in the doorway*) Thanksgiving weekend in Larchmont. Well, aren't we grand!

LIAM. Won't the dinner be formal, Mary?

MARY. Don't worry, Paddy. Your suit's all you'll need.

PADDY. What suit?

OWEN. He hasn't got a suit.

MARY. You haven't got a suit?

PADDY. Fuck no, I haven't got a suit! I never had a suit!

MARY. Easy now, Paddy. My friend, Tommy, works with me has a black suit. He's about your size and I know he won't be needing it this weekend.

PADDY. Well ...

MARY. Oh, come on, Paddy. He's just up the street. (*Mary and Paddy exit quickly*)

OWEN. This booklet says I can bake potatoes in five minutes and a chocolate cake in ten. Frosted and all.

LIAM. Sure, Owen. I figure if you're going to have your own restaurant, you'll want to familiarize yourself with the latest technology. Where's Desmond?

OWEN. In there, reading. (*He goes to the refrigerator and gets two beers for them*) I don't know, Liam. This here microwave oven seems sound enough. But wouldn't it take the pleasure out of cooking? I mean to say, for me, the pleasure is in watching the food, smelling it and tasting it. If you've one of these here jobs ... seems like all the pride would go out of it. I like to think I have a talent for it, Liam. But what good would it do me? (*He takes a drink of beer and sits at the table*) Then there's the pots, Liam. A good cook pot is a wonder to behold. With this here thing, all you need is a piece of paper. No. It's not for me.

LIAM. (*Sitting at the table*) We can use it to dry the socks, then. How's Des?

OWEN. Reading. That's all I know or care to know.

LIAM. At least he's not sleeping. I never knew anyone to sleep so much. They say that's a sign of depression, Owen.

OWEN. He got a letter there, from home. It's from his girl, Kathleen. That'll cheer him up.

LIAM. Mario says there's a high rate of depression back home.

OWEN. How does that dago come by the news?

LIAM. He read it in the papers. (*He thinks a minute*) Dago?

OWEN. (*Lowering his voice*) There's nothing the matter with Des that work won't cure. He was always on the dark side. Too much reading will do that to you. As far back as I can remember, that's all he ever wanted to do. If Des went missing, you could always find him in the library. He never got on with his father, so I wasn't surprised when he wrote me, saying he was coming over. But, he told no one in the family. Not even Kathleen, and they to be married. Just went off to the airport one day and nicked on the plane. That's irresponsible behavior, Liam. That should have been the tip-off right there . . . but I was glad enough to have him here. (*Silence*) He was full of it when he first come over. This was it for him. America! Heaven on earth for Desmond. He went everywhere and couldn't get there fast enough. Museums, plays, concerts. I never saw him so happy. Then his money ran out. He'd get a job and he couldn't keep it. There was always something wrong. The boss was an eedjit. The wages too low. The work demeaning.

LIAM. Maybe that was true.

OWEN. It was true. It *is* true. But, Christ, Liam, the bottom line here, the cold reality is . . . we're immigrants! It's a time-honored tradition in America . . . or anywhere. Exploit the immigrants. You have to know that before you come. And accept it. If you don't like it . . . save your money and go back home.

LIAM. You can't save what you don't have.

OWEN. Exactly! Have you heard him yet? Going on about Man's Inhumanity to Man and World Injustice. I tell him there's no hope wanting to change the world if he's power-less to improve his own lot. Nothing I say makes any difference. He doesn't want a job. He'd rather moon about, feeling sorry for himself. Well, cousin, or no, I'm about at the end of my rope. (*Pause*) Maybe Kathleen will convince him to go back home. That might be best. (*There's noise from the hallway and Mary and Paddy return. Paddy's carrying the suit*) That was fast.

LIAM. Are you fixed up then, Paddy?

PADDY. You'd think I was carrying off his mother!

MARY. You can't blame him, Paddy, he makes his living with that suit. (*She gets herself a beer from the refrigerator*)

PADDY. (*Checking the clock*) Would youse look at the time! Deirdre will be here any minute.

MARY. She can wait a bit. She's lucky to have you. (*Paddy*

scoops everything into his suitcase) Now, don't forget your necktie. (*Paddy looks panicked and betrayed*) Oh, jaysus, Paddy ... I never thought you didn't have a necktie!

PADDY. Why would I have a necktie?!!

LIAM. (*Going back to the chest of drawers*) Not to worry, Paddy. Here's one of mine with the shirts and socks.

PADDY. Ah, thanks, Gizmo.

LIAM. Don't thank me, thank me mother. She'd be happy someone's getting the good of them. (*The doorbell rings*)

PADDY. That's Deirdre!

MARY. Isn't she coming up for you?

OWEN. Yeah, Paddy. I think we should meet her. We wouldn't feel right about you driving off with a strange woman.

LIAM. With my clothes in your bag.

PADDY. There's not time, mates. We can't be late. (*He's at the door, suitcase in hand. They gather around him. He pauses*) You'll meet her another time, I promise youse.

OWEN. Four days and nights of posh living and you'll not be the same man.

PADDY. Well. Wish me luck. (*They all shout their good luck after Paddy as he goes down the hall. They return to the apartment and close the door. Mary runs to the window*)

MARY. Come on ... let's have a look at this. There she is! A blonde!

LIAM. Would you look at that car! That's a Jaguar! Nice color.

OWEN. Nice woman! (*Returning to the kitchen counter*) Looks like the farmer's got himself a prize heifer.

MARY. I hope he's all right.

LIAM. He looks all right to me.

MARY. I wouldn't want to see him hurt.

OWEN. Quit your worrying, Mary. Nothing can hurt Paddy ... as long as he stays out of the trees.

LIAM. What could happen to him, Mary? A weekend in the countryside. A good feed. You know how he likes to eat.

OWEN. A dip in the pool. Billiards, maybe. Some tennis.

MARY. Paddy can't play tennis.

OWEN. There's always a first time.

LIAM. They might teach him.

MARY. I don't know. That kind of people can make you feel

pretty small, if they want to. I've seen it happen. Poor Paddy could end up being the butt of their jokes the whole time. (*Desmond enters from the bedroom and stands listening at the door. He's wearing a "Save the Whales" T-shirt*)

OWEN. Look. What's the worst that could happen up there? They find out that he works for them ... which they will ... it won't be too bad. The old mother wants to win her prize, doesn't she? They won't dismiss him. They'll put a good face on. He'll have a grand time and come back to a letter from little Deirdre, explaining that Daddy and Mummy think it best, et cetera. They'll probably send her away someplace for the winter. The Riviera, maybe. He'll get some postcards. He's only known her for a month. I doubt his heart'll be broken.

MARY. Ah, Owen. Your scenario is possible, but boring.

LIAM. Well, I want him to bring back a good yarn. I want to hear all about it. Don't you?

MARY. I do. It's like Paddy's going for the pot of gold at the end of the rainbow. He believes in it. He wants it. And I hope he gets it. If he does, then we all have a chance.

DESMOND. You sound like an American, Mary ... talking about the luck of the Irish. Well, here we all are. Where's the luck?

MARY. That's what I mean, Des. One of us has to be lucky.

OWEN. Yer right, yer right. Let's all have a drink to Paddy's successful conquest of the Morrisseys. (*He moves to the refrigerator and gets out more beer*) Matter of fact, we're all lucky to be here. It's been raining at home for two weeks straight.

DESMOND. You had a letter, Owen?

OWEN. Yeah. From Emer. There's one for you there, on the press, Des. She said Uncle Matt's off to Belfast again.

DESMOND. Thanks for tellin' us! (*Desmond runs to the chest of drawers and eagerly reads his letter*)

OWEN. Our Uncle Matt's in love with a woman lives in Belfast. They're both in their seventies. They've been in love for over thirty years.

MARY. Isn't it about time your Uncle Matt popped the question? (*Suddenly Desmond wads the letter up and throws it down*)

OWEN. What is it, Des? Dead whales off Dublin Bay?

DESMOND. I'm going to the bar.

MARY. Was it bad news, Des?

DESMOND. Oh, everything's fine. Just grand. Kathleen's getting married! (*He slams out of the apartment*)

MARY. Oh no! (*Pause*) But that's terrible.

OWEN. Maybe that's what he needs. It's his own fault. He's been up to nothing.

MARY. Owen, go after him.

OWEN. I'm hungry. I want to try out the microwave.

LIAM. Why did your Uncle Matt never marry the woman, Owen?

OWEN. I remember when I was about sixteen, I asked him that. He says to me, real quiet: "Ah my boy, my boy ... there are irreconcilable differences."

LIAM. She's a Protestant, is she?

MARY. Des shouldn't be alone now, Owen. That's terrible news to get ... in a letter like that.

OWEN. For jaysus' sake, Mary! Ah, maybe you're right. I'll go talk to him. (*Gets his jacket and leaves*)

MARY. Suddenly ... I don't know why ... I feel so ... sad.

LIAM. Come on, Mary. Let's nuke us up some grub. (*Starts to clear the table and picks up the book Desmond has been reading. He notes the title*) Leaves of Grass by Walt Whitman?

MARY. Dessie's. (*He passes the book to Mary and begins to prepare the meal. Mary flips through the book. Reading aloud*) Wait'll ya hear this, Liam. "I sing the body electric ..." (*She reads to herself for a bit, then puts the book down. As Liam plugs in the microwave, there's a flash of light, screams in reaction and the lights fade out. Music*)

SCENE FIVE

Liam is alone in the apartment. There is a large "ghetto blaster" kind of radio on the top of the refrigerator. Liam is trying on his latest acquisition, a pair of ornate cowboy boots. He poses in them. Throughout the scene, he is preoccupied with the boots. There's a tap at the door. It's Breda. She stands there, awkwardly.

BREDA. Hello, Liam

LIAM. Breda. (*She enters*) Well. Come on in.

BREDA. I can't stay.

LIAM. No.

BREDA. I only want a bit of company. (*Liam moves to the couch and polishes the boots. She follows him. Silence*)

LIAM. How do you like my new boots?

BREDA. I only want a bit of quiet.

LIAM. Authentic Tony Lama's they are ... according to Tyrone. (*Silence*) Well. There's some tea in the pot. Help yourself.

BREDA. Oh. Thanks.

LIAM. You'll find a clean cup in the rack.

BREDA. Yes.

LIAM. Watch out for the radio there.

BREDA. (*Gets a cup and returns*) Are we alone?

LIAM. Afraid so. (*Breda spills some tea*) Owen's off to Gaelic Park. Paddy's not back yet. I don't know where Des is.

BREDA. I'm used to that crowded apartment. They say people get TB from that. (*She sits at table*)

LIAM. From crowded apartments?

BREDA. Oh, yes! Overcrowding can actually cause TB.

LIAM. If that's the case, TB must be rampant in the Bronx.

BREDA. Oh, it is! It's making a comeback, TB is. Rose said so.

LIAM. Well, I'm not going to lose sleep worrying about that. How's the job, Breda?

BREDA. It's all ... ah, it's ... it's all right.

LIAM. (*Moving to the table and putting a foot up on a chair*) See this here? Genuine ostrich-skin vamps. (*More silence. Soon, though, he's aware that Breda is sobbing quietly*) Breda! What's wrong?! (*Her sobs build in intensity. She makes some awful sounds*) What is it, Breda? What? Have you got TB?! (*She shakes her head negatively*) Would you please stop crying and tell me what's the matter with you? (*Breda looks at Liam*) See this detail here? That's flame-stitching, that is.

BREDA. I'm so ashamed! (*She lunges at Liam and throws her arms around his neck*)

LIAM. Look out for the boots, will ya!!

BREDA. Oh, Liam! I was used! A man used me for his pleasure!

LIAM. Let go of me, Breda! Wait, now! Are you sure?

BREDA. Didn't he put his hand up my jumper?

LIAM. Who did?!

BREDA. I can't tell it! Oh, God, I can't tell who did this to me!

LIAM. Well ... why don't you just go to confession and ...

BREDA. How can I!?! What shall I do now? (*Breda grabs on to Liam again. As he tries to resist her, they fall over onto the couch*)

LIAM. Jeez, will you look out what ... ooooh! Get a hold of yourself, can't you?!! You'll scratch the boots. (*He works desperately to separate himself from Breda and save his boots*)

BREDA. The cook. It was the cook. He's Greek! We were in the kitchen. I thought he was passing me another cutlet for the dinner at table five and before I knew it, the hand was up the jumper. A Greek, Liam! The cook! I had hand prints all over my back. I quit. I had to. I couldn't go back there. He's had me!

LIAM. (*Picks up a set of headphones that were on the couch*) Bollocks!

BREDA. What about my family?!

LIAM. They're bent!

BREDA. I'll have to tell them, Liam.

LIAM. (*Standing*) The headphones are bent!

BREDA. I couldn't possibly go back and not tell them. That would be dishonest. I'd be living a lie! (*She grabs at Liam again. He moves back*) Tell me, Liam ... what should I do?

LIAM. How the fuck should I know?!

BREDA. Don't curse, Liam!

LIAM. Sit down, Breda. Just sit down, will ya? (*Breda sits*) I can't tell you what to do.

BREDA. (*Jumping up*) You're telling me to sit down!

LIAM. Because you're crowding me. Get back from my boots. Can you tell me how I can straighten these, now? Huh? Can you?!!

BREDA. No, but ...

LIAM. Then don't expect me to tell you anything about your situation. What'd you quit for, anyway? That was dumb.

BREDA. I had to!

LIAM. Yeah, and now you've no job. Just because some Greek made a grab for your body.

BREDA. Don't you talk about my body!

LIAM. You're the one who came in here talking about your body. What's so special about your body, anyway, I'd like to know?

BREDA. I should have known better than to expect any sympathy or understanding from you, Liam

LIAM. What about my body?! Huh?!! You were just grabbing at my body!

BREDA. You're a man!

LIAM. What's that got to do with it?

BREDA. That was innocent! There was no lust in my heart.

LIAM. Nevertheless, you grabbed me and pulled me down on the couch.

BREDA. We fell.

LIAM. Yeah, we fell on the headphones and now they're bajanxed.

BREDA. (*Moves about the apartment*) Well, I'm sorry.

LIAM. Get away from that radio!

BREDA. I only wanted ... to feel ... I wanted ... protection.

LIAM. What would I protect you from? The Greek?

BREDA. (*Moving back toward Liam*) It's just ... back home, I have my brothers. I'm used to that, see? If anything happened to me, they'd protect me.

LIAM. Breda, listen to yourself. If anything happened to you ... you wouldn't need protecting, would ya?

BREDA. Something *did* happen to me!

LIAM. Correct! And what did you do?

BREDA. (*Sitting at the table again*) I dropped the cutlet.

LIAM. More than that, Breda. You quit your job.

BREDA. I had to!

LIAM. Why did you have to?! Why didn't you tell the Greek to mind his own bleeding business and keep his hands to himself? Who do you think you are, anyway ... Helen of Troy?! What's so special about you?

BREDA. Don't say that, Liam!!

LIAM. I will say it! It's fucking important!

BREDA. Don't curse, Liam! I'll leave if you curse!

LIAM. Leave, then! Just fucking leave! I didn't ask you to come in here, with your problems?! Look around you. We've all got problems. You come here for a lark. It's easy for you.

If you don't like your job, you can just quit it. What about the others? Huh?! What about Rose or Paula or Mary? What about Des . . . and Tyrone? They can't even get jobs and you're throwing yours away. If you wanted your family's protection, you should have stayed at home. (*Silence*)

BREDA. Liam!

LIAM. Well, what're you looking at me like that for?

BREDA. I never heard you talk so much.

LIAM. Just because I don't talk, doesn't mean I don't think. You talk all the time, but you don't think. That's your problem. You should think more, Breda. It's good for you. Your family did your thinking for you. (*Silence*)

BREDA. Those are lovely boots.

LIAM. Thanks. (*He sits on the couch and resumes polishing his boots*)

BREDA. I think I'll go home now.

LIAM. Well, wash your cup before you go.

BREDA. I mean to Ireland. I don't like it here.

LIAM. That's up to you.

BREDA. Thanks for the tea, Liam. (*She puts her cup in the sink and moves to the door*)

LIAM. No problem.

BREDA. (*Standing at the door*) Liam?

LIAM. (*Exasperated*) What is it now?

BREDA. Well, are you just going to let me leave like this?

LIAM. Goodbye, then.

BREDA. That's not what I meant.

LIAM. What should I say?

BREDA. (*She starts moving in on Liam again*) Liam, I just said I was going back home.

LIAM. That's your decision. I mean. What do you want me to say? (*Jumping up from the couch*) There you go! You're doing it again!

BREDA. What am I doing?

LIAM. You're crowding me! Back off, Breda! I can't breathe when you crowd me like that!

BREDA. (*Crossing to table*) Oh, stop with the boots a minute! This may be our last chance to talk.

LIAM. I don't want to talk. (*Silence*)

BREDA. (*Sitting at the table*) Will you be going home for Christmas?

LIAM. No! I haven't the money.

BREDA. Owen and Paddy are going back.

LIAM. Des will be here. Just him and me. (*Pause*) He's pretty intense, Des is. I like him though.

BREDA. He scares me. He keeps to himself.

LIAM. (*Sitting at the table*) That's because he's a poet, Breda. You know? He feels things more than the others.

BREDA. Mary told us his girl left him.

LIAM. Yeah. She just wrote him in a letter she was getting married ... to some fella he doesn't even know.

BREDA. Well, but he must have known that might happen. You can't leave a girl to just sit and wait at home.

LIAM. What're you talking about?

BREDA. Besides, Mary's in love with him.

LIAM. Don't be daft!

BREDA. Oh, she is too! Can't you see it? She's always mooning around after him.

LIAM. She didn't say she was, did she? Did she tell you?

BREDA. A girl doesn't have to say it. Her actions speak for her. Honestly, Liam, you're so naive. Can't you tell?

LIAM. Tell what?

BREDA. When a girl loves you?

LIAM. What would I want to know that for?

BREDA. Well, if you ever want to get married, you'll need to know.

LIAM. (*Getting angry*) What would I want to get married for?!

BREDA. You're just being silly, Liam. Most people get married. After a certain age ...

LIAM. I'm not most people!

BREDA. ... you want to think about starting a family. It's natural.

LIAM. No!

BREDA. You're just being stubborn. I know I want to get married. I've been thinking about it a lot since I've been over. I don't like being on my own.

LIAM. I like it fine!

BREDA. Most of my friends back home are married now. I

have everything planned. It will be lovely . . . a big wedding with masses of flowers and that. I know exactly how my dress will be. Mam will sew it up for me. I'll have two wee babies. A boy and a girl. The girl will be Grainne and the boy will be named for his da. (*She looks over to Liam, who's been staring at her in disbelief. He jumps up and makes for the door*)

LIAM. Bleeding hell!

BREDA. (*Jarred out of her reverie*) Where are you off to, Liam?

LIAM. The bar! (*He exits leaving a startled Breda. Music. Lights out*)

SCENE SIX

Mary and Owen are at the kitchen counter, preparing a meal. Mary shows him what she's doing . . . wrapping truffles in bacon and brown paper. Owen sits on counter top.

OWEN. (*Laughing*) Wait'll ya hear . . . so, she fell on him and he fell on her . . .

MARY. Could you picture the face on Breda?

OWEN. Give us a beer there, Mary.

MARY. (*Opening the refrigerator*) And one for meself. (*She hands beer to Owen*) And, tell us, what did your last maid die of?

OWEN. (*Reaching for Mary*) Not doing what she was told. (*They kiss. Mary breaks away, laughing, and goes back to truffles*)

MARY. How's this, Owen?

OWEN. (*Looking*) That's about right. I tell you, Mary, I can't wait to get back home and have my own place.

MARY. What kind of food will you have? Fish and chips or pizza?

OWEN. None of that! I'm opening me a diner. I've already talked to the railways people in Dublin. I'm getting a good deal on an old railway carriage that I'll convert. They said they'll even move it onto the site . . . once I've bought the land, that is. Only thing . . . I'm stumped for a name for the place. I'm leaning toward "The Erie-Lackawanna." What do you think?

MARY. Eerie Lackawanna? What's that, a haunted lake?

OWEN. It's an American railway line. Now, I could also name it after a particular train. They give them names too. There's the Silver Chief, the Twentieth Century Limited and the Wabash Cannonball.

MARY. Why limit yourself to railways, Owen? Why not get totally fantastical and call your place "The Cross-Bronx Expressway"?

OWEN. Not bad, Mary! For a fast food restaurant, that's not bad at all. But I've me heart set on the railway dining car angle. Uncle Matt told Des and me about some great-granduncle who came over and worked on the Pennsylvania Railroad. I had half an idea I'd try to locate that side of the family when I first came over, but sure, he never kept in touch. The last Matt heard, he was out in the West somewhere ... and that was before I was born. (*Pause*) Let's toss these wee buggers in the oven. (*Mary puts the pan in the oven. Liam enters cautiously with a box under his arm*) Liam! What have you got this time?

MARY. Yeah ... what diabolical scientific breakthrough have you brought us?

OWEN. One of these days, you'll come in and the cops will be right behind you.

LIAM. It's only an answering machine for the telephone. Where's Breda?

MARY. (*Exchanging looks with Owen*) She went to a film with Paula. Why?

LIAM. No reason. What's cooking? (*He puts the box on the couch and goes to get beer*)

MARY. Truffles.

OWEN. Another grand experiment in the culinary art.

MARY. I worked a demo, Liam, and I got my hands on some of these lovely black Perigord truffles. They were selling for $50 a pound! Can you believe it?!

OWEN. Each and every one guaranteed kissed by a pig.

LIAM. How'd the pigs get in the picture?

OWEN. The French keep these special trick pigs that can sniff the truffles and then they root them out of the ground with their lovely delicate snouts.

LIAM. You're pulling me leg.

MARY. No, it's the truth, Liam. I looked up a recipe and so tonight we are having roast truffles wrapped in bacon.

LIAM. So much for the pig. (*He returns to couch and begins setting up the answering machine*)

OWEN. That's where brains'll get you.

MARY. With champagne, mind.

LIAM. Too bad we haven't something to celebrate.

OWEN. Oh, but we have, mates.

MARY. We do? And what might that be, Owen?

OWEN. Youse'll have to wait until the food is on the table and the drinks in our hands.

MARY. You found Desmond a job!

OWEN. Ah, give over, Mary! He's a lost cause, he is.

LIAM. Has he been back today?

OWEN. He has not. That's two days missing.

MARY. I can't help worrying about him.

LIAM. I'll go out later and ask Mario if he's seen him.

OWEN. I wouldn't mention it ...

LIAM. Mario's all right, Owen. Really.

MARY. Well, Paddy's due back anytime now, I expect. Oh, I just thought! Supposing it went wrong for him up there and he comes in to find us with champagne and all?

OWEN. Don't be spreading gloom around the place. If that's the case, we'll cheer him up. Them three bottles ought to do the job.

LIAM. After his posh weekend, he'll take it all in stride. He might even have had his fill of the bubbly and be bored with our little layout.

MARY. I just hope he gets back all right. Tommy needs his suit tomorrow.

LIAM. How long does it take truffles to cook? I'm starved.

OWEN. Patience, my boyo. Art takes time. (*Owen tosses a salad while Mary sets the table*) Have you got your ticket home yet, Mary?

MARY. I'm not going home for Christmas. I've decided not to go back.

OWEN. I thought you were taking the plane with Paddy and me.

LIAM. You're really going then, Owen? But how will you get

back in?

OWEN. I've not missed a Christmas home since I've been over. There are ways ... if you have the will. (*To Mary*) What's got into you?

MARY. I've changed my mind, is all. I'm in no mood to face them at home. Ever again. I'd rather live in Outer Mongolia.

OWEN. What are you going on about? Are you turned feminist on us, Mary?

MARY. (*Defensively*) Well ... maybe I have ... (*Paddy enters. They grow quiet, watching him*)

OWEN. Well, here's the jumped-up Paddy back from Larchmont!

PADDY. (*Suddenly grinning*) No more Paddy, mates. Paddy's dead and buried. It's Padraig from here out.

OWEN. Can you spell that?

LIAM. What are you talking?

MARY. Oh, whatever you are, come the hell in here and sit down and tell us everything!

OWEN. Wait, now. Let's crack open a bottle. (*He displays the bottle on his arm for Paddy's approval*)

PADDY. (*Noticing the label*) That's good stuff.

MARY. Listen to him, will ya?

PADDY. Haven't I been swilling it all weekend?

LIAM. Ah, I knew it.

PADDY. Didn't they put it in the orange juice at breakfast?

MARY. So what's it like in Larchmont? (*Paddy checks his appearance in the mirror. Owen opens and pours champagne for everyone. He raises his glass*)

OWEN. First, we drink to Paddy!

LIAM AND MARY. Slante!

OWEN. Go n-eiri leat! (*They all laugh and drink*) Ah. This is the stuff all right.

PADDY. They put it in the Guinness.

MARY. Black Velvet! I love it!

OWEN. Now, tell us what happened to you up there in heaven. (*They gather around the table, with Paddy sitting in the center*)

MARY. What are the Morrisseys like?

PADDY. (*Settling down*) Well. Deirdre and me got up there in good time. Swear to God she drives like she rides a horse. Anyway ... the parents weren't there. They come the next day. Flew in from Houston. Your man's in the oil business.

LIAM. Oh, jaysus, Paddy!

OWEN. Liquid gold!

PADDY. Anyway, in they come. Old Maureen and the Duke.

LIAM. He's a duke too?!

OWEN. Hold on, Liam. This is America.

PADDY. They just call him that ... like John Wayne, see? So, in they come first thing Thursday morning and the party's on. People were coming out of the woodwork. And the servants. I give up trying to count them. It was all very grand, you know? The Thanksgiving dinner was amazing. The table was almost as long as the room itself, all covered with lace and silver and there were these wee cards telling you where to sit. I was next to the grandparents. There were candles all up and down the table and three roast turkeys and a couple of hams. Owen, you should have been there! They had food I never even heard of. I never did finish counting how many people they fed around that table. And, matter a damn if the food was contaminated, I went to sleep that night a happy man. Anyway, most of the guests stayed over and on Saturday, they laid on another big spread in a tent out in the back. There's a brother named Jamie, has a rock band. Not bad. They were all there. Her sister, Louisa, come home from college. She's studying to be a veterinarian. All day long, the Duke's business friends kept cornering me, wanting to know what did I think of the situation in the North. At first, I didn't know what they were going on about.

OWEN. Well, did they wise up to your game, Paddy?

PADDY. Ah, they don't know who they've got working for them. I had a desperate moment there, when old Dukie took it in his head to go down to the greenhouse with a bottle of his best and toast the gardeners. On the way down, I was sweating, lads. And there's Devlin. The sly old dog, not a word out of him. As cool as you please when they introduced us. Deirdre's collapsed in the shrubbery, laughing.

MARY. But did they like you, Paddy?

PADDY. Ah, they couldn't get enough of me. All of them but the mother. Old Maureen was a tough nut to crack. Very stand-offish. But, late Saturday night, they dragged me up to sing with the band. I sang a lot of traditional stuff, ending up with "Four Green Fields" . . . and she started to come 'round. I saw my chance, so I tried a bit of the Irish on her and it worked like a charm. Before long, I was calling her my dark Roisin and I had her in the palm of me hand, lads. By one in the morning, the band was jumping buck naked into the pool.˙ (*Silence. They stare at Paddy*) So, up I went to Duke and I come clean with him about the gardening and all. And I told him how it is with Deirdre and me. He's all for the marriage.

MARY. Marriage?!

OWEN. So soon?!

PADDY. He told me he'd like nothing better than to see her settled down and raising a family.

MARY. Oh, Paddy!

PADDY. Yeah. There's nothing left but to pop the question.

LIAM. You mean, you haven't asked her yet?

PADDY. I was going to . . . this weekend, you know. But it was so wild up there. I never seen anything like it. You shoulda been there. (*Pause*) The house was full of dogs and cats. (*Silence. They all continue to stare at him. He shrugs*) And that's the lot. Well, mates, what have I missed? (*It's as though a spell has been broken. Suddenly, they all begin to talk at once*)

LIAM. I got us an answering machine.

MARY. And Owen's got some mysterious news he's been withholding 'til you returned.

OWEN. Ah, right! My turn, Paddy. This morning I sent the wife my last installment. I now have all I need to capitalize my restaurant and I can bloody well kiss America goodbye. So let's drink to the "Erie-Lackawanna Diner" and to all the paddys who built the railways. (*Everyone but Mary shows surprise and pleasure*)

MARY. So you'll not be back after the holidays.

OWEN. Oh, I'll be back, Mary. There are some loose ends to

tie up. (*He moves to the stove*)

MARY. Loose ends?

OWEN. And now, time for the feast! (*Owen puts the salad on the table and Mary brings the truffles*)

LIAM. It's truffles and bacon, Paddy. You ever heard of them? A pig roots them out of the ground and then they kill him for the bacon.

PADDY. Where's this?

LIAM. In France someplace.

PADDY. Barbarians! (*They all gather round the table, looking at the food*)

MARY. Ah, the smell of the little buggers! Oooh, done to a turn.

OWEN. Gather round, mates! Here's more champers.

PADDY. I will now propose another toast. Let's drink to the Irish, my friends. The Irish saved me arse this weekend. (*They raise their glasses*) Go mbeimís beo ar an am seo arís!

ALL. Slante! (*They drink, then, look to the door as Desmond enters. He stands there swaying, all beaten and bloodied*)

MARY. Dessie!

OWEN. Bloody Christ!

PADDY. Who did this?

LIAM. Jaysus, Des!

OWEN. Did the cops see youse? Get him in here!

MARY. I'll get Rose.

OWEN. Shut the door! Shut the door!

MARY. Rose! (*Runs out into the hallway*)

OWEN. Shut that feckin door! (*Paddy and Liam help Des to the table*)

LIAM. (*Brings a glass of champagne*) Have this, Des. (*Music. Lights out*)

act 2

SCENE ONE

Lights up on Christmas Eve day, in the apartment. Carols are softly playing on the radio. Desmond is curled up under many blankets, asleep on the couch. Liam is fiddling around with wires connected to a decorated Christmas tree. Desmond turns over and wakes up. He wears a "Free The Carriage Horses" T-shirt.

LIAM. Happy Christmas, Des!

DESMOND. Who trimmed the tree?

LIAM. Mary and Paula were over last night. We did it while you slept. You never even stirred.

DESMOND. What's that there?

LIAM. A dimmer switch.

DESMOND. And what's that in aid of?

LIAM. Hold on 'til I show you. (*He plugs in the tree and does some fancy light work with the dimmer switch. The colored lights grow bright, then dim; they flash, etc. Silence*)

DESMOND. Bloody Christmas!

LIAM. Wait now, 'til you have some eggnog. (*He goes over to the refrigerator and brings back a pitcher and a frothy cupful*) This will set you right. Get you in the proper spirit.

DESMOND. (*Drinks*) Mmmmm. Not bad. What time is it, anyway?

LIAM. Half-three. (*He sits at the table*)

DESMOND. The tree looks good. (*Silence*)

LIAM. I've been sitting here, thinking of home. The Christmas goose is a pile of bones by now. Mam's in the kitchen with Frances doing the washing up. Me da and the brothers will be on about politics. This is the first I've been away on Christmas.

DESMOND. Ah, give over, Liam.

LIAM. It's a kid's holiday, isn't it, Des?

DESMOND. Yeah.

LIAM. Mam always cries on Christmas. She says it's from happiness ... having us all 'round the table.

DESMOND. You'll be sobbing yourself in a minute. Give us some more of that eggnog. It takes the edge off.

LIAM. (*Refills his glass and pours some for himself*) I guess what it is, is ... I'm homesick, Des. I suddenly miss them all. Everything.

DESMOND. A lot of good that'll do ya.

LIAM. It's the first time I've really thought of them since I've been over.

DESMOND. (*Getting up and crossing to the kitchen*) I'm hungry. Is there anything to eat in this kip?

LIAM. There's Mary's mother's Christmas cake. And she worked a party last night so we've got some turkey and the trimmings. (*Desmond gets a slice of Christmas cake from the refrigerator. Liam begins to fold blankets and put couch away*) We're going to midnight mass at St. Pat's. Do you want to come along?

DESMOND. Whose idea was that?

LIAM. Mary's ma asked her would she go and write her what it's like.

DESMOND. You've seen one, you've seen them all. That's one of the holy mysteries of the Catholic Church.

LIAM. Rose and Paula are coming too.

DESMOND. Paula? I'll pass.

LIAM. Look, Des, you shouldn't be so hard on her. She likes you, is all.

DESMOND. I see the look in Paula's eye. She's like a stray cat looking for a plate of milk.

LIAM. What are you talking about? She's not like that at all. (*He takes blankets into the bedroom*)

DESMOND. (*Goes to packages under the tree, picks one up and shakes it. Then he goes to the window and looks out*) Come over here and look at this, Liam! It's snowing! (*He opens the window and sits on the sill*)

LIAM. (*Returning from the bedroom*) Jaysus, look out now, Des!

DESMOND. I could slip over the edge and do a free fall through the snowflakes. They say you pass out before you hit the ground.

LIAM. Will you come away from there and shut that window. It's freezing! (*Desmond laughs and leans way out. Liam, frightened, grabs him and pulls him back into the room. He slams the window shut. Desmond keeps on laughing*) You eedjit! We're seven stories up off the ground!

DESMOND. Ah. I've always hated Christmas. All holidays. They're only there to get you looking forward to something. When they come, they're always a disappointment. Here.

Let's have a toast. (*He refills their glasses with eggnog*) Let's have a toast to an ordinary day. I raise my glass to January 21st.

LIAM. That's the parents' anniversary. (*Pause*) I'm sorry, Des. I can't help it. I'm homesick.

DESMOND. Ah, what's home for anybody, these days? (*They sit at the table*)

LIAM. Sure, you must feel something, being away over here ... with Owen home and all.

DESMOND. Sorry, old sod. I feel nothing. I might be homesick, if I knew where home was. It's not Ireland for me anymore. I'm glad to be out of it. I sit here, night after night, and watch all of youse. You're all on a tear over here ... free at last to do whatever you want, with no one watching you. But you're never free of the place. Whether you stay or go back. It clings to you like seaweed, pulling you back, pulling you down. Just look at all the bloody Yanks. Mention Ireland and they're crying in their beer. Matter a damn if they're only half or a quarter or a tenth Irish. The sight of green turns them all soft and silly in the head. Even the ones who've never been there. Off they go on the suffering, all the bloody injustices done over the centuries. What do they know? Huh? What the bloody hell do they know about us or Ireland now? It's Cromwell and the Famine. They don't give a flying fuck about us ... you and me ... here and now. Thousands of us, washed up on the shores of America. In and out with the tides.

LIAM. I've been talking to Peter Kelly about that.

DESMOND. You're always on about Peter Kelly.

LIAM. He's been very good to me.

DESMOND. Peter Kelly's glad to have you. What's he pay you? Huh? He pays you $7 an hour. Straight up. That's it. No unemployment compensation. No hospitalization. That's it.

LIAM. Easy now, Des. He didn't have to hire me. Didn't have to pay my fare over. He give me a chance I wouldn't have had.

DESMOND. Don't easy me, Liam. You know it's true what I'm saying. (*Pause*) The Yanks are in love with the idea of

Ireland. They don't want to know the truth.

LIAM. The truth is their people first come here in coffin ships. They want to remember that. It's their history.

DESMOND. What's history, for fuck sake?! It's yesterday, is all. Nobody learns from history. We're still fighting wars, aren't we? Killing each other over land and money.

LIAM. Sometimes over freedom, Des. Over human rights.

DESMOND. Yeah. But what happens when the fuckers get their human rights? Huh? They turn around and grab somebody else's. Oh, not right away. There's always a decent interval 'til they get on their feet. Then they deliver the old drop-kick to the crotch of some other miserable poor bugger. My own cousin is no exception. Owen. We grew up together. Suddenly Owen's big time, Mr. Success. You haven't known him very long, Liam. You haven't seen the change in him. I'm ashamed to say he's a racist pig. And his wife and kids mean nothing to him.

LIAM. I don't believe that.

DESMOND. And look at the others! Paula, for example. She goes from minding her sister's kids at home to minding some stranger's here for $4 an hour ... and she thinks her lot's improved.

LIAM. That's more than her sister paid her. And she's on her own, free to do as she likes.

DESMOND. And what does she like? Huh? She likes me! (*They laugh*) See what I'm saying, Liam? She's not a free woman! She's looking to marry ... to find some man to make decisions for her. None of youse are free. Because you won't face the truth. It's the truth that makes you free.

LIAM. And what is this truth?

DESMOND. Ah ... I don't know. (*Pause*) The truth is, there's no more home, Liam. I know that. We can't go home. There's no place for us there. We have to break with the past. (*Silence. Suddenly, Liam jumps up and goes to the Christmas tree*)

LIAM. Come on, now. Let's open our presents!

DESMOND. You know as well as I do ... there's fags and socks in those boxes.

LIAM. (*He drops a present and returns to the table*) Ah, you spoil everything, Desmond. (*Silence*)

DESMOND. I'm sorry, Gizmo. Fuck me. You're right. I'm just a little down.

LIAM. You've been down since I met you.

DESMOND. It's just that ... I can't seem to get it together. When I first come over, I couldn't get enough of the place. In and out of the subways. I'd just get on one and ride to the end of the line to see where I'd end up. Went up the World Trade Center for the overview. Been in all the museums. It seemed like ... there was so much excitement here, ya know? The place was wide open! (*Pause*) But after you've seen it all, you start to take a closer look. And that's when you see what it all costs.

LIAM. How do you mean?

DESMOND. I mean, who's paying for all the excitement? Huh? Who pays for the gleaming skyscrapers and the parades and the limos that are clogging the streets? Just have a look at the rest of the South Bronx. We're just more cheap labor for them, Liam. Playing right into their hands. Think about it. What would happen if we all just stayed home? What would happen here and what would happen in Ireland? (*Silence*)

LIAM. (*Beginning to show the effects of the eggnog*) Des. Maybe you should see a psychiatrist.

DESMOND. What the bloody hell for?!!

LIAM. For help. I think you're depressed. And depression is a kind of disease. Maybe Rose could help you. Or Mary.

DESMOND. I'm not depressed! I'm unemployed in the Land of Opportunity. That's all. Jaysus, the last thing I need to do is ask those women across the hall for help. They'd drown me with all their talk of love. (*He refills their cups with eggnog*)

LIAM. No they wouldn't. Rose is a nurse.

DESMOND. It's bad enough around this place with Paddy mooning about. That woman he's got hasn't the brains of a donkey. Does he care? He does not. For all his talk of love. This is the Land of Opportunity and Paddy is marrying land.

LIAM. If she'll have him.

DESMOND. Why wouldn't she? He's an Irishman! (*Silence*) And you, Liam. Just look at yourself. You've bought the American Dream too. The dream of ownership. Look at all the stuff you've dragged in here. Do you really need a battery-operated, automatic toothpaste dispenser? Ask yourself.

LIAM. I don't just use all these things. I take them apart and see how they work, Des. It's amazing how easy it is. What a simple mechanism is behind all this stuff. I'm learning something from it, Des.

DESMOND. Yeah. Well, where's it going to get you? In the end. (*Silence. Desmond crosses to sit on the back of the couch. He winces with pain*)

LIAM. Still hurts, does it?

DESMOND. A bit.

LIAM. We were lucky to have Rose across the hall to do for that broken rib. What happened when they mugged you, Des? You never said.

DESMOND. Ah, it was nothing. The beating itself, I mean. There was no reason for it. I only wanted to talk to them, see? About what I've been thinking about the system over here. Owen's always on about the "narrowbacks" and "donkey hunting." He gets that from the other guys on the job. They're always ragging him. So, that night I went in a bar I was never in before. I just wanted to talk about it, you know? You have to admit, we live a pretty isolated existence over here. We're in a ghetto up here in the Bronx. Anyway ... I'm in this bar and I get in conversation with these guys and we start buying each other drinks and ... I don't know ... listening to them, I suddenly felt such love in my heart for them. You know? They were just like me brothers. I guess I was fairly well gone with the drink by then. I started in on the system, how it can lock you in, no matter where you are. I wanted to tell them, make them understand that it's the same with us, back home. No work, no future. But, friendly like, you know? I meant nothing. (*Silence*)

LIAM. What happened?

DESMOND. I was talking to them all right ... and I kind of got lost ... I looked in their eyes and ... I saw this hate. It didn't scare me, but ... I suddenly thought I was going to cry. So I left. I just walked out, no goodbye, nothing. (*Silence*) Anyway. They followed me and they jumped me. Dragged me in an alley and beat the bejaysus out of me. (*Moves back to the table and starts to laugh*) Jaysus, Liam ... they called me a fag! They thought I was a homosexual. (*Desmond pours more eggnog for himself and Liam. It's strong stuff and they're beginning to be drunk. Silence. Desmond sits*) That look of hatred. I saw the same thing in my father's eyes. You think you get used to it but you never do. I've always been afraid, Liam. (*Pause*) Well, drink up, Gizmo.

LIAM. Better go easy, Desmond. I don't want to be down on me arse when Mary and Paula come over.

DESMOND. And why not? Gets the spirit of Christmas into you. You'll need it for midnight mass. You'll be hours breathing in all that incense. Are you sure you want to go?

LIAM. I promised Mary.

DESMOND. Ah, fuck me then ... I'll go along with you. You'll need a chaperone with them two women. We'll give thanks with the Yanks. We'll sing their hosannas and hallelujahs with the great mob of them. (*He drinks his eggnog and urges Liam to drink up as well; He refills their glasses*) Ah ... you want to read philosophy, Liam. The Greeks had it all figured out thousands of years ago.

LIAM. Ah ... (*Hic*) don't be talking to me about Greeks.

DESMOND. Thales said "Water is Truth."

LIAM. It's not water we're drinking here.

DESMOND. Yeah ... like, if you think of all of humanity as one vast body of water. Doesn't matter a damn what the political system is at the top. Governments come and go. They can get into all manner of corruption and violence ... but still, people survive. The people go on. Like water, Liam. The human tide finds a way around or over ... or under ... any obstacle. Take immigration.

LIAM. (*Hic!*) Immigration?

DESMOND. Yeah. Governments are always trying to stop it, contain it in some way. They've divided the world up into little pieces, borders you can't cross over. What happens?

LIAM. Whaa-at?

DESMOND. People cross them. They go where they want to go. One way or another. They find a way. Yeah. Water is the truth, Liam. That's it. (*Pause*) For instance, now, you take an American astronaut.

LIAM. An astronaut?!!

DESMOND. Right. Just to show you how crazy governments can get. An American astronaut can go to the moon, for fuck's sake. But not to Cuba.

LIAM. If he wanted to go. (*Hic!*)

DESMOND. If he wanted to go. It's ridiculous!

LIAM. Ridi . . . redik (*Hic!*) . . . dikalis (*Desmond notices Liam's state of inebriation and laughs*)

DESMOND. Ah . . . Gizmo. You're a great lad to talk to. You know that?

LIAM. I'm snackered.

DESMOND. (*Not too sober himself*) I love you, Liam. You know that? I'd never say it when we're sober . . . it wouldn't do. Ah . . . you're like a brother, you are. (*Pause*) I love you. And that's the truth. Hey, Liam! Let's open the presents! (*Desmond gets up and pats Liam on the shoulder as he goes to the presents. Liam falls over. Desmond picks up some presents, turns back to Liam and finds him passed out cold on the floor. Music. Lights fade to black*)

SCENE TWO

It's Christmas morning in the apartment and all is quiet. The lights on the Christmas tree are still on. Suddenly, Liam enters from the bedroom. He's hung over. He puts the kettle on. He's restless, keeps prowling around the apartment, looking toward the bedroom. He sits on couch. Church bells ring and the kettle whistles. The noise seems deafening to him. He quickly makes tea, pours a cup and sits at table. Finally, Mary comes to the bedroom door. She smiles, tiptoes up behind him and kisses him.

MARY. Happy Christmas, Liam.

LIAM. (*Suddenly shy*) Christmas.

MARY. What's the matter?

LIAM. I . . . nothing. I'm hung over, is all. There's tea there.

MARY. Oh, lovely. Shall I make breakfast?

LIAM. I . . . think I'll just have the tea, thanks.

MARY. Ah, you'll need more than tea. I'll make us a nice Christmas breakfast. There's still some of Mam's Christmas cake here. (*Mary busies herself at the counter. Liam watches her*) Wasn't last night lovely, with the snow and all? I can't wait to tell my mam how beautiful St. Patrick's was. I like to think I'm a liberated woman but, to tell you the truth, I've still a soft spot in my heart for the Church. It's all that pageantry, I guess. They do know how to put on a show. Wasn't the music and all the singing glorious? And I was so happy you got Desmond to come along. Rose and Paula really got him going. I've never see him laugh so much. What are you staring at, Liam?

LIAM. Nothing.

MARY. There's brown bread. Will you have brown bread as well?

LIAM. Suit yourself. It's funny, seeing you make breakfast.

MARY. Owen's not the only one can cook. (*Silence. Liam continues to watch her*) You know, I think maybe Des is finally working his way out of his funk. Paula will help him. Paula's great. Wasn't it fun in the park, after? I haven't laughed like that in ages! And wasn't it sweet of Mario to treat us to all that cognac? That really warmed up the old bones, didn't it. (*She laughs*)

LIAM. Mary?

MARY. Yes, Liam?

LIAM. I . . . what happened last night . . .

MARY. Don't you remember, Liam?

LIAM. (*Embarrassed*) I remember . . . of course I remember. I just don't . . .

MARY. It was nice, wasn't it?

LIAM. Yeah . . . well, I mean . . . I just don't know how . . .

MARY. Don't think about it now, Liam. Sometimes things happen and you just have to let them happen. It was Christmas Eve.

LIAM. You think so?

MARY. (*Laughing*) Wait 'til Breda wakes up and finds Desmond in the bed with her! It was such a lovely time and what a shame to just ... I thought somehow that it wouldn't have been right for you to be all alone here, you know. With the others across the hall, why shouldn't we be together too? We're old friends now.

LIAM. That's what I'm trying to say, Mary. I mean, I like you a lot. I've never, you know ... well, I never slept with anyone ... with a girl before.

MARY. It was nice. Wasn't it?

LIAM. Yes. I mean ... yes, it was.

MARY. Here now, have some breakfast. Look, Liam. It's still snowing. (*They sit down to eat. They're ravenous*) Oh, this is delicious!

LIAM. Wait, now. There's some jam here, too. (*He jumps up and gets a new jar from the refrigerator*)

MARY. Raspberry jam! Oh, Liam ... I'm in heaven! This reminds me of the time my granny sent my sister and me out to pick raspberries. We used to stay with her in the summers out in the country. There were ducks and chickens and we'd have to gather the eggs for her. She kept some geese, too. They were mean old things that would chase us. We always had to keep a sharp lookout for them. They'd come rushing at us out of nowhere, hissing. But they loved granny. Once a year, she'd catch them up and hold them in her lap with their heads tucked under her arm and she'd pluck out their down and make pillows. We loved to be there when the raspberries were ripe, because that's when granny made the jam. We'd be so full of raspberries.

LIAM. Mary. I love you, Mary.

MARY. Oh, Liam. I love you too.

LIAM. No. I mean ... I think ... I really love you.

MARY. Ah, Liam. I think you shouldn't say that.

LIAM. But I do.

MARY. You don't really mean that. You don't know me well enough.

LIAM. I do know you. Haven't we been together a lot? You said yourself ...

MARY. Yes, but that's different. I only live across the hall. It's natural that we'd see so much of each other.

LIAM. But ... I've been watching you, too, Mary. You're so kind and ... you always think of us, bring us things.

MARY. It's like a family situation here, Liam. We're all away from our own homes so we have to stay together here and sort of look out for each other. You all are like my brothers. You're probably just saying that because I remind you of your sister.

LIAM. My sister? Frances?!

MARY. It's true, isn't it?

LIAM. Well, I never thought of you as being like Frances.

MARY. Well, if you stop and think about it ... you'll see what I mean. Oh, I'm so glad I'm not working tomorrow! I've been so busy ... I haven't had time to bless myself. Tomorrow, I'll rest up for New Year's ... all that end of the year madness. (*Silence*)

LIAM. My visa's almost up.

MARY. So's mine.

LIAM. Are you still set on staying?

MARY. I told you, Liam, I'll never go back there.

LIAM. Not even to see your family?

MARY. If they want to see me, they can come here. There's nothing for me back home. What kind of job could I get? And nobody looks at you here in that funny way they do if you're a woman and you're alone. And there's privacy here, Liam. Think if we did what we did back home. People would know ... they always do. There'd be talk. There are more opportunities for women here. I'm going to start a course in graphic design in January. I'm so excited about it. Now! Come on ... let's get dressed and go for a walk in the snow. Tell you what ... let's go to the zoo! Do you think the zoo will be open? (*Suddenly, Breda screams from across the hall*) Breda! (*They laugh. Lights out*)

SCENE THREE

Paddy is alone, leaning against the refrigerator and listening to the end of a sad country western song. Announcer: "A little bit of country for you city folks on this fine spring day. It's 70° in Central

Park with not a cloud in the sky. And now for all you Mets fans on the way to Shea, here's one of my all-time favorites . . ." Another song comes on and Paddy sits on the back of the couch and stares out the window. Liam, Des and Mary enter the apartment, their arms full of boxes and bags. They're very happy. They begin opening the purchases and taking out clothes for Des.

DESMOND. Well, look who's here!

MARY. Hello, Paddy! Wait till you see what we've got.

LIAM. Paddy! Ah, there's great news this day. Desmond has a job at last!

MARY. Oh, Paddy, you shoulda been with us. We all went up the Fordham Road and . . .

LIAM. With my excellent sartorial guidance . . . and the loan of some cash . . .

MARY. . . . we have outfitted Des for his new position in the world. From the skin out . . . it was formidable.

LIAM. He was as bad as you were, Paddy . . . only the clothes on his back.

MARY. Come on now. Des . . . give us a show.

LIAM. Get them jeans off you, man.

DESMOND. Ah, go on.

LIAM. No . . . we want the full effect. I've a right to see the fruits of my investment.

MARY. Right! Off with the jeans and into the casual elegance of these grey flannels. (*Mary and Liam corner Des behind the counter*) Oh, don't be so shy, Desmond. I'll tie your necktie. (*Desmond gives her a shocked look as they help him into his new clothes*)

LIAM. Well, you've been scarce around here, Paddy.

DESMOND. Yeah. What brings you home to us . . . is it raining in Larchmont?

PADDY. (*Sighing deeply*) Ah, everything's blooming up there. Old Devlin and me, we've got the place roaring with flowers. Tiger lilies, snapdragons, you name it and we've got it. (*They all look at each other. It is clear that something is wrong with Paddy. They stare at him. Mary turns off the radio. He moans loudly*) Ah, jaysus . . . I haven't felt like this since my calf strayed into the bog.

LIAM. What's up, Paddy?

DESMOND. What're you so long in the face for? I thought you'd be happy for me.

MARY. Is it something about Deirdre? (*Paddy sighs and shrugs his shoulders. They gather around him. Mary sits on the couch*)

LIAM. She won't marry you.

MARY. Oh, Paddy!

LIAM. You asked her, didn't you, Paddy?

MARY. Ah, but how did you ask her, Paddy? It's all in the asking.

PADDY. Of course I asked her. What do you take me for?!

LIAM. What's your problem, then?

DESMOND. She refused you. Ah, I knew this would happen, Paddy. You were swimming out of your depth.

PADDY. She didn't bloody refuse me at all! She said yes. She'll have me. (*The others all look at each other. They can't figure out what his trouble is*) She thinks I'll take her back. She wants to live in Ireland, mates. (*Silence*) I told her I thought maybe we'd settle here. I like America fine. But, she'll have none of it. It's back to the roots for Deirdre. Ireland or nothing. (*Silence*) I tried to tell her how it is, you know, with the three brothers and the wee farm. I tried to explain how I come here hoping for a fresh start. Jeez, here I am dreaming of a ranch in Colorado or Wyoming.

MARY. What'd she say to all that?

PADDY. (*Crosses to center*) Nothing will do but a farm with wee cottages. She wants thatched roofs and turf fires, lads. A leprechaun under every bush. And Barry Fitzgerald coming up the lane.

DESMOND. That's Hollywood for ya. Hollywood and the Tourist Board.

PADDY. And horses. She wants to raise horses and ride to the hounds.

DESMOND. That'll take money. Would she forget about the horses and just raise the hounds?

PADDY. Money's no problem. She's already talked to Duke. It's all worked out. Duke will set us up as a wedding present. He's made contact with an agent and it seems there's a big place in Roscommon can be had. I tell you, lads, these Yanks are something else!

LIAM. What are ya on about?! Go for it, man!!

PADDY. That's not what's worrying me, Liam.

LIAM. Sure, it's a gift, Paddy!

PADDY. But ... how's it going to look if I go back and set myself up in style? Huh?! What'll they say back home?

MARY. They'll come 'round, Paddy. Sure, it's your family.

PADDY. Ah, I know them, the begrudgers. I can just imagine what they'll be saying.

DESMOND. Forget about them.

LIAM. It's your life, Paddy.

MARY. It they want to be small about it, that's their lookout.

PADDY. I wanted to make it in America. Be a Yank! I like the music. I like the cars. It's big here. Room for everybody. The cities are big. There's space. The way Duke talks about Texas ... sure, the whole of Ireland is only as big as Texas.

MARY. Look at it this way. With her family here, you'll be coming back for holidays. You'll be a regular jet-setter.

PADDY. (*Sits at table*) At least I'll see Texas before I go back. Duke said he'd take me with him in a few weeks when he goes down on business. Well, those are fine feathers, Des. What about you? What's the new job?

LIAM. Go on. Tell him, Des.

DESMOND. I'm going to be a nanny.

PADDY. A what?!

DESMOND. A nanny.

PADDY. Oh, jaysus, has the world gone mad entirely?! Deirdre's suddenly talking blood lines like a man and now this.

MARY. Paula got him the job through the people she works for. That ought to make Owen happy at last.

DESMOND. I doubt that. It's not a bad gig, Paddy. Two boys. One's five and the other's eight. I'll tutor them a bit. Nice little lads they are. The parents are never there and they need a bit of company. They love baseball and they say they'll teach me how to play it.

BREDA. (*Runs into the apartment*) Tommy has the loan of a van and he's going to Orchard Beach. He says we can come along.

MARY. Smashing! It's only half-one. We can have a picnic.

PADDY. The lot of us?

BREDA. He'll be glad of the company. It's just him and his girl friend, Wanda.

PADDY. Wanda? Which one's she, then?

MARY. Oh, come on now ... it's been so long since we've all been together. I'll get Rose and Paula, too. They'll be going home soon. The weather's perfect.

BREDA. Will I tell him we're going?

PADDY. I've nothing better to do. Are you game, Des?

DESMOND. Well, for the love of me I can't think why not.

MARY. Listen to him! I believe old Dessie's back among the living.

LIAM. (*Still wary of Breda*) What about Owen? Shouldn't we wait for Ownie?

MARY. Ah, Owen's no fun anymore. We'll just go make a picnic lunch. Come on, Breda! (*Breda runs out and Mary follows*)

PADDY. (*Shouting after them*) Make us some ham sandwiches! (*Mary bumps into Owen as he enters*)

OWEN. What's the rush?

MARY. We're off to the beach. Are ya coming?

OWEN. I've been stuck in that bleedin' subway for almost an hour. (*He slumps down on the couch*)

MARY. Owen, wait'll you hear. Des has himself a job!

OWEN. Does he now? Well, that's news.

MARY. We're after buying out the Fordham Road. What gas!

OWEN. It's true then? You've a job?

DESMOND. It is, yeah.

OWEN. When do you start?

DESMOND. Monday.

OWEN. And none too soon. It's time you started to pull your weight around here. I've been carrying you too long. (*He goes to the refrigerator for a beer*)

DESMOND. I will now, Owen.

OWEN. That's right, boyo. I've been keeping careful count. And you'll pay back the money you owe me. (*Desmond moves away from Owen, over to the chest of drawers*)

MARY. So ... we're off to the beach to celebrate ...

OWEN. What's the job, then? Construction?

DESMOND. No.

MARY. Come with us, Owen. It's a lovely day.

OWEN. What's the job?

MARY. You lads get ready, now! (*Exits*)

OWEN. What manner of work is it?

DESMOND. I'm to be a nanny.

OWEN. What?

LIAM. It's a sort of a tutor. He's to look after two young lads.

OWEN. A fecking nanny?

PADDY. Ah, it's an honest job, now, Ownie.

OWEN. What's it pay?

DESMOND. Six-fifty an hour. (*Owen moves down from counter. Paddy moves closer to him*)

OWEN. When I offered to get you on the site, you said the pay wasn't good enough. He turned up his nose at twelve dollars an hour. And now, he'll settle for six-fifty.

PADDY. That's a high-rise you're working on there, Ownie. We're not all in love with heights, you know.

OWEN. I want an explanation! I want to know why my job isn't good enough for him. Why he'd rather chase after a pair of young boys for six bloody fifty an hour.

LIAM. Leave it, Owen, it's his choice. (*He moves toward Desmond*)

OWEN. You stay out of this! What do you know, ya little fool. Letting every black in the neighborhood sell you a line of junk. Shooting yer mouth off to everyone you meet.

LIAM. I don't shoot me mouth off . . .

DESMOND. Leave him out of this, Owen.

OWEN. (*Mocking*) "Leave him out of this." Listen to him, Paddy. Now he has a job, he'll be telling us what to say.

PADDY. Ah, give over . . .

DESMOND. I'm not telling you anything. I'm just saying Liam's got nothing to do with this.

OWEN. I hope he doesn't. Liam's a good lad. I wouldn't care to think Liam's mixed up in anything.

DESMOND. Mixed up in what?

LIAM. I'm not mixed up in anything . . .

PADDY. Will we go to the beach, for feck sake?!

DESMOND. No! I want to hear this. Mixed up in what, Owen?

What's the implication here? (*Desmond and Owen move toward each other. Paddy and Liam are between them*)

OWEN. Oh, no implication, cousin. Fact! I ran into some friends of yours ... from last November.

PADDY. You met the bastards who worked on Des?!

OWEN. I did, indeed. And they had some news for me.

LIAM. What news, Owen? Jaysus, I'm surprised you spoke to them at all!

DESMOND. I told you what they said, Liam.

OWEN. They said our mate here ... my own cousin ... is a queer!

DESMOND. I've had about enough of this, Owen!

LIAM. That's crazy talk, Owen! You don't believe that?!

OWEN. A prancer!

DESMOND. I didn't know the bar, Owen, I told you ...

OWEN. A little pouf ...

DESMOND. If you don't shut your mouth, I'll ...

OWEN. You'll what? Huh?

PADDY. Wait now, wait now ... I say we get the bastards ...

DESMOND. You've a nerve, coming in here, accusing me without hearing the whole story! You've known me all my life ...

OWEN. My own cousin ... Madame bleedin' Butterfly (*By now, Liam and Paddy are holding the other two away from each other*)

DESMOND. You bastard! I'll kill you!

OWEN. Come ahead, I've been waiting a year for this!

DESMOND. You fuckin' hypocrite! What of yourself. What about you and Mary?

OWEN. At least I'm a healthy man with healthy appetites! (*At this, Liam turns away from all of them*)

DESMOND. And that goes for the little wifey as well, I'm told. Wait'll you hear mates ... the little wifey has an appetite for the whole of Dublin ...

OWEN. Let go of me, Paddy!

PADDY. Easy, now, easy ...

DESMOND. What's she get, Owen ... $12 an hour, same as you? You two must be rolling in green.

LIAM. (*Turning back*) Stop, Dessie!

OWEN. *Get off me*, Paddy!

DESMOND. Ah, but it's never enough is it, Owen? Once you've the smell of the money on ya . . . you must have more. Am I right, Ownie?

OWEN. You filthy pig, I'll rip your guts out! (*Owen lunges at Des and lands a punch. Des falls on the couch. Paddy pulls Owen away and shoves him to the counter. Des recovers and jumps back up*)

DESMOND. Where's the diner, Owen? I thought you were gone from here . . . the dream come true! So where's that diner you were always whining about? It was the money got you, wasn't it? Forget the diner! You just can't stay away from the golden trough. What about the diner, Owen? What are you back here for? Or can't you stand the stinking mess you left back home while you went in search of the holy green! (*Owen comes apart. He smashes his pots and kicks the stove, then breaks down and cries. Liam curls up on the couch with his head in his arms*)

PADDY. Jaysus! (*Silence*)

OWEN. She give it away, Dessie! I found out at Christmas. She give all the money to her family. There'll be no diner. Ever. After three bloody, fucking years slaving my guts out over here. There's nothing. (*Silence, while Owen cries*)

PADDY. Easy, mate.

DESMOND. Jeez, I'm sorry, Owen. (*Silence. Desmond sits on arm of couch*) I say we all made a mistake coming to the states. We all shoulda gone to feckin' Romania. For all the good it's done us. (*Mary and Breda return in high spirits and see the situation*)

MARY. Owen!

BREDA. It's all set. Tommy's downstairs with the car. Will you look at the faces on ya?!

MARY. What in the name a God's going on here?! Owen?

BREDA. Will youse get your gear, then. The sun's fading . . . I want to work on my tan. (*Exits*)

MARY. Paddy! What's happened?

PADDY. It's nothing to do with you, Mary. Just leave it.

MARY. I will not leave it! The lunch is packed. I can't believe what I'm seeing. Not ten minutes ago, you were wild to get to the beach. And now look at youse. Des? Liam! You've been here nearly a year. It's time to celebrate. It's springtime, you slaggers!

PADDY. Ah, come on now. Will we go, lads? This is our chance to see Breda in a bathing outfit. Picture that, Owen.

OWEN. A cheering thought. (*Suddenly, Owen starts to laugh uncontrollably*) Romania! Fucking Romania! Jaysus, Des! Could ya see us?! (*Paddy laughs as well. Des smiles*)

MARY. Well, whatever you're on about, that's more like it. Tommy's waiting, Paddy.

PADDY. All right, now, where's my Christian Dior beach towel?

MARY. Well, aren't we posh. Don't be sitting there, Liam. You come, too.

LIAM. Ah, piss on all a youse! (*Liam slams out the door. They all stare after him. Music. Lights out*)

SCENE FOUR

Later in The Old Sod, Mario is behind the bar watching a baseball game on TV. Liam sleeps quietly, his head resting on his arms.

MARIO. HoJo! Don't do this to me!

LIAM. (*Wakes and looks up*) What's happening?

MARIO. McReynolds and Teufel are on and Strawberry's up. Bottom of the ninth. Three-two, Pirates. (*Liam drinks and stares glumly at the TV*) HoJo fanned, man. (*Silence, except for the sound of the game*)

LIAM. The place is so empty today.

MARIO. Everybody's at Shea or fishing. The blues are running off Sheepshead. Come on, Darryl . . . show 'em how, baby! Yeah. Just me and Mr. Costelloe, here. Mr. Costelloe don't fish. What's a matter, Liam? You got a problem?

LIAM. Why?

MARIO. You're not interested in the game.

LIAM. I'm interested. I'm just tired, is all.

MARIO. (*Goes back to the TV*) Okay now. This is it . . . this is the pitch, Darryl. (*Strawberry hits a home run*) Alllriiiight!! Look at that? Ain't that beautiful?! It's poetry, that is. (*He turns the sound down on the TV*) I had money on that game. I tell you, Liam. I think they'll take the pennant this year. It might be close . . . Pittsburgh's got a good team, but I think the Mets have got it this year. (*Silence*)

LIAM. Everybody went to Orchard Beach today.

MARIO. Why didn't you go with them? You could use a little color, Liam. Your color's off.

LIAM. Ahhh, I don't know.

MARIO. What is it . . . Breda been after you again?

LIAM. No, none of that. It's just . . .

MARIO. I only ask because, I see a guy come in here looks the way you do . . . nine out of ten times, it's some kind of woman troubles. (*Liam sighs loudly*) So, what have you got here?

LIAM. I don't know. Maybe I . . . I guess it is a woman . . .

MARIO. Don't make a problem for yourself. You love somebody, there's no problem in that. Let it be that way.

LIAM. Let it be?

MARIO. Yeah. Have yourself another beer and think about playing ball. What position you want?

LIAM. Huh?

MARIO. Sports, my friend. Some of the guys are thinking about starting up a softball team. We could play Saturday's over on Randall's Island.

MARIO. (*Puts another beer down in front of Liam and takes a pad and pencil from his back pocket*) So, what position you wanna play?

LIAM. I never played softball.

MARIO. You want second or you want the field? I think you'd be better on second. You're quick with your hands, Liam. In the field you gotta think ahead more. And think fast. I'll put you down for second base. (*He returns behind bar*)

LIAM. I haven't seen Tyrone around.

MARIO. Last I heard, he went South.

LIAM. He said he might go down for Christmas and I haven't seen him since.

MARIO. He'll do that from time to time . . . just disappear.

LIAM. I like Tyrone.

MARIO. Hell of a guy.

LIAM. I don't know if you should put me down for the softball team, Mario. I might be going home soon.

MARIO. Get an extension. We could have a World Series here

to go to, Liam.

LIAM. There doesn't seem much point in an extension. The work's slowing down for Peter Kelly. I wouldn't want him to feel obligated to carry me, you know? (*Pause*) I'd hate to leave without saying goodbye to Tyrone.

MARIO. You could always work here. I'd teach you the ropes. We could use an extra barkeep in the summer.

LIAM. I don't know.

MARIO. You could do worse. A bar's not a bad place to work. A bar's a place of hope ... the place where you go at night, before you surrender to the next day. (*Pause*) I'll keep your name on the list anyhow. In case you change your mind.

LIAM. Mary says she's staying on.

MARIO. Yeah?

LIAM. She'll take her chances. She likes it here. Says it's better for women. She may be right.

MARIO. She'll probably marry some guy here.

LIAM. Who?

MARIO. Who? I don't know! I'm just saying it could happen. She's a good looking woman.

LIAM. Yeah. (*Silence*) I could get a six-month extension, I suppose.

MARIO. Think about it.

LIAM. It'll be strange going back, now. I feel different. I don't know what to do. I feel a little bit like Des must feel. Stay or go. And does it matter at all what I do? It's a kind of a lonely feeling. (*Silence*) Did I tell you that Breda's got religion?

MARIO. She didn't have enough?

LIAM. I mean, she's being reborn. She goes twice a week and gets submerged in a tub of water. Breathes through a straw and all. She says that her childhood flashes before her and she relives it all.

MARIO. Go figure. (*Owen enters the bar*) Owen!

LIAM. How was the beach? (*Mario gets a beer and puts it down in front of Owen. He drinks and joins Liam at the table*)

OWEN. Jeez, Liam ... Dessie's gone missing. We were all out on the beach, having a great time eating and drinking.

And Des says he's going for a walk. I wanted to go with him, you know? But he said he wanted to be alone. Well ... it was hot, you know and we'd been drinking beer ... so, we all lay down. I must have fallen asleep. Anyway ... I woke up real sudden like. I couldn't have been asleep for more than twenty minutes. And ... I woke up and ... the first thing I thought of was Des. But he wasn't back. No sign of him anywhere.

MARIO. Did you check the concession stand?

OWEN. First thing. And I asked the lifeguard had he seen him and he said no.

LIAM. What about up under the trees, out of the sun?

OWEN. Paddy checked there. We thought maybe he went up there to take a nap. But ... nothing.

LIAM. I don't see what you're worried for ... maybe he decided to walk home.

OWEN. That's what Mary thought. Breda got hysterical. She wanted to get the police to search for him. But we couldn't do that ... they'd ask a lot of questions. No point in making a bad situation worse.

MARIO. He probably just took a walk and got lost. He'll show up. (*He joins them at the table*)

LIAM. He's disappeared before.

OWEN. That's what I figure. But why did I wake up like that, with him on my mind? I had an awful feeling something was wrong. I feel rotten, Liam.

MARIO. A sleep in the sun can do that to you. He'll show up.

LIAM. He might be back at the apartment. Did you check there?

OWEN. First thing. The others are still there, waiting for him. The Pogues are in town. (*He's talking to Mario*) We all planned to go to the concert. Des loves the Pogues.

MARIO. Maybe you'll see him there.

OWEN. (*To Liam*) Do you think we should go?

LIAM. What if he's in trouble somewhere?

OWEN. That's what I mean. I told Mary I'd be down here, looking for you. She said she'd call if there was any word from him. I'm worried, Liam. He's such a crazy bastard. (*Pause*) Just gone, like that.

LIAM. You never know what he'd get into.

MARIO. (*Returning to bar*) If anything happened to him, the cops would notify you.

OWEN. He has no identification on him.

LIAM. We might have to go to the police, Ownie.

OWEN. I'd hate that. I never meant all them things I said, Liam. I have to go back. I have to know. Will you go with me?

LIAM. (*Touching Owen's arm*) Let's go, then. (*Liam and Owen start out the door*)

MARIO. I'll hold the fort here. Let me know if you find him.

OWEN. First thing.

LIAM. We'll stop back, Mario. (*They exit. Music. Lights fade*)

SCENE FIVE

The apartment. Paddy is asleep on the couch. Liam and Breda are sitting at the table. Liam is looking through a book from a small pile on the table. Breda is flipping through the "Irish Times."
Mary is taking Desmond's clothes from the dresser and putting them in a box. Breda finds something in the paper and stops her paging.

BREDA. Look at this. It's in the paper from home already. "Young Dublin Man Drowns While Visiting New York."

LIAM. (*Scornfully*) Visiting!

MARY. Don't read it, Breda. We know the details. (*Owen enters with a bag. He hands it to Mary*) What's this?

OWEN. The clothes he was wearing. (*Pause*) I didn't like to leave them there. With strangers. (*Owen pats Paddy and sits on a chair at the table. Paddy snores on*) The Sleep of the Innocent.

LIAM. He cried most of the night.

MARY. (*Sitting on arm of the couch*) What did they say, Owen?

OWEN. We're to make arrangements for him as soon as possible. (*Pause*) Jeez. I don't know what you do, exactly.

LIAM. You should have asked, Owen.

OWEN. I did, Gizmo. I just didn't hear what they said.

MARY. I'll call the Irish Consulate. They'll tell as what to do. Will we pack his books?

OWEN. Yeah. Everything. I want to leave nothing behind us.

LIAM. You'll need to buy the casket, Owen. :

OWEN. When I called home ... the news was bad enough. I didn't want to ask could they wire me some cash to cover the expenses. They haven't much to spare themselves. (*Silence. They all sit staring*) Growing up we were like brothers. I used to look after him, ya know? I told him to come over. What a wind-up. Washed up on the beach like that. All covered with sand, he was. We nearly missed him, in the dark. Didn't we, Gizmo?

LIAM. (*Moves out of the apartment scene and into The Old Sod. He leans on the bar from behind it*) I'm standing in for Mario today, Mr. Costelloe. He's gone with Owen to help him arrange things. The Yanks came through for Dessie in the end. When Peter Kelly and the owner here heard what happened, they put up the money for his casket and all. Owen'll be going home with him. (*Owen stands, looks at Mary, touches Breda on the shoulder and exits. Pause*) Poor Ownie. Blames himself, he does. But it was an accident, sure. We figure, he must have walked out on the rocks and slipped. (*Pause*) He was a good old skin, was Desmond. (*Pause*) My friend Tyrone stopped by today. He offered me the loan of some cash. When he heard. To go home, you know? (*Pause*) I'm thinking I'll chance my arm here for a bit. It's just Paddy and me now ... 'til the wedding. We're looking for another mate, if you hear of anyone. (*Breda stands, touches Paddy on the head as she passes and exits*) Breda's going home, too ... wearing black, no doubt. And Mary's moving to Manhattan soon. (*She stands, wakes Paddy and they exit. Mary having one last look before she goes*) She's found another share ... it's close to her design class. (*Pause*) Yeah. We're all going to Kennedy tomorrow, to see Des off. (*He begins to wipe the bar vigorously*) Hard to believe I've been here nearly a year ... on Bainbridge Avenue. "The Irish Mile," they call it. (*Just then a fierce-looking young woman comes through the door. She carries a heavy backpack. She looks around, notices Liam staring at her and drops her pack*)

YOUNG WOMAN. I'm looking for Seamus. (*Lights out*)

about the authors

DAVID BUDBILL was born in Cleveland, Ohio, in 1940 to a streetcar driver and a minister's daughter. He is the author of five plays, five books of poems, a collection of short stories, a novel, and a picture book for children. Among his prizes and honors are a National Endowment for the Arts Playwriting Fellowship in 1991, a Guggenheim Fellowship in Poetry in 1981, and The Dorothy Canfield Fisher Award for Fiction in 1978.

In 1991 Chelsea Green Publishing Company published *Judevine: The Complete Poems*, a book that spans an arc of twenty years in the lives and struggles of the people in a mythic town in northern Vermont called Judevine. This book includes Budbill's previous books *The Chain Saw Dance, From Down to the Village*, and *Why I Came to Judevine*; his poem/play *Pulp Cutters' Nativity*; and a hundred pages of new uncollected and unpublished material. *Judevine: The Complete Poems* serves as the foundation for Budbill's acclaimed and widely produced play *Judevine*, which has played to enthusiastic audiences at Arena Stage in Washington, DC, The Theatre Project in Brunswick, Maine, Florida Studio Theatre in Sarasota, McCarter Theatre in Princeton, New Jersey, American Conservatory Theatre in San Francisco (where it won the 1990 Bay Area Theatre Critics Circle Award for Ensemble Performance), Texas Wesleyan University in Fort Worth, and Perseverance Theatre in Juneau, Alaska, among many other places.

Budbill's newest play, *Thingy World!*, is a play about America's consuming and self-centered materialistic way of life and how it has created a culture of waste and destruction that now threatens to destroy the world. Through the mediums of song, dance, comedy, and satire, *Thingy World!* not only lays bare the American way of life but offers some entertaining and constructive suggestions regarding how we might live our lives differently.

JO CARSON lives and works in Johnson City, Tennessee, where she writes plays, short stories, essays, and poems. She has authored a series of monologues and dialogues that she has performed for audiences at music festivals; theatres in Cleveland, San Francisco, and New York; an Appalachian Festival in Italy; and Wednesday-night dinners at the Baptist church in Johnson City. A collection of this material, *Stories I Ain't Told Nobody Yet*, is available from Orchard Books in New York. She has written two books for children, co-organized the founding meeting of Alternate Regional Organization Of Theatres, South, and has been an occasional commentator on National Public Radio's *All Things Considered* for five years. She has written and performed on and off for fourteen years with The Road Company, a small theatre in Johnson City focusing on developing its own material. Carson won awards in 1984 from the Center for Appalachian Studies and Services and in 1986 from the Kentucky Foundation for Women, both of which provided stipends to work on scripts outside of her work with The Road Company. The second of those scripts is *Daytrips*, which received the 1989 Joseph P. Kesselring Award. *Daytrips* has been produced at The Los Angeles Theatre Center, Hartford Stage, and The Women's Project among other prestigious regional theatres. The acting edition has been published by Dramatists Play Service. In the spring of 1991 Carson was commissioned to write a full-length play about the life of Davy Crockett.

SAMUEL L. KELLEY grew up on a small farm his family rented in Marvell (Turkey Scratch), Arkansas. His first-grade teacher started him on the stage as an actor at age six and he has been fascinated with the theatre every since. He is a 1990 graduate of the Yale School of Drama. While there, he received the 1989–90 Molly Kuhn Award for Best Play (*Pill Hill*), the William Morris Agency Fellowship in Playwriting, and the 1988–89 Lemist Esler Fellowship in Playwriting. He was recently commissioned by the Arena Stage in Washington, DC, to write a play for that company.

Pill Hill has been produced at the Penumbra Theatre Company in Saint Paul, MN, the Philadelphia Theatre Company, and the National Black Theatre Festival in Winston-Salem, North Carolina. There have been readings and/or productions of his plays at the Manhattan Theatre Club, Yale Repertory Theatre, Yale Cabaret Theatre, and Yale African American Heritage Ensemble; in Syracuse, New York, with the Paul Robeson Company for the Performing Arts in conjunction with the Salt City for the Performing Arts; at the First Street Theatre in Ithaca, New York; and at the State University of New York at Cortland.

Publications include *The Evolution of Character Portrayals in the Films of Sidney Poitier: 1950—1970* (Garland Publishers, 1983) and "Sidney Poitier: heros integrationniste" (*CINE-MACTION*, Paris, France, 1988).

In addition to an M.F.A. in playwriting from Yale, he has a B.A. degree in speech and drama from the University of Arkansas at Pine Bluff, an M.A. in public speaking from the University of Arkansas at Fayetteville, and a Ph.D. in radio, television and film from the University of Michigan. He is currently on the faculty at the State University of New York at Cortland, where he teaches communication studies.

JANET NOBLE was born in Grover's Mills, New Jersey, a year after Orson Welles's *The War of the Worlds* radio broadcast interrupted her parents' pinochle game with the startling news that Martians had landed in the neighborhood.

Since 1963 she has been living and working in New York City. She has worked as a professional actress in regional and off-off-Broadway theatres and is especially happy to have appeared in *The Grand Tarot* with Charles Ludlam and his Ridiculous Theatre Company. She has had plays included in The Ensemble Studio Theatre's annual Octoberfests of New One Act Plays and, in 1984, was a resident at Edward Albee's William Flanagan Memorial Foundation for Creative Persons in Montauk, New York.

Noble has maintained a long and fruitful association with The Irish Arts Center in New York City, where she has acted as well as directed and co-produced. Her first full-length play, *Kiss My Blarney Stone*, premiered there in 1987. She was named one of the top one hundred Irish Americans in 1990 by *Irish American Magazine*.